C-1288   CAREER EXAMINATION SERIES

*This is your*
*PASSBOOK for...*

# Fire Inspector

*Test Preparation Study Guide*
*Questions & Answers*

**NATIONAL LEARNING CORPORATION** ®

# COPYRIGHT NOTICE

This book is SOLELY intended for, is sold ONLY to, and its use is RESTRICTED to individual, bona fide applicants or candidates who qualify by virtue of having seriously filed applications for appropriate license, certificate, professional and/or promotional advancement, higher school matriculation, scholarship, or other legitimate requirements of education and/or governmental authorities.

This book is NOT intended for use, class instruction, tutoring, training, duplication, copying, reprinting, excerption, or adaptation, etc., by:

1) Other publishers
2) Proprietors and/or Instructors of "Coaching" and/or Preparatory Courses
3) Personnel and/or Training Divisions of commercial, industrial, and governmental organizations
4) Schools, colleges, or universities and/or their departments and staffs, including teachers and other personnel
5) Testing Agencies or Bureaus
6) Study groups which seek by the purchase of a single volume to copy and/or duplicate and/or adapt this material for use by the group as a whole without having purchased individual volumes for each of the members of the group
7) Et al.

Such persons would be in violation of appropriate Federal and State statutes.

PROVISION OF LICENSING AGREEMENTS – Recognized educational, commercial, industrial, and governmental institutions and organizations, and others legitimately engaged in educational pursuits, including training, testing, and measurement activities, may address request for a licensing agreement to the copyright owners, who will determine whether, and under what conditions, including fees and charges, the materials in this book may be used them. In other words, a licensing facility exists for the legitimate use of the material in this book on other than an individual basis. However, it is asseverated and affirmed here that the material in this book CANNOT be used without the receipt of the express permission of such a licensing agreement from the Publishers. Inquiries re licensing should be addressed to the company, attention rights and permissions department.

All rights reserved, including the right of reproduction in whole or in part, in any form or by any means, electronic or mechanical, including photocopying, recording, or by any information storage and retrieval system, without permission in writing from the Publisher.

Copyright © 2024 by
# National Learning Corporation

212 Michael Drive, Syosset, NY 11791
(516) 921-8888 • www.passbooks.com
E-mail: info@passbooks.com

PUBLISHED IN THE UNITED STATES OF AMERICA

# PASSBOOK® SERIES

THE *PASSBOOK® SERIES* has been created to prepare applicants and candidates for the ultimate academic battlefield – the examination room.

At some time in our lives, each and every one of us may be required to take an examination – for validation, matriculation, admission, qualification, registration, certification, or licensure.

Based on the assumption that every applicant or candidate has met the basic formal educational standards, has taken the required number of courses, and read the necessary texts, the *PASSBOOK® SERIES* furnishes the one special preparation which may assure passing with confidence, instead of failing with insecurity. Examination questions – together with answers – are furnished as the basic vehicle for study so that the mysteries of the examination and its compounding difficulties may be eliminated or diminished by a sure method.

This book is meant to help you pass your examination provided that you qualify and are serious in your objective.

The entire field is reviewed through the huge store of content information which is succinctly presented through a provocative and challenging approach – the question-and-answer method.

A climate of success is established by furnishing the correct answers at the end of each test.

You soon learn to recognize types of questions, forms of questions, and patterns of questioning. You may even begin to anticipate expected outcomes.

You perceive that many questions are repeated or adapted so that you can gain acute insights, which may enable you to score many sure points.

You learn how to confront new questions, or types of questions, and to attack them confidently and work out the correct answers.

You note objectives and emphases, and recognize pitfalls and dangers, so that you may make positive educational adjustments.

Moreover, you are kept fully informed in relation to new concepts, methods, practices, and directions in the field.

You discover that you are actually taking the examination all the time: you are preparing for the examination by "taking" an examination, not by reading extraneous and/or supererogatory textbooks.

In short, this PASSBOOK®, used directedly, should be an important factor in helping you to pass your test.

# FIRE INSPECTOR

## DUTIES
Inspects buildings to determine compliance with fire codes and safety standards. Investigates complaints of fire hazards in order to correct them. Reports violations of fire prevention code to property owner. Inspects storage facilities for inflammable liquids and explosives. Refers repeat violations to supervisors.

## SCOPE OF EXAMINATION
The written test will be designed to cover knowledge, skills, and/or abilities in the following areas:
1. Fire prevention, including fire inspections and fire hazards;
2. Understanding and interpreting fire prevention laws and codes; and
3. Preparation of written material.

# HOW TO TAKE A TEST

## I. YOU MUST PASS AN EXAMINATION

### A. WHAT EVERY CANDIDATE SHOULD KNOW

Examination applicants often ask us for help in preparing for the written test. What can I study in advance? What kinds of questions will be asked? How will the test be given? How will the papers be graded?

As an applicant for a civil service examination, you may be wondering about some of these things. Our purpose here is to suggest effective methods of advance study and to describe civil service examinations.

Your chances for success on this examination can be increased if you know how to prepare. Those "pre-examination jitters" can be reduced if you know what to expect. You can even experience an adventure in good citizenship if you know why civil service exams are given.

### B. WHY ARE CIVIL SERVICE EXAMINATIONS GIVEN?

Civil service examinations are important to you in two ways. As a citizen, you want public jobs filled by employees who know how to do their work. As a job seeker, you want a fair chance to compete for that job on an equal footing with other candidates. The best-known means of accomplishing this two-fold goal is the competitive examination.

Exams are widely publicized throughout the nation. They may be administered for jobs in federal, state, city, municipal, town or village governments or agencies.

Any citizen may apply, with some limitations, such as the age or residence of applicants. Your experience and education may be reviewed to see whether you meet the requirements for the particular examination. When these requirements exist, they are reasonable and applied consistently to all applicants. Thus, a competitive examination may cause you some uneasiness now, but it is your privilege and safeguard.

### C. HOW ARE CIVIL SERVICE EXAMS DEVELOPED?

Examinations are carefully written by trained technicians who are specialists in the field known as "psychological measurement," in consultation with recognized authorities in the field of work that the test will cover. These experts recommend the subject matter areas or skills to be tested; only those knowledges or skills important to your success on the job are included. The most reliable books and source materials available are used as references. Together, the experts and technicians judge the difficulty level of the questions.

Test technicians know how to phrase questions so that the problem is clearly stated. Their ethics do not permit "trick" or "catch" questions. Questions may have been tried out on sample groups, or subjected to statistical analysis, to determine their usefulness.

Written tests are often used in combination with performance tests, ratings of training and experience, and oral interviews. All of these measures combine to form the best-known means of finding the right person for the right job.

## II. HOW TO PASS THE WRITTEN TEST

### A. NATURE OF THE EXAMINATION

To prepare intelligently for civil service examinations, you should know how they differ from school examinations you have taken. In school you were assigned certain definite pages to read or subjects to cover. The examination questions were quite detailed and usually emphasized memory. Civil service exams, on the other hand, try to discover your present ability to perform the duties of a position, plus your potentiality to learn these duties. In other words, a civil service exam attempts to predict how successful you will be. Questions cover such a broad area that they cannot be as minute and detailed as school exam questions.

In the public service similar kinds of work, or positions, are grouped together in one "class." This process is known as *position-classification*. All the positions in a class are paid according to the salary range for that class. One class title covers all of these positions, and they are all tested by the same examination.

### B. FOUR BASIC STEPS

#### 1) Study the announcement

How, then, can you know what subjects to study? Our best answer is: "Learn as much as possible about the class of positions for which you've applied." The exam will test the knowledge, skills and abilities needed to do the work.

Your most valuable source of information about the position you want is the official exam announcement. This announcement lists the training and experience qualifications. Check these standards and apply only if you come reasonably close to meeting them.

The brief description of the position in the examination announcement offers some clues to the subjects which will be tested. Think about the job itself. Review the duties in your mind. Can you perform them, or are there some in which you are rusty? Fill in the blank spots in your preparation.

Many jurisdictions preview the written test in the exam announcement by including a section called "Knowledge and Abilities Required," "Scope of the Examination," or some similar heading. Here you will find out specifically what fields will be tested.

#### 2) Review your own background

Once you learn in general what the position is all about, and what you need to know to do the work, ask yourself which subjects you already know fairly well and which need improvement. You may wonder whether to concentrate on improving your strong areas or on building some background in your fields of weakness. When the announcement has specified "some knowledge" or "considerable knowledge," or has used adjectives like "beginning principles of…" or "advanced … methods," you can get a clue as to the number and difficulty of questions to be asked in any given field. More questions, and hence broader coverage, would be included for those subjects which are more important in the work. Now weigh your strengths and weaknesses against the job requirements and prepare accordingly.

#### 3) Determine the level of the position

Another way to tell how intensively you should prepare is to understand the level of the job for which you are applying. Is it the entering level? In other words, is this the position in which beginners in a field of work are hired? Or is it an intermediate or advanced level? Sometimes this is indicated by such words as "Junior" or "Senior" in the class title. Other jurisdictions use Roman numerals to designate the level – Clerk I, Clerk II, for example. The word "Supervisor" sometimes appears in the title. If the level is not indicated by the title, check the description of duties. Will you be working under very close supervision, or will you have responsibility for independent decisions in this work?

**4) Choose appropriate study materials**

Now that you know the subjects to be examined and the relative amount of each subject to be covered, you can choose suitable study materials. For beginning level jobs, or even advanced ones, if you have a pronounced weakness in some aspect of your training, read a modern, standard textbook in that field. Be sure it is up to date and has general coverage. Such books are normally available at your library, and the librarian will be glad to help you locate one. For entry-level positions, questions of appropriate difficulty are chosen -- neither highly advanced questions, nor those too simple. Such questions require careful thought but not advanced training.

If the position for which you are applying is technical or advanced, you will read more advanced, specialized material. If you are already familiar with the basic principles of your field, elementary textbooks would waste your time. Concentrate on advanced textbooks and technical periodicals. Think through the concepts and review difficult problems in your field.

These are all general sources. You can get more ideas on your own initiative, following these leads. For example, training manuals and publications of the government agency which employs workers in your field can be useful, particularly for technical and professional positions. A letter or visit to the government department involved may result in more specific study suggestions, and certainly will provide you with a more definite idea of the exact nature of the position you are seeking.

## III. KINDS OF TESTS

Tests are used for purposes other than measuring knowledge and ability to perform specified duties. For some positions, it is equally important to test ability to make adjustments to new situations or to profit from training. In others, basic mental abilities not dependent on information are essential. Questions which test these things may not appear as pertinent to the duties of the position as those which test for knowledge and information. Yet they are often highly important parts of a fair examination. For very general questions, it is almost impossible to help you direct your study efforts. What we can do is to point out some of the more common of these general abilities needed in public service positions and describe some typical questions.

1) General information

Broad, general information has been found useful for predicting job success in some kinds of work. This is tested in a variety of ways, from vocabulary lists to questions about current events. Basic background in some field of work, such as sociology or economics, may be sampled in a group of questions. Often these are principles which have become familiar to most persons through exposure rather than through formal training. It is difficult to advise you how to study for these questions; being alert to the world around you is our best suggestion.

2) Verbal ability

An example of an ability needed in many positions is verbal or language ability. Verbal ability is, in brief, the ability to use and understand words. Vocabulary and grammar tests are typical measures of this ability. Reading comprehension or paragraph interpretation questions are common in many kinds of civil service tests. You are given a paragraph of written material and asked to find its central meaning.

3) Numerical ability

Number skills can be tested by the familiar arithmetic problem, by checking paired lists of numbers to see which are alike and which are different, or by interpreting charts and graphs. In the latter test, a graph may be printed in the test booklet which you are asked to use as the basis for answering questions.

4) Observation

A popular test for law-enforcement positions is the observation test. A picture is shown to you for several minutes, then taken away. Questions about the picture test your ability to observe both details and larger elements.

5) Following directions

In many positions in the public service, the employee must be able to carry out written instructions dependably and accurately. You may be given a chart with several columns, each column listing a variety of information. The questions require you to carry out directions involving the information given in the chart.

6) Skills and aptitudes

Performance tests effectively measure some manual skills and aptitudes. When the skill is one in which you are trained, such as typing or shorthand, you can practice. These tests are often very much like those given in business school or high school courses. For many of the other skills and aptitudes, however, no short-time preparation can be made. Skills and abilities natural to you or that you have developed throughout your lifetime are being tested.

Many of the general questions just described provide all the data needed to answer the questions and ask you to use your reasoning ability to find the answers. Your best preparation for these tests, as well as for tests of facts and ideas, is to be at your physical and mental best. You, no doubt, have your own methods of getting into an exam-taking mood and keeping "in shape." The next section lists some ideas on this subject.

IV. KINDS OF QUESTIONS

Only rarely is the "essay" question, which you answer in narrative form, used in civil service tests. Civil service tests are usually of the short-answer type. Full instructions for answering these questions will be given to you at the examination. But in case this is your first experience with short-answer questions and separate answer sheets, here is what you need to know:

**1) Multiple-choice Questions**

Most popular of the short-answer questions is the "multiple choice" or "best answer" question. It can be used, for example, to test for factual knowledge, ability to solve problems or judgment in meeting situations found at work.

A multiple-choice question is normally one of three types—
- It can begin with an incomplete statement followed by several possible endings. You are to find the one ending which *best* completes the statement, although some of the others may not be entirely wrong.
- It can also be a complete statement in the form of a question which is answered by choosing one of the statements listed.

- It can be in the form of a problem – again you select the best answer.

Here is an example of a multiple-choice question with a discussion which should give you some clues as to the method for choosing the right answer:

When an employee has a complaint about his assignment, the action which will *best* help him overcome his difficulty is to
- A. discuss his difficulty with his coworkers
- B. take the problem to the head of the organization
- C. take the problem to the person who gave him the assignment
- D. say nothing to anyone about his complaint

In answering this question, you should study each of the choices to find which is best. Consider choice "A" – Certainly an employee may discuss his complaint with fellow employees, but no change or improvement can result, and the complaint remains unresolved. Choice "B" is a poor choice since the head of the organization probably does not know what assignment you have been given, and taking your problem to him is known as "going over the head" of the supervisor. The supervisor, or person who made the assignment, is the person who can clarify it or correct any injustice. Choice "C" is, therefore, correct. To say nothing, as in choice "D," is unwise. Supervisors have and interest in knowing the problems employees are facing, and the employee is seeking a solution to his problem.

## 2) True/False Questions

The "true/false" or "right/wrong" form of question is sometimes used. Here a complete statement is given. Your job is to decide whether the statement is right or wrong.

SAMPLE: A roaming cell-phone call to a nearby city costs less than a non-roaming call to a distant city.

This statement is wrong, or false, since roaming calls are more expensive.

This is not a complete list of all possible question forms, although most of the others are variations of these common types. You will always get complete directions for answering questions. Be sure you understand *how* to mark your answers – ask questions until you do.

## V. RECORDING YOUR ANSWERS

Computer terminals are used more and more today for many different kinds of exams.

For an examination with very few applicants, you may be told to record your answers in the test booklet itself. Separate answer sheets are much more common. If this separate answer sheet is to be scored by machine – and this is often the case – it is highly important that you mark your answers correctly in order to get credit.

An electronic scoring machine is often used in civil service offices because of the speed with which papers can be scored. Machine-scored answer sheets must be marked with a pencil, which will be given to you. This pencil has a high graphite content which responds to the electronic scoring machine. As a matter of fact, stray dots may register as answers, so do not let your pencil rest on the answer sheet while you are pondering the correct answer. Also, if your pencil lead breaks or is otherwise defective, ask for another.

Since the answer sheet will be dropped in a slot in the scoring machine, be careful not to bend the corners or get the paper crumpled.

The answer sheet normally has five vertical columns of numbers, with 30 numbers to a column. These numbers correspond to the question numbers in your test booklet. After each number, going across the page are four or five pairs of dotted lines. These short dotted lines have small letters or numbers above them. The first two pairs may also have a "T" or "F" above the letters. This indicates that the first two pairs only are to be used if the questions are of the true-false type. If the questions are multiple choice, disregard the "T" and "F" and pay attention only to the small letters or numbers.

Answer your questions in the manner of the sample that follows:

32. The largest city in the United States is
    A. Washington, D.C.
    B. New York City
    C. Chicago
    D. Detroit
    E. San Francisco

1) Choose the answer you think is best. (New York City is the largest, so "B" is correct.)
2) Find the row of dotted lines numbered the same as the question you are answering. (Find row number 32)
3) Find the pair of dotted lines corresponding to the answer. (Find the pair of lines under the mark "B.")
4) Make a solid black mark between the dotted lines.


## VI. BEFORE THE TEST

Common sense will help you find procedures to follow to get ready for an examination. Too many of us, however, overlook these sensible measures. Indeed, nervousness and fatigue have been found to be the most serious reasons why applicants fail to do their best on civil service tests. Here is a list of reminders:

- Begin your preparation early – Don't wait until the last minute to go scurrying around for books and materials or to find out what the position is all about.
- Prepare continuously – An hour a night for a week is better than an all-night cram session. This has been definitely established. What is more, a night a week for a month will return better dividends than crowding your study into a shorter period of time.
- Locate the place of the exam – You have been sent a notice telling you when and where to report for the examination. If the location is in a different town or otherwise unfamiliar to you, it would be well to inquire the best route and learn something about the building.
- Relax the night before the test – Allow your mind to rest. Do not study at all that night. Plan some mild recreation or diversion; then go to bed early and get a good night's sleep.
- Get up early enough to make a leisurely trip to the place for the test – This way unforeseen events, traffic snarls, unfamiliar buildings, etc. will not upset you.
- Dress comfortably – A written test is not a fashion show. You will be known by number and not by name, so wear something comfortable.

- Leave excess paraphernalia at home – Shopping bags and odd bundles will get in your way. You need bring only the items mentioned in the official notice you received; usually everything you need is provided. Do not bring reference books to the exam. They will only confuse those last minutes and be taken away from you when in the test room.
- Arrive somewhat ahead of time – If because of transportation schedules you must get there very early, bring a newspaper or magazine to take your mind off yourself while waiting.
- Locate the examination room – When you have found the proper room, you will be directed to the seat or part of the room where you will sit. Sometimes you are given a sheet of instructions to read while you are waiting. Do not fill out any forms until you are told to do so; just read them and be prepared.
- Relax and prepare to listen to the instructions
- If you have any physical problem that may keep you from doing your best, be sure to tell the test administrator. If you are sick or in poor health, you really cannot do your best on the exam. You can come back and take the test some other time.

## VII. AT THE TEST

The day of the test is here and you have the test booklet in your hand. The temptation to get going is very strong. Caution! There is more to success than knowing the right answers. You must know how to identify your papers and understand variations in the type of short-answer question used in this particular examination. Follow these suggestions for maximum results from your efforts:

### 1) Cooperate with the monitor

The test administrator has a duty to create a situation in which you can be as much at ease as possible. He will give instructions, tell you when to begin, check to see that you are marking your answer sheet correctly, and so on. He is not there to guard you, although he will see that your competitors do not take unfair advantage. He wants to help you do your best.

### 2) Listen to all instructions

Don't jump the gun! Wait until you understand all directions. In most civil service tests you get more time than you need to answer the questions. So don't be in a hurry. Read each word of instructions until you clearly understand the meaning. Study the examples, listen to all announcements and follow directions. Ask questions if you do not understand what to do.

### 3) Identify your papers

Civil service exams are usually identified by number only. You will be assigned a number; you must not put your name on your test papers. Be sure to copy your number correctly. Since more than one exam may be given, copy your exact examination title.

### 4) Plan your time

Unless you are told that a test is a "speed" or "rate of work" test, speed itself is usually not important. Time enough to answer all the questions will be provided, but this does not mean that you have all day. An overall time limit has been set. Divide the total time (in minutes) by the number of questions to determine the approximate time you have for each question.

### 5) Do not linger over difficult questions

If you come across a difficult question, mark it with a paper clip (useful to have along) and come back to it when you have been through the booklet. One caution if you do this – be sure to skip a number on your answer sheet as well. Check often to be sure that you have not lost your place and that you are marking in the row numbered the same as the question you are answering.

### 6) Read the questions

Be sure you know what the question asks! Many capable people are unsuccessful because they failed to *read* the questions correctly.

### 7) Answer all questions

Unless you have been instructed that a penalty will be deducted for incorrect answers, it is better to guess than to omit a question.

### 8) Speed tests

It is often better NOT to guess on speed tests. It has been found that on timed tests people are tempted to spend the last few seconds before time is called in marking answers at random – without even reading them – in the hope of picking up a few extra points. To discourage this practice, the instructions may warn you that your score will be "corrected" for guessing. That is, a penalty will be applied. The incorrect answers will be deducted from the correct ones, or some other penalty formula will be used.

### 9) Review your answers

If you finish before time is called, go back to the questions you guessed or omitted to give them further thought. Review other answers if you have time.

### 10) Return your test materials

If you are ready to leave before others have finished or time is called, take ALL your materials to the monitor and leave quietly. Never take any test material with you. The monitor can discover whose papers are not complete, and taking a test booklet may be grounds for disqualification.

## VIII. EXAMINATION TECHNIQUES

1) Read the general instructions carefully. These are usually printed on the first page of the exam booklet. As a rule, these instructions refer to the timing of the examination; the fact that you should not start work until the signal and must stop work at a signal, etc. If there are any *special* instructions, such as a choice of questions to be answered, make sure that you note this instruction carefully.

2) When you are ready to start work on the examination, that is as soon as the signal has been given, read the instructions to each question booklet, underline any key words or phrases, such as *least, best, outline, describe* and the like. In this way you will tend to answer as requested rather than discover on reviewing your paper that you *listed without describing*, that you selected the *worst* choice rather than the *best* choice, etc.

3) If the examination is of the objective or multiple-choice type – that is, each question will also give a series of possible answers: A, B, C or D, and you are called upon to select the best answer and write the letter next to that answer on your answer paper – it is advisable to start answering each question in turn. There may be anywhere from 50 to 100 such questions in the three or four hours allotted and you can see how much time would be taken if you read through all the questions before beginning to answer any. Furthermore, if you come across a question or group of questions which you know would be difficult to answer, it would undoubtedly affect your handling of all the other questions.

4) If the examination is of the essay type and contains but a few questions, it is a moot point as to whether you should read all the questions before starting to answer any one. Of course, if you are given a choice – say five out of seven and the like – then it is essential to read all the questions so you can eliminate the two that are most difficult. If, however, you are asked to answer all the questions, there may be danger in trying to answer the easiest one first because you may find that you will spend too much time on it. The best technique is to answer the first question, then proceed to the second, etc.

5) Time your answers. Before the exam begins, write down the time it started, then add the time allowed for the examination and write down the time it must be completed, then divide the time available somewhat as follows:
    - If 3-1/2 hours are allowed, that would be 210 minutes. If you have 80 objective-type questions, that would be an average of 2-1/2 minutes per question. Allow yourself no more than 2 minutes per question, or a total of 160 minutes, which will permit about 50 minutes to review.
    - If for the time allotment of 210 minutes there are 7 essay questions to answer, that would average about 30 minutes a question. Give yourself only 25 minutes per question so that you have about 35 minutes to review.

6) The most important instruction is to *read each question* and make sure you know what is wanted. The second most important instruction is to *time yourself properly* so that you answer every question. The third most important instruction is to *answer every question*. Guess if you have to but include something for each question. Remember that you will receive no credit for a blank and will probably receive some credit if you write something in answer to an essay question. If you guess a letter – say "B" for a multiple-choice question – you may have guessed right. If you leave a blank as an answer to a multiple-choice question, the examiners may respect your feelings but it will not add a point to your score. Some exams may penalize you for wrong answers, so in such cases *only*, you may not want to guess unless you have some basis for your answer.

7) Suggestions
    a. Objective-type questions
        1. Examine the question booklet for proper sequence of pages and questions
        2. Read all instructions carefully
        3. Skip any question which seems too difficult; return to it after all other questions have been answered
        4. Apportion your time properly; do not spend too much time on any single question or group of questions

5. Note and underline key words – *all, most, fewest, least, best, worst, same, opposite*, etc.
6. Pay particular attention to negatives
7. Note unusual option, e.g., unduly long, short, complex, different or similar in content to the body of the question
8. Observe the use of "hedging" words – *probably, may, most likely*, etc.
9. Make sure that your answer is put next to the same number as the question
10. Do not second-guess unless you have good reason to believe the second answer is definitely more correct
11. Cross out original answer if you decide another answer is more accurate; do not erase until you are ready to hand your paper in
12. Answer all questions; guess unless instructed otherwise
13. Leave time for review

b. Essay questions
1. Read each question carefully
2. Determine exactly what is wanted. Underline key words or phrases.
3. Decide on outline or paragraph answer
4. Include many different points and elements unless asked to develop any one or two points or elements
5. Show impartiality by giving pros and cons unless directed to select one side only
6. Make and write down any assumptions you find necessary to answer the questions
7. Watch your English, grammar, punctuation and choice of words
8. Time your answers; don't crowd material

8) Answering the essay question

Most essay questions can be answered by framing the specific response around several key words or ideas. Here are a few such key words or ideas:

M's: manpower, materials, methods, money, management
P's: purpose, program, policy, plan, procedure, practice, problems, pitfalls, personnel, public relations

   a. Six basic steps in handling problems:
      1. Preliminary plan and background development
      2. Collect information, data and facts
      3. Analyze and interpret information, data and facts
      4. Analyze and develop solutions as well as make recommendations
      5. Prepare report and sell recommendations
      6. Install recommendations and follow up effectiveness

   b. Pitfalls to avoid
      1. *Taking things for granted* – A statement of the situation does not necessarily imply that each of the elements is necessarily true; for example, a complaint may be invalid and biased so that all that can be taken for granted is that a complaint has been registered

2. *Considering only one side of a situation* – Wherever possible, indicate several alternatives and then point out the reasons you selected the best one
3. *Failing to indicate follow up* – Whenever your answer indicates action on your part, make certain that you will take proper follow-up action to see how successful your recommendations, procedures or actions turn out to be
4. *Taking too long in answering any single question* – Remember to time your answers properly

## IX. AFTER THE TEST

Scoring procedures differ in detail among civil service jurisdictions although the general principles are the same. Whether the papers are hand-scored or graded by machine we have described, they are nearly always graded by number. That is, the person who marks the paper knows only the number – never the name – of the applicant. Not until all the papers have been graded will they be matched with names. If other tests, such as training and experience or oral interview ratings have been given, scores will be combined. Different parts of the examination usually have different weights. For example, the written test might count 60 percent of the final grade, and a rating of training and experience 40 percent. In many jurisdictions, veterans will have a certain number of points added to their grades.

After the final grade has been determined, the names are placed in grade order and an eligible list is established. There are various methods for resolving ties between those who get the same final grade – probably the most common is to place first the name of the person whose application was received first. Job offers are made from the eligible list in the order the names appear on it. You will be notified of your grade and your rank as soon as all these computations have been made. This will be done as rapidly as possible.

People who are found to meet the requirements in the announcement are called "eligibles." Their names are put on a list of eligible candidates. An eligible's chances of getting a job depend on how high he stands on this list and how fast agencies are filling jobs from the list.

When a job is to be filled from a list of eligibles, the agency asks for the names of people on the list of eligibles for that job. When the civil service commission receives this request, it sends to the agency the names of the three people highest on this list. Or, if the job to be filled has specialized requirements, the office sends the agency the names of the top three persons who meet these requirements from the general list.

The appointing officer makes a choice from among the three people whose names were sent to him. If the selected person accepts the appointment, the names of the others are put back on the list to be considered for future openings.

That is the rule in hiring from all kinds of eligible lists, whether they are for typist, carpenter, chemist, or something else. For every vacancy, the appointing officer has his choice of any one of the top three eligibles on the list. This explains why the person whose name is on top of the list sometimes does not get an appointment when some of the persons lower on the list do. If the appointing officer chooses the second or third eligible, the No. 1 eligible does not get a job at once, but stays on the list until he is appointed or the list is terminated.

## X. HOW TO PASS THE INTERVIEW TEST

The examination for which you applied requires an oral interview test. You have already taken the written test and you are now being called for the interview test – the final part of the formal examination.

You may think that it is not possible to prepare for an interview test and that there are no procedures to follow during an interview. Our purpose is to point out some things you can do in advance that will help you and some good rules to follow and pitfalls to avoid while you are being interviewed.

*What is an interview supposed to test?*

The written examination is designed to test the technical knowledge and competence of the candidate; the oral is designed to evaluate intangible qualities, not readily measured otherwise, and to establish a list showing the relative fitness of each candidate – as measured against his competitors – for the position sought. Scoring is not on the basis of "right" and "wrong," but on a sliding scale of values ranging from "not passable" to "outstanding." As a matter of fact, it is possible to achieve a relatively low score without a single "incorrect" answer because of evident weakness in the qualities being measured.

Occasionally, an examination may consist entirely of an oral test – either an individual or a group oral. In such cases, information is sought concerning the technical knowledges and abilities of the candidate, since there has been no written examination for this purpose. More commonly, however, an oral test is used to supplement a written examination.

*Who conducts interviews?*

The composition of oral boards varies among different jurisdictions. In nearly all, a representative of the personnel department serves as chairman. One of the members of the board may be a representative of the department in which the candidate would work. In some cases, "outside experts" are used, and, frequently, a businessman or some other representative of the general public is asked to serve. Labor and management or other special groups may be represented. The aim is to secure the services of experts in the appropriate field.

However the board is composed, it is a good idea (and not at all improper or unethical) to ascertain in advance of the interview who the members are and what groups they represent. When you are introduced to them, you will have some idea of their backgrounds and interests, and at least you will not stutter and stammer over their names.

*What should be done before the interview?*

While knowledge about the board members is useful and takes some of the surprise element out of the interview, there is other preparation which is more substantive. It *is* possible to prepare for an oral interview – in several ways:

### 1) Keep a copy of your application and review it carefully before the interview

This may be the only document before the oral board, and the starting point of the interview. Know what education and experience you have listed there, and the sequence and dates of all of it. Sometimes the board will ask you to review the highlights of your experience for them; you should not have to hem and haw doing it.

### 2) Study the class specification and the examination announcement

Usually, the oral board has one or both of these to guide them. The qualities, characteristics or knowledges required by the position sought are stated in these documents. They offer valuable clues as to the nature of the oral interview. For example, if the job involves supervisory responsibilities, the announcement will usually indicate that knowledge of modern supervisory methods and the qualifications of the candidate as a supervisor will be tested. If so, you can expect such questions, frequently in the form of a hypothetical situation which you are expected to solve. NEVER go into an oral without knowledge of the duties and responsibilities of the job you seek.

### 3) Think through each qualification required

Try to visualize the kind of questions you would ask if you were a board member. How well could you answer them? Try especially to appraise your own knowledge and background in each area, *measured against the job sought*, and identify any areas in which you are weak. Be critical and realistic – do not flatter yourself.

### 4) Do some general reading in areas in which you feel you may be weak

For example, if the job involves supervision and your past experience has NOT, some general reading in supervisory methods and practices, particularly in the field of human relations, might be useful. Do NOT study agency procedures or detailed manuals. The oral board will be testing your understanding and capacity, not your memory.

### 5) Get a good night's sleep and watch your general health and mental attitude

You will want a clear head at the interview. Take care of a cold or any other minor ailment, and of course, no hangovers.

*What should be done on the day of the interview?*

Now comes the day of the interview itself. Give yourself plenty of time to get there. Plan to arrive somewhat ahead of the scheduled time, particularly if your appointment is in the fore part of the day. If a previous candidate fails to appear, the board might be ready for you a bit early. By early afternoon an oral board is almost invariably behind schedule if there are many candidates, and you may have to wait. Take along a book or magazine to read, or your application to review, but leave any extraneous material in the waiting room when you go in for your interview. In any event, relax and compose yourself.

The matter of dress is important. The board is forming impressions about you – from your experience, your manners, your attitude, and your appearance. Give your personal appearance careful attention. Dress your best, but not your flashiest. Choose conservative, appropriate clothing, and be sure it is immaculate. This is a business interview, and your appearance should indicate that you regard it as such. Besides, being well groomed and properly dressed will help boost your confidence.

Sooner or later, someone will call your name and escort you into the interview room. *This is it.* From here on you are on your own. It is too late for any more preparation. But remember, you asked for this opportunity to prove your fitness, and you are here because your request was granted.

*What happens when you go in?*

The usual sequence of events will be as follows: The clerk (who is often the board stenographer) will introduce you to the chairman of the oral board, who will introduce you to the other members of the board. Acknowledge the introductions before you sit down. Do not be surprised if you find a microphone facing you or a stenotypist sitting by. Oral interviews are usually recorded in the event of an appeal or other review.

Usually the chairman of the board will open the interview by reviewing the highlights of your education and work experience from your application – primarily for the benefit of the other members of the board, as well as to get the material into the record. Do not interrupt or comment unless there is an error or significant misinterpretation; if that is the case, do not hesitate. But do not quibble about insignificant matters. Also, he will usually ask you some question about your education, experience or your present job – partly to get you to start talking and to establish the interviewing "rapport." He may start the actual questioning, or turn it over to one of the other members. Frequently, each member undertakes the questioning on a particular area, one in which he is perhaps most competent, so you can expect each member to participate in the examination. Because time is limited, you may also expect some rather abrupt switches in the direction the questioning takes, so do not be upset by it. Normally, a board member will not pursue a single line of questioning unless he discovers a particular strength or weakness.

After each member has participated, the chairman will usually ask whether any member has any further questions, then will ask you if you have anything you wish to add. Unless you are expecting this question, it may floor you. Worse, it may start you off on an extended, extemporaneous speech. The board is not usually seeking more information. The question is principally to offer you a last opportunity to present further qualifications or to indicate that you have nothing to add. So, if you feel that a significant qualification or characteristic has been overlooked, it is proper to point it out in a sentence or so. Do not compliment the board on the thoroughness of their examination – they have been sketchy, and you know it. If you wish, merely say, "No thank you, I have nothing further to add." This is a point where you can "talk yourself out" of a good impression or fail to present an important bit of information. Remember, *you close the interview yourself*.

The chairman will then say, "That is all, Mr. _____, thank you." Do not be startled; the interview is over, and quicker than you think. Thank him, gather your belongings and take your leave. Save your sigh of relief for the other side of the door.

*How to put your best foot forward*

Throughout this entire process, you may feel that the board individually and collectively is trying to pierce your defenses, seek out your hidden weaknesses and embarrass and confuse you. Actually, this is not true. They are obliged to make an appraisal of your qualifications for the job you are seeking, and they want to see you in your best light. Remember, they must interview all candidates and a non-cooperative candidate may become a failure in spite of their best efforts to bring out his qualifications. Here are 15 suggestions that will help you:

1) **Be natural – Keep your attitude confident, not cocky**

If you are not confident that you can do the job, do not expect the board to be. Do not apologize for your weaknesses, try to bring out your strong points. The board is interested in a positive, not negative, presentation. Cockiness will antagonize any board member and make him wonder if you are covering up a weakness by a false show of strength.

2) **Get comfortable, but don't lounge or sprawl**

Sit erectly but not stiffly. A careless posture may lead the board to conclude that you are careless in other things, or at least that you are not impressed by the importance of the occasion. Either conclusion is natural, even if incorrect. Do not fuss with your clothing, a pencil or an ashtray. Your hands may occasionally be useful to emphasize a point; do not let them become a point of distraction.

3) **Do not wisecrack or make small talk**

This is a serious situation, and your attitude should show that you consider it as such. Further, the time of the board is limited – they do not want to waste it, and neither should you.

### 4) Do not exaggerate your experience or abilities

In the first place, from information in the application or other interviews and sources, the board may know more about you than you think. Secondly, you probably will not get away with it. An experienced board is rather adept at spotting such a situation, so do not take the chance.

### 5) If you know a board member, do not make a point of it, yet do not hide it

Certainly you are not fooling him, and probably not the other members of the board. Do not try to take advantage of your acquaintanceship – it will probably do you little good.

### 6) Do not dominate the interview

Let the board do that. They will give you the clues – do not assume that you have to do all the talking. Realize that the board has a number of questions to ask you, and do not try to take up all the interview time by showing off your extensive knowledge of the answer to the first one.

### 7) Be attentive

You only have 20 minutes or so, and you should keep your attention at its sharpest throughout. When a member is addressing a problem or question to you, give him your undivided attention. Address your reply principally to him, but do not exclude the other board members.

### 8) Do not interrupt

A board member may be stating a problem for you to analyze. He will ask you a question when the time comes. Let him state the problem, and wait for the question.

### 9) Make sure you understand the question

Do not try to answer until you are sure what the question is. If it is not clear, restate it in your own words or ask the board member to clarify it for you. However, do not haggle about minor elements.

### 10) Reply promptly but not hastily

A common entry on oral board rating sheets is "candidate responded readily," or "candidate hesitated in replies." Respond as promptly and quickly as you can, but do not jump to a hasty, ill-considered answer.

### 11) Do not be peremptory in your answers

A brief answer is proper – but do not fire your answer back. That is a losing game from your point of view. The board member can probably ask questions much faster than you can answer them.

### 12) Do not try to create the answer you think the board member wants

He is interested in what kind of mind you have and how it works – not in playing games. Furthermore, he can usually spot this practice and will actually grade you down on it.

### 13) Do not switch sides in your reply merely to agree with a board member

Frequently, a member will take a contrary position merely to draw you out and to see if you are willing and able to defend your point of view. Do not start a debate, yet do not surrender a good position. If a position is worth taking, it is worth defending.

### 14) Do not be afraid to admit an error in judgment if you are shown to be wrong

The board knows that you are forced to reply without any opportunity for careful consideration. Your answer may be demonstrably wrong. If so, admit it and get on with the interview.

### 15) Do not dwell at length on your present job

The opening question may relate to your present assignment. Answer the question but do not go into an extended discussion. You are being examined for a *new* job, not your present one. As a matter of fact, try to phrase ALL your answers in terms of the job for which you are being examined.

*Basis of Rating*

Probably you will forget most of these "do's" and "don'ts" when you walk into the oral interview room. Even remembering them all will not ensure you a passing grade. Perhaps you did not have the qualifications in the first place. But remembering them will help you to put your best foot forward, without treading on the toes of the board members.

Rumor and popular opinion to the contrary notwithstanding, an oral board wants you to make the best appearance possible. They know you are under pressure – but they also want to see how you respond to it as a guide to what your reaction would be under the pressures of the job you seek. They will be influenced by the degree of poise you display, the personal traits you show and the manner in which you respond.

## ABOUT THIS BOOK

This book contains tests divided into Examination Sections. Go through each test, answering every question in the margin. We have also attached a sample answer sheet at the back of the book that can be removed and used. At the end of each test look at the answer key and check your answers. On the ones you got wrong, look at the right answer choice and learn. Do not fill in the answers first. Do not memorize the questions and answers, but understand the answer and principles involved. On your test, the questions will likely be different from the samples. Questions are changed and new ones added. If you understand these past questions you should have success with any changes that arise. Tests may consist of several types of questions. We have additional books on each subject should more study be advisable or necessary for you. Finally, the more you study, the better prepared you will be. This book is intended to be the last thing you study before you walk into the examination room. Prior study of relevant texts is also recommended. NLC publishes some of these in our Fundamental Series. Knowledge and good sense are important factors in passing your exam. Good luck also helps. So now study this Passbook, absorb the material contained within and take that knowledge into the examination. Then do your best to pass that exam.

# EXAMINATION SECTION

# EXAMINATION SECTION
# TEST 1

DIRECTIONS: Each question or incomplete statement is followed by several suggested answers or completions. Select the one that BEST answers the question or completes the statement. *PRINT THE LETTER OF THE CORRECT ANSWER IN THE SPACE AT THE RIGHT.*

1. A television receiver has a greater inherent fire hazard than a conventional radio receiver because

    A. of greater electrical leakage
    B. cabinets are inadequately ventilated
    C. higher voltage is used in the system
    D. they are operated for longer periods of time
    E. the coaxial cable lead-in is covered with a highly flammable coating

    1.____

2. Of the following, the MOST frequent factor contributing to conflagrations in the United States and Canada in the last 25 years has been

    A. high winds
    B. lack of exposure protection
    C. delayed alarms
    D. congestion of hazardous occupancies
    E. inadequate water distribution system

    2.____

3. If, upon reinspection of a plant which has 30 days to comply with a previous order, you find that the order has not been completely obeyed but that some work has taken place, you should

    A. report to proper authorities to obtain legal action
    B. assume the delay is unavoidable and check again in 30 days
    C. inform the person in charge that a 10-day extension will be granted and that legal action will be taken if the order has not been followed
    D. none of the above

    3.____

4. An analysis of loss records in one city showed that one-third of the total loss in building fires was in residence buildings and that, of the total loss in such buildings, in the year under study, nearly 80 percent was in multiple dwelling buildings.
The one of the following courses of action for the fire department which should be taken *immediately* on the basis of this report is to

    A. relocate companies
    B. recommend sprinkler protection for multiple dwellings
    C. institute special training fighting multiple dwelling fires
    D. reduce the protection given to other than multiple dwelling residences
    E. inspect multiple dwellings more thoroughly

    4.____

5. It is good practice to so install heating devices that under conditions of maximum heat (long-continued exposure) they will not cause the temperature of exposed woodwork to exceed 160° F.
This practice is

    5.____

1

A. *correct* because of the possibility that wood and other combustible materials, after long-continued exposure to relatively moderate heat, may ignite at temperatures far below their usual ignition temperatures
B. *not correct* because no wood in ordinary use will ignite at a temperature of less than 400° F. and, consequently, the requirement is needlessly severe
C. *correct* because oxidation proceeds much more rapidly at higher temperatures
D. *not correct* because oxidation proceeds much more slowly at higher temperatures
E. *correct* because, under prolonged heating, the temperature of the air in the room will build up until the ignition point is reached unless the applied temperature is kept sufficiently low

6. Analysis of the causes of fires is important, as only by knowing the causes of fires is it possible to effectively prevent fire.
An analysis of fires in rooms used for spraying flammable paints and finishes has shown that the MOST important of the following causes is

   A. smoking by employees
   B. defective electrical equipment
   C. spontaneous ignition of paint deposits, rubbish, wiping rags
   D. static electricity resulting from friction
   E. cutting and welding operations

7. The flammability or combustibility of radioactive materials has little or no direct effect on the fire hazard of a laboratory PRIMARILY because

   A. the unusual structural characteristics of such a laboratory serve to limit possible fire spread from such hazards
   B. water or water spray are effective on most radioactive substances
   C. the quantities of such material in any one laboratory are usually small
   D. laboratory fire prevention and firefighting facilities usually exceed maximum fire hazards
   E. such materials are inherently of a low order of combustibility

8. Comparison of the burning qualities of foam rubber and cotton mattresses shows that, generally,

   A. a cotton mattress burns faster but cooler
   B. a foam rubber mattress burns slower but hotter
   C. a foam rubber mattress burns faster and hotter
   D. a cotton mattress burns faster and hotter
   E. the potential fire hazard of a foam rubber mattress is higher

9. During Christmas and other holiday shopping seasons, it is required that frequent inspections shall be made of department stores, at irregular intervals.
Of the following, the MOST important reason for this inspection procedure is to

   A. prevent unnecessary interference with store operations
   B. check characteristic holiday operations
   C. permit more frequent and thorough coverage of the stores in question
   D. avoid delay in urgent fire operations
   E. permit more flexible scheduling of inspection

10. The fire load computation of a building indicates, for the most part, the    10._____

   A. risk of a fire breaking out
   B. rate at which a fire is likely to grow
   C. combustibility of the various parts of the building rather than its contents
   D. amount of combustibles and the method of protection
   E. maximum fire stress to which the building might be subjected

11. It is far more important that escape routes from multistory buildings should be protected    11._____
   against smoke and hot gases than from direct flame or heat.
   This statement is

   A. *not correct;* resistive construction is likely to be smoke-resistive as well
   B. *correct;* adequate means for ventilation is essential to prevent cutting off escape routes
   C. *not correct;* unless corridors and escape stairs are constructed of fire resistive materials, progress of fire cannot be blocked
   D. *correct;* unless properly protected from smoke and hot gases, escape stairs would be unusable by occupants
   E. *not correct;* unless properly protected against direct flame or heat, escape routes cannot resist smoke or hot gases

12. The minimum width of exit usually required for a single file of persons is MOST NEARLY    12._____
   _____ inches.

   A. 15-17    B. 18-20    C. 21-23    D. 24-27    E. 27-30

13. The MOST pronounced method of reducing the fire and life hazards in public buildings is    13._____
   by

   A. ample exits of any type
   B. ample stairways inside the buildings
   C. the use of exit signs and panic locks
   D. fire-resisting construction suitable for the occupancy

14. From all viewpoints, the MOST hazardous materials that could be stored, constituting a    14._____
   life as well as a fire hazard, would be

   A. second-hand niter bags
   B. used motor vehicles
   C. loose or baled vegetable fibers
   D. pyroxylin and pyroxylin plastic products

15. The CHIEF fire hazard of welding and cutting operations is    15._____

   A. flames of the torch igniting nearby material
   B. broken hose line
   C. flying sparks
   D. back-firing of torch

16. Of the following items associated with motion picture theatres, the PRIMARY hazard is    16._____

   A. misuse of electricity           B. heating defects
   C. smoking and matches             D. projection booth fires

17. The MOST hazardous method of fumigation is by the use of

    A. heat (125° F.)
    B. carbon tetrachloride mixture with flammable fumigant
    C. carbon dioxide mixture with flammable fumigant
    D. carbon bisulphide

17.____

18. The combined use of inspections, periodic reports of activities, follow-up procedures, special reports from subordinates, and a rating system comprise a system of

    A. coordination                 B. command
    C. control                         D. representation
    E. on-the-job training

18.____

19. What should be provided in air conditioning ducts to *prevent* the spread of fire and smoke through a property?

    A. Automatic dampers          B. Intake screens
    C. Steel wool air filters           D. Heat actuated devices

19.____

20. The *outstanding* fire hazard of boarding and rooming houses is

    A. misuse of electricity           B. smoking and matches
    C. heating defects                D. incendiary

20.____

21. The SIMPLEST and MOST feasible method of avoiding the overheating of woodwork near any high temperature heating appliance is by

    A. filling the intervening space with insulating material
    B. covering the woodwork with sheet metal
    C. providing an air space between the woodwork and the appliance
    D. covering the woodwork with asbestos sheets

21.____

22. The PRINCIPAL source of fire hazard in connection with heating equipment in mercantile buildings comes from

    A. defective wiring
    B. insufficient clearance from combustible materials
    C. the storage and handling of fuel
    D. defective motors

22.____

23. More ink has been spilled on the item of smoking as a cause of fire than on any other, but the total result has been negligible.
This situation is BEST accounted for by the fact that

    A. smoking is generally an automatic act performed unthinkingly
    B. truly effective facilities for elimination of smoking hazards are exceedingly cumbersome or expensive
    C. most people regard smoking as a personal prerogative and resent control measures
    D. smoking is practiced by many individuals with defective intelligence and social attitudes

23.____

24. There are two basic factors in assessing building construction from the fire prevention standpoint. One is the combustibility of materials.
    The other is

    A. extinguishment facilities
    B. excess structural strength
    C. ventilation control
    D. limitation of fire spread
    E. means of access and egress

25. The LEAST accurate statement concerning the protection of openings in walls and partitions is:

    A. Protection of wall openings may prevent either the horizontal or the vertical spread of fire
    B. The general features of a building have no bearing on the extent to which such protection is necessary
    C. The protection secured by fire doors and fire windows cannot be better than the fire resistant value of the walls
    D. Good solid walls are preferable to those with fire doors in restricting the spread of fire

## KEY (CORRECT ANSWERS)

| | | | |
|---|---|---|---|
| 1. C | | 11. D | |
| 2. A | | 12. C | |
| 3. A | | 13. D | |
| 4. E | | 14. D | |
| 5. A | | 15. C | |
| 6. C | | 16. D | |
| 7. C | | 17. D | |
| 8. C | | 18. C | |
| 9. B | | 19. A | |
| 10. E | | 20. C | |

21. C
22. B
23. A
24. D
25. B

# TEST 2

DIRECTIONS: Each question or incomplete statement is followed by several suggested answers or completions. Select the one that BEST answers the question or completes the statement. *PRINT THE LETTER OF THE CORRECT ANSWER IN THE SPACE AT THE RIGHT.*

1. The materials of which a building are constructed and the opportunities for the spread of fire are important, but the GREATEST single hazard is usually that of   1.___

    A. occupancy
    B. location
    C. fire protective measures
    D. construction

2. A warehouse with a leaky roof contains a large amount of building material.   2.___
   The one of the following materials which is MOST likely to set fire to the warehouse is

    A. gasoline    B. crude oil    C. lime    D. kerosene

3. For the most effective results in conducting a Fire Prevention Week campaign, it would be DESIRABLE to emphasize fire prevention   3.___

    A. in its broader community aspects
    B. as a means of lowering insurance rates
    C. as it applies to the individuals' own homes
    D. as a means of lowering operating costs of the fire department
    E. as a means of assuring the uninterrupted operation of busines

4. Floor or wall openings sometimes prevent the banking up of heated air.   4.___
   This condition, with respect to sprinklers, is considered

    A. advantageous
    B. unimportant
    C. detrimental
    D. good ventilation

5. The BEST all-round fireproofing material, due to its high resistance to heat, its lightness, its great strength, its adaptability to any shape, and which is also very easily repaired when damaged by a severe fire, is   5.___

    A. brick
    B. hollow clay tile
    C. gypsum
    D. concrete

6. Commercial storage and industrial occupancies are classified in the Fire Code as _____ hazardous.   6.___

    A. highly
    B. moderately
    C. lightly
    D. all of the above

7. An unusually large number of fires of *unknown cause* is characteristic of the fires involving   7.___

    A. restaurants
    B. warehouses
    C. mercantile stores
    D. hospitals

8. It is obvious that where a division wall is not continued through the roof, and where the roof is combustible on both sides of the wall, fire is almost certain to spread beyond the wall if the fire is of any duration. According to the foregoing statement, there is *need* of   8.___

    A. parapets
    B. more resistive division walls
    C. fire-stopping of roof spaces
    D. fire-stopping division walls

9. The hazard of flammable gases is generally _____ to that of flammable liquids. The above missing word is

   A. opposite   B. dissimilar   C. similar   D. identical

10. The MOST important factor that would materially decrease large-loss supermarket fires is

    A. education of the general public
    B. separating the utility area from the rest of the building by a fire-resistive wall
    C. maintenance of an adequate supply of fire extinguishers
    D. keeping all aisles clear of merchandise and storage
    E. fireproof disposal containers for matches, cigarettes, etc. in the sales area

11. The PRIMARY difference between the large number of small fires that produces a small percentage of total losses, and the smaller number of large fires that accounts for 95 percent of the total loss in the United States is usually

    A. the nature of the material involved in the fire
    B. the type of structure involved
    C. early discovery
    D. availability of personnel to fight the fire
    E. availability of adequate apparatus

12. From the fire prevention standpoint, air conditioning and air blower systems are of concern MAINLY because they

    A. provide a means for the spread of fire through the building served
    B. severely limit adequate ventilation in case of fire
    C. intensify fires from other sources by providing abnormally large amounts of air
    D. characteristically accumulate hazardous quantities of dust and lints which are subject to spontaneous ignition

13. At what interval of time should rubbish and waste material be removed from piers, docks, and wharves?

    A. At least daily
    B. Once per week
    C. As often as needed to prevent dangerous conditions
    D. As fast as accumulated

14. Of the various rooms found in the average school building, which two places deserve MORE consideration from a point of view of preventing personal injuries that may result from panic?
    The

    A. auditorium and the boiler room
    B. classroom on the highest floor and the room in the lowest (basement) part of the building
    C. auditorium and the cafeteria
    D. classroom nearest the auditorium exit and the auditorium itself

15. The underlying reason behind routine periodic and frequent fire-prevention inspection is:

    A. Occupants, hazards, and code compliances may vary considerably in given buildings over a short period
    B. The need for favorable public opinion
    C. A large city usually has many new buildings being constructed
    D. Most individuals continually and consciously try to evade the fire regulations

16. The FIRST objective of all fire prevention is

    A. safeguarding life against fire
    B. reducing insurance rates
    C. preventing property damage
    D. confining fire to a limited area

17. Which one of the following is the cause of the GREATEST number of fires?

    A. Electrical wiring           B. Spontaneous ignition
    C. Sparks on roofs             D. Smoking and matches

18. The type of occupancy in which the LARGEST number of fires occurs is

    A. restaurants and other mercantile establishments
    B. hospitals, theatres, and other public buildings
    C. dwellings, including apartments and hotels
    D. bakeries, cleaning establishments, and other manufacturing plants

19. Which one of the following factors generally should be given the GREATEST right in estimating the fire risk in a general or mixed public warehouse?

    A. Availability of water hydrants to the warehouse
    B. Location of warehouse with respect to other buildings in the area
    C. Intensity and direction of prevailing winds in the area
    D. Kind of merchandise stored in warehouse

20. Of the following, the one which is perhaps the MOST important year-round element in fire prevention in residences is

    A. proper and regular disposal of combustible waste
    B. care in the operation of heating systems
    C. periodic inspections by members of the fire department
    D. radio announcements calling attention to fire hazards in the home

21. The fire-prevention and fire-protection problem resolves itself into three phases, each of which must receive attention. The possibility of human or mechanical failure makes it unsafe to place sole reliance on any one method.
    If two of these phases are preventing the outbreak of fire and preventing the serious spread of fire, then the third phase would be providing for

    A. extensive research in the cause and prevention of non-incendiary fires
    B. the specialized training of fire department personnel at all levels
    C. the prompt detecting and extinguishing of fires
    D. ample modern firefighting equipment

22. The LARGEST cause of apartment and tenement house fires is 22._____

    A. smoking and matches
    B. electrical
    C. gas stoves and explosions
    D. heating equipment

23. Fire-loss statistics show that 90 percent of the losses occur at _____ percent of the fires. 23._____

    A. 10          B. 15          C. 20          D. 30

24. To best analyze the fire prevention and protection problem in a certain section of the city, the MOST basic thing that is necessary to know is the _____ the area. 24._____

    A. number of fire companies in
    B. structural and occupancy data of
    C. number of people living in
    D. available water supply for

25. Of the following, the GREATEST fire hazard in furniture and cabinet shops is 25._____

    A. spontaneous ignition
    B. heating systems in buildings
    C. exposure
    D. misuse of electricity

# KEY (CORRECT ANSWERS)

| | | | |
|---|---|---|---|
| 1. A | | 11. C | |
| 2. C | | 12. A | |
| 3. C | | 13. A | |
| 4. C | | 14. C | |
| 5. B | | 15. A | |
| 6. D | | 16. A | |
| 7. B | | 17. D | |
| 8. A | | 18. C | |
| 9. C | | 19. D | |
| 10. B | | 20. A | |

21. C
22. A
23. A
24. B
25. A

# EXAMINATION SECTION
# TEST 1

DIRECTIONS: Each question or incomplete statement is followed by several suggested answers or completions. Select the one that BEST answers the question or completes the statement. *PRINT THE LETTER OF THE CORRECT ANSWER IN THE SPACE AT THE RIGHT.*

1. Assume that you are making an inspection at a plastics manufacturing factory. The plant manager discusses fire safety procedures with you and tells you that he will be having small-scale bench tests made in order to measure various properties of plastics exposed to fire. The manager tells you he expects to gain certain information from these tests. Of the following, you would be correct in telling him that these tests will be MOST effective in evaluating the

    A. tendency of the plastic to melt and drip
    B. relative combustibility of plastics
    C. composition of products of combustion
    D. methods of installation of plastic parts

    1._____

2. Assume that your division commander has asked you to prepare a report on minimizing the hazard of dust explosions. This is one in a series of reports to be used to guide industrial plant managers in your division on fire safety precautions.
Of the following, it would be MOST appropriate for you to point out that generally

    A. a high level of moisture in the air will be effective in raising the ignition temperature of most dusts and reducing the deflagration once ignition has occurred
    B. relatively small amounts of inert solid powder will be effective in preventing explosions by reducing the combustibility of a dust through heat absorption
    C. removal of high-temperature sources of ignition will be effective in reducing the possibility of explosion because common ignition sources generally do not provide ignition temperatures required for dust explosions
    D. inert gas will be effective in preventing explosions because it dilutes the oxygen to a concentration too low to support combustion

    2._____

3. The selection of smoke removal and venting procedures in hi-rise buildings depends to a large extent on the factors which affect smoke movement in these structures, such as the *stack effect.*
Which one of the following statements about the stack effect is MOST NEARLY correct?

    A. When the outside temperature is much lower than the inside temperature and a fire occurs some distance below the neutral pressure plane, the stack effect will not overcome the fire pressure.
    B. The stack effect will cause smoke and toxic gases to flow through stairwells and elevator shafts, except when the doors of these shafts remain closed.
    C. When the outside temperature is greater than the inside temperature, a reverse stack effect occurs with the upper building opening becoming the inlet and the lower opening the outlet.
    D. The magnitude of the stack effect is a function of building height, air leakage between floors, and the differences between inside and outside temperatures, but is not affected by the air leakage through exterior walls.

    3._____

4. Warehouse fires often present a severe challenge to firefighters. A fire officer inspecting a storage warehouse should be aware of proper indoor storage practices and the use of racks and pallets in such storage.
Which one of the following statements regarding storage practices in warehouses is generally CORRECT?

   A. The arrangement of commodities stored in racks generally provides greater flue spaces both horizontally and vertically than palletized general storage.
   B. Storage of empty plastic pallets within warehouses should be in piles limited to eight feet in height.
   C. Stacking idle pallets in piles is unlikely to promote rapid spread of fire, heat release, and complete combustion.
   D. Storage of empty wood pallets in an unsprinklered warehouse containing other storage should be limited to buildings of fireproof construction.

5. The Fire Code provides that, in a dry cleaning establishment, each room where a washing tank is located must be provided with an approved fire extinguishing system.
The type of system which is specified is a(n) _____ system.

   A. steam                B. carbon dioxide
   C. foam                 D. ordinary sprinkler

6. According to the Fire Code, the MAXIMUM quantity of calcium carbide which may be lawfully stored without a permit is _____ lbs.

   A. 60        B. 80        C. 100        D. 120

7. A Class C refrigerating system, as defined in the Fire Code, is one in which the quantity of refrigerant does NOT exceed _____ lbs.

   A. 20        B. 25        C. 30        D. 35

8. According to the Building Code, a tank used to provide the required primary water supply to a standpipe system may also be used as a supply for an automatic sprinkler system

   A. in all cases where both have been installed
   B. where there are other acceptable sources of water supply for the sprinkler system
   C. only when the standpipe system has a direct connection to the public water system
   D. provided that its capacity is at least five thousand gallons greater than that required for the sprinkler system

9. For computing the capacity of water supplies other than the fire pump, the Building Code assumes that the average discharge, in gallons per minute, from a standard one-half inch sprinkler head is

   A. 20        B. 25        C. 30        D. 35

10. The door that can be closed to separate the bedrooms from the rest of the apartment is the door between the

    A. entrance hall and the bedroom hall
    B. living room and the entrance hall
    C. kitchen and the living room
    D. dining room and the living room

Questions 11-25.

DIRECTIONS: Questions 11 through 25 are to be answered SOLELY on the basis of the following facts and Building Inspection Form. Each box on the form is numbered. Read the facts and review the form before answering the questions.

Firefighters are required to inspect all buildings within their assigned area of the city. They check conditions within the building for violations of fire safety laws. While inspecting a building, they must fill out a Building Inspection Form as a record of the conditions they observed.

On June 12, 2015, Firefighter Edward Gold, assigned to Engine Company 82, is ordered by Captain John Bailey to inspect the building at 1400 Compton Place as part of the engine company's monthly building inspection duty. The building is a one-story brick warehouse where books of the S & G Publishing Company are stored before shipment to stores.

Firefighter Gold enters the warehouse through the main entrance door in the front of the building. Though an exit sign is present above the door, the sign is unlit because of a burned-out bulb. There is a small office to one side of the main entrance area where Firefighter Gold goes to meet the warehouse manager, Mr. Stevens. The firefighter explains the purpose of the inspection.

Firefighter Gold tells the manager that he will check the automatic sprinkler system first because if a fire got started in a warehouse full of stored books, the fire could spread rapidly. He asks Mr. Stevens for the Certificate of Fitness issued to the company employee certified to maintain the sprinkler system in working order. The certificate is dated June 1, 2002, and Gold observes that it has expired. The manager promises to have the certificate renewed as soon as possible.

The firefighter wants to locate the main control valve of the sprinkler system. He asks Mr. Stevens to go with him and show him its location. Gold and the manager leave through an office door which leads into the main working area of the warehouse. They locate the main sprinkler control valve on the wall in a corner of the work area behind high shelves stocked with books. The firefighter observes that the main control valve is sealed in the open position. Gold next climbs a ladder lying against the storage shelves and measures the distance between the top of the stack of books on the highest shelf and the sprinkler heads suspended on pipes below the ceiling. The distance is three feet.

Firefighter Gold next inspects the remaining exits from the building. A large fire door leads out to the loading dock in the rear of the warehouse. A small door on the side of the warehouse that is used by employees when they leave for the day is partially obstructed by cartons. Lighted exit signs can be clearly seen above both doors. During working hours, only the main entrance door and the fire door to the loading dock are unlocked. Mr. Stevens says he keeps the side door locked to keep employees from leaving early and only unlocks it at closing time.

Firefighter Gold and the manager then walk through the main work area. Gold observes that fireproof rubbish receptacles are placed at frequent intervals. However, they are not covered and the contents are overflowing, resulting in several piles of litter on the floor. *No Smok-*

*ing* signs are on the walls of the work area, but are difficult to see behind the rows of high storage shelves.

The two fire extinguishers in the work area are found lying on the floor rather than hung on wall racks. The two other fire extinguishers in the warehouse, one in the office and one in the employee lounge, are both correctly hung on wall racks. All four fire extinguishers are fully charged. According to their tags, they were last inspected on March 11, 2015.

Firefighter Gold continues the inspection by checking on the electrical wiring, which appears to be generally in good condition. However, four switch boxes lack covers. The main junction box has a cover, but it cannot be closed because the cover is corroded.

The inspection is now complete, so Firefighter Gold thanks Mr. Stevens for his cooperation and leaves the building. Gold checks that all required information is entered on the Building Inspection Form, including information concerning building violations. Firefighter Gold signs and dates the Building Inspection Form and then submits it to Captain Bailey for his review. After reviewing Firefighter Gold's report, Captain Bailey signs the Building Inspection Form.

5 (#1)

BUILDING INSPECTION FORM

| DIVISION (1) | BATTALION (2) | COMPANY (3) | |
|---|---|---|---|
| BUILDING INFORMATION | Name of Business (4) | | Address (5) |
| | Type of Business (6) | | Occupancy Code Number (7) |
| CONDITION OF EXITS | Number of Exits (8) | Exits Obstructed (9) | Exits unlocked (10) |
| | Exit Signs (11) | Exit Sign Lights (12) | Fire Doors (13) |
| HOUSEKEEPING CONDITIONS | Rubbish Receptacles (14) | | No Smoking Signs (15) |
| | Clearance of stock in Feet from Sprinkler Heads (16) | | |
| | Electrical Wiring (17) | Switches (18) | Junction Box (19) |
| CONDITION OF FIRE EXTINGUISHERS | Charged (20) | Placement (21) | Date of Last Inspection (22) |
| CONDITION OF AUTOMATIC SPRINKLER SYSTEM | Color of Siamese (23) | Main Control Valve (24) | Shut-off sign (25) |
| | Certificate of Fitness (26) | | Date of Last Inspection (27) |
| SPECIAL CONDITIONS | Rubbish/Obstructions (28) | | Certificate of Occupancy (29) |
| | | | Heavy Load Signs (30) |
| FIRE DEPARTMENT INFORMATION | Inspector Name_____ Signature _____ (31) | | Rank (32) | Date (33) |
| | Officer Name_____ (34) Signature _____ | | Rank (35) | Date (36) |

11. Which one of the following should be entered in Box 3?    11.____

    A.  Ladder Company 79         B.  Engine Company 12
    C.  Ladder Company 140        D.  Engine Company 82

12. Which one of the following should be entered in Box 4? _____ Company.   12.____

    A.  G & R Printing            B.  S & G Printing
    C.  R & G Publishing          D.  S & G Publishing

13. Which one of the following should be entered in Box 8?    13.____

    A.  2        B.  3        C.  4        D.  5

14. Which one of the following should be entered in Box 9? _____ door.    14.____

    A.  Office   B.  Side     C.  Main     D.  Fire

15. Which one of the following should be entered in Box 10? _____ door and _____ door.   15.____

    A.  Fire; main                B.  Side; office
    C.  Fire; side                D.  Main; cellar

16. The entry in Box 12 should show that replacement bulbs are needed for _____ light(s).   16.____

    A.  one      B.  two      C.  three    D.  all

17. The entry in Box 14 should show that covers are missing from _____ of the rubbish receptacles.   17.____

    A.  two      B.  three    C.  four     D.  all

18. Which one of the following should be entered in Box 16?   18.____

    A.  One and one-half          B.  Two
    C.  Two and one-half          D.  Three

19. Which one of the following should be entered in Box 19?   19.____

    A.  Faulty circuits           B.  Exposed wiring
    C.  Corroded cover            D.  Good condition

20. Which one of the following entries about the placement of fire extinguishers should appear in Box 21?   20.____

    A.  One on the floor; three hung on wall racks
    B.  Two on the floor; two hung on wall racks
    C.  Three on the floor; one hung on wall rack
    D.  Four hung on wall racks

21. Which one of the following should be entered in Box 22?   21.____

    A.  June 1, 2012              B.  May 21, 2014
    C.  March 11, 2015            D.  May 1, 2015

22. The entry in Box 24 should show that the position of the main control valve is   22.____

    A.  open                      B.  half open
    C.  one-third closed          D.  closed

23. Which one of the following should be entered in Box 26?    23._____

    A. Expired                B. Missing from file
    C. Never issued           D. Current

24. Which one of the following should be entered in Box 28?    24._____

    A. Ceiling plaster cracked
    B. Rubbish piles litter work floor
    C. Second floor stairway blocked
    D. Open paint cans on loading dock

25. Which one of the following should be entered in Box 34?    25._____

    A. John Bailey            B. Edward Gold
    C. John Gold              D. Edward Bailey

---

# KEY (CORRECT ANSWERS)

| | | | |
|---|---|---|---|
| 1. | D | 11. | D |
| 2. | A | 12. | D |
| 3. | D | 13. | B |
| 4. | C | 14. | B |
| 5. | A | 15. | A |
| 6. | D | 16. | A |
| 7. | A | 17. | D |
| 8. | D | 18. | D |
| 9. | A | 19. | C |
| 10. | A | 20. | B |

21. C
22. A
23. A
24. B
25. A

---

# TEST 2

DIRECTIONS: Each question or incomplete statement is followed by several suggested answers or completions. Select the one that BEST answers the question or completes the statement. *PRINT THE LETTER OF THE CORRECT ANSWER IN THE SPACE AT THE RIGHT.*

1. The materials of which a building are constructed and the opportunities for the spread of fire are important, but the GREATEST single hazard is usually that of     1._____

   A. occupancy            B. location
   C. fire protective measures   D. construction

2. A warehouse with a leaky roof contains a large amount of building material. The one of the following materials which is MOST likely to set fire to the warehouse is     2._____

   A. gasoline   B. crude oil
   C. lime       D. kerosene

3. For the most effective results in conducting a Fire Prevention Week campaign, it would be DESIRABLE to emphasize fire prevention     3._____

   A. in its broader community aspects
   B. as a means of lowering insurance rates
   C. as it applies to the individuals' own homes
   D. as a means of lowering operating costs of the fire department

4. Floor or wall openings sometimes prevent the banking up of heated air. This condition, with respect to sprinklers, is considered     4._____

   A. advantageous   B. unimportant
   C. detrimental    D. good ventilation

5. The BEST all-round fireproofing material, due to its high resistance to heat, its lightness, its great strength, its adaptability to any shape, and which is also very easily repaired when damaged by a severe fire, is     5._____

   A. brick     B. hollow clay tile
   C. gypsum    D. concrete

6. Commercial storage and industrial occupancies are classified in the Fire Code as     6._____

   A. highly hazardous     B. moderately hazardous
   C. lightly hazardous    D. all of the above

7. An unusually large number of fires of *unknown cause* is characteristic of the fires involving     7._____

   A. restaurants        B. warehouses
   C. mercantile stores  D. hospitals

8. It is obvious that where a division wall is not continued through the roof, and where the roof is combustible on both sides of the wall, fire is almost certain to spread beyond the wall if the fire is of any duration. According to the above statement, there is NEED of     8._____

   A. parapets                      B. more resistive division walls
   C. fire-stopping of roof spaces  D. fire-stopping division walls

9. The hazard of flammable gases is generally _____ to that of flammable liquids.    9._____

   A. opposite           B. dissimilar
   C. similar            D. identical

10. The MOST important factor that would materially decrease large-loss supermarket fires is    10._____

    A. education of the general public
    B. separating the utility area from the rest of the building by a fire-resistive wall
    C. maintenance of an adequate supply of fire extinguishers
    D. keeping all aisles clear of merchandise and storage

11. The PRIMARY difference between the large number of small fires that produces a small percentage of total losses, and the smaller number of large fires that accounts for 95 percent of the total loss in the United States is usually    11._____

    A. the nature of the material involved in the fire
    B. the type of structure involved
    C. early discovery
    D. availability of personnel to fight the fire

12. From the fire prevention standpoint, air conditioning and air blower systems are of concern MAINLY because they    12._____

    A. provide a means for the spread of fire through the building served
    B. severely limit adequate ventilation in case of fire
    C. intensify fires from other sources by providing abnormally large amounts of air
    D. characteristically accumulate hazardous quantities of dust and lints which are subject to spontaneous ignition

13. At what interval of time should rubbish and waste materials be removed from piers, docks, and wharves?    13._____

    A. At least daily
    B. Once per week
    C. As often as needed to prevent dangerous condition
    D. As fast as accumulated

14. Of the various rooms found in the average school building, which two places deserve MORE consideration from a point of view of preventing personal injuries that may result from panic?    14._____
    The

    A. auditorium and the boiler room
    B. classroom on the highest floor and the room in the lowest (basement) part of the building
    C. auditorium and the cafeteria
    D. classroom nearest the auditorium exit and the auditorium itself

15. The underlying reason behind routine periodic and frequent fire prevention inspection is:

    A. Occupants, hazards, and code compliances may vary considerably in given buildings over a short period
    B. The need for favorable public opinion
    C. A large city usually has many new buildings being constructed
    D. Most individuals continually and consciously try to evade the fire regulations

16. The FIRST objective of all fire prevention is

    A. safeguarding life against fire
    B. reducing insurance rates
    C. preventing property damage
    D. confining fire to a limited area

17. Which one of the following is the cause of the GREATEST number of fires?

    A. Electrical wiring         B. Spontaneous ignition
    C. Sparks on roofs           D. Smoking and matches

18. The type of occupancy in which the LARGEST number of fires occurs is

    A. restaurants and other mercantile establishments
    B. hospitals, theatres, and other public buildings
    C. dwellings, including apartments and hotels
    D. bakeries, cleaning establishments, and other manufacturing plants

19. Which one of the following factors generally should be given the GREATEST right in estimating the fire risk in a general or mixed public warehouse?

    A. Availability of water hydrants to the warehouse
    B. Location of warehouse with respect to other buildings in the area
    C. Intensity and direction of prevailing winds in the area
    D. Kind of merchandise stored in the warehouse

20. Of the following, the one which is perhaps the MOST important year-round element in fire prevention in residences is

    A. proper and regular disposal of combustible waste
    B. care in the operation of heating systems
    C. periodic inspections by members of the fire department
    D. radio announcements calling attention to fire hazards in the home

21. The fire prevention and fire protection problem resolves itself into three phases, each of which must receive attention. The possibility of human or mechanical failure makes it unsafe to place sole reliance on any one method. If two of these phases are preventing the outbreak of fire and preventing the serious spread of fire, then the third phase would be providing for

    A. extensive research in the cause and prevention of non-incendiary fires
    B. the specialized training of fire department personnel at all levels
    C. the prompt detecting and extinguishing of fire
    D. ample modern firefighting equipment

22. The LARGEST cause of apartment and tenement house fires is 22.____
    A. smoking and matches
    B. electrical
    C. gas stoves and explosions
    D. heating equipment

23. Fire loss statistics show that 90 percent of the losses occur at _____ percent of the fires. 23.____
    A. 10   B. 15   C. 20   D. 30

24. To best analyze the fire prevention and protection problem in a certain section of the city, the MOST basic thing that is necessary to know is the _____ the area. 24.____
    A. number of fire companies in
    B. structural and occupancy data of
    C. number of people living in
    D. available water supply for

25. Of the following, the GREATEST fire hazard in furniture and cabinet shops is 25.____
    A. spontaneous ignition
    B. heating systems in buildings
    C. exposure
    D. misuse of electricity

## KEY (CORRECT ANSWERS)

| | | | |
|---|---|---|---|
| 1. A | | 11. C | |
| 2. C | | 12. A | |
| 3. C | | 13. A | |
| 4. C | | 14. C | |
| 5. B | | 15. A | |
| 6. D | | 16. A | |
| 7. B | | 17. D | |
| 8. A | | 18. C | |
| 9. C | | 19. D | |
| 10. B | | 20. A | |

21. C
22. A
23. A
24. B
25. A

# TEST 3

DIRECTIONS: Each question or incomplete statement is followed by several suggested answers or completions. Select the one that BEST answers the question or completes the statement. *PRINT THE LETTER OF THE CORRECT ANSWER IN THE SPACE AT THE RIGHT.*

1. On inspection of a 5-story building, you find that only half of the required stairways serving the top floor continue to the roof.
   This condition is legal if the building is a(n)

   A. warehouse
   B. school
   C. office building
   D. department store

   1._____

2. In order to determine whether a building in a county is within the fire limits, one of the sources you should check is the maps that are part of the

   A. Administrative Code
   B. most recent zoning resolution
   C. zoning resolution in force
   D. Sanborn maps

   2._____

3. During inspection of a motion picture theatre, you find 6 reels of safety film in closed containers in the manager's office.
   This condition is

   A. *legal* because the film is safety film
   B. *illegal* because film may not be kept in an office
   C. *legal* because there is less than 25,000 feet of film
   D. *illegal* because the film must be kept in a vented metal cabinet

   3._____

4. A two-story, two-family dwelling has been converted to three-family use. There is only one stairway to the street. There is no fire escape. The stairs are not enclosed with fire-regarded partitions. The doors to the apartments are self-closing, but are not fireproof. Of the following statements, the one that is MOST complete and accurate is that the condition described

   A. *conforms* to the requirements of the Multiple Dwelling Law
   B. *does not conform* to the requirements of the Multiple Dwelling Law because the apartment doors should be fireproof
   C. *does not conform* to the requirements of the Multiple Dwelling Law because the apartment doors should be fireproof and the stair hall should be enclosed
   D. *does not conform* to the requirements of the Multiple Dwelling Law because the apartment doors should be fireproof, the stair hall should be enclosed, and a second means of egress should be provided

   4._____

5. On fire prevention inspection, you find a revolving door being used as a required means of egress from the lobby of a hospital.
   This condition is

   A. *illegal*
   B. *legal* only if the door is a type A revolving door
   C. *legal* only if the door is a type B revolving door
   D. *legal* only if all other required means of egress are swinging doors

   5._____

6. The time of day when the GREATEST number of fires occur is from  6.____

   A. Midnight to 6 A.M.  B. 6 A.M. to 12 Noon
   C. 12 Noon to 6 P.M.  D. 6 P.M. to Midnight

7. Of the following types of industrial organizations, the one in which the GREATEST number of fires occur is  7.____

   A. newspaper and printing shops
   B. carpet and rug factories
   C. foundries, metal works, and machine shops
   D. paint, oil, and varnish factories

8. The fire department and the United States Coast Guard have agreed on a program for coordinating their fire prevention activities on the city waterfront.  8.____
   Part of this agreement provides for notification of the other party whenever

   A. any violation is discovered
   B. any serious violation is discovered
   C. any violation is discovered and is not abated within 10 days
   D. any violation is discovered involving a matter under the jurisdiction of the other party

9. A company on AFID makes a complete inspection of a 12-story commercial building occupied as follows:  9.____

   Alpha Co. - floors 1 through 5 and half of 6
   Beta Co. - half of 6 and all of 7
   Delta Co. - part of 8
   Gamma Co. - part of 8
   Epsilon Co. - part of 8

   All other floors - each occupied by single companies According to Regulations, the number of inspections to be recorded on reports for statistical purposes is MOST NEARLY

   A. 12  B. 13  C. 16  D. 18

10. The division coordinator is authorized to discontinue the use of individual inspectors for inspections generally performed by companies on AFID. This action is to be taken when the company  10.____

    A. is up to date on its inspection schedule for the year
    B. is 10 percent ahead of its inspection schedule for the year
    C. has completed sufficient number of inspections to assure completion of its schedule for the year
    D. has completed its regular inspection schedule for the year

Questions 11-15.

DIRECTIONS: Column I lists five properties of fire extinguishers. Column II lists various types of fire extinguishers. For each property in Column I, select the fire extinguisher from Column II having that property and place the letter next to the extinguisher in the properly numbered space.

| COLUMN I | COLUMN II | |
|---|---|---|
| 11. Contains aluminum sulphate in solution | A. Water gas cartridge expelled | 11.____ |
| 12. Water in extinguishing agent will cause corrosion of container | B. Antifreeze (water mixed with antifreeze chemical) | 12.____ |
| 13. Usually contains sodium chloride | C. Carbon dioxide | 13.____ |
|  | D. Foam |  |
| 14. Produces a mass of bubbles filled with $CO_2$ gas | E. Carbon tetrachloride | 14.____ |
| 15. Inspection check by weighing extinguisher only |  | 15.____ |

16. Of the following categories by means of which structured fires were extended during the last few years, the MOST common involved was

    A. cocklofts
    B. partitions
    C. stairways
    D. doors

17. The one of the following which is NOT required by the housing maintenance code for the protection of openings into public halls in old-law tenements less than four stories high is that *every*

    A. door opening into the public hall shall be fireproof, having a fire-resisting rating of at least one hour
    B. door opening into the public hall shall be self-closing
    C. glazed panel in a door opening into a public hall shall be glazed with wire glass
    D. transom opening upon any public hall shall be glazed with wire glass and firmly secured in a closed position

18. Firestopping of the space above a hung ceiling into areas not exceeding 3,000 square feet is REQUIRED when the

    A. structural members within the concealed space are individually protected with materials having the required fire resistance
    B. concealed space is sprinklered
    C. ceiling contributes to the required fire resistance of the floor or roof assembly
    D. ceiling is not an essential part of the fire-resistive assembly

19. When a deluge sprinkler system is provided around the perimeter of a theater stage, manual operating devices as well as automatic controls are required by the building code.
    The MOST complete and accurate statement concerning these manual operating devices is that they should be located

    A. at the emergency control station
    B. adjacent to one exit from the stage
    C. at the emergency control station and adjacent to one exit from the stage
    D. at the emergency control station, adjacent to one exit from the stage, and at the deluge valve

20. Yellow painted Siamese caps on office buildings will indicate that the Siamese serves ONLY

    A. the standpipe in pressurized stairs
    B. the sprinklers in sub-basement locations
    C. a combination standpipe and sprinkler system
    D. as a supply line to the fire pump for the upper level standpipe outlets

21. A fireman, on his way to work, is stopped by a citizen who complains that the employees of a nearby store frequently pile empty crates and boxes in a doorway, blocking passage.
    The one of the following which would be the MOST appropriate action for the fireman to take is to

    A. assure the citizen that the fire department's inspectional activities will eventually *catch up* with the store
    B. obtain the address of the store and investigate to determine whether the citizen's complaint is justified
    C. obtain the address of the store and report the complaint to his superior officer
    D. ask the citizen for specific dates on which this practice has occurred to determine whether the complaint is justified

22. In the Halon coding system, each digit represents the number of atoms while the position of the digit in the number represents a specific chemical element.
    For Halon number 1202, the number 1 indicates that the molecule contains one atom of

    A. bromine    B. carbon    C. chlorine    D. fluorine

23. A street vault incident described in a department safety bulletin explains how two persons were asphyxiated when they descended into the vault.
    Tests of the atmosphere of the vault showed that the hazard was due to

    A. light smoke and flames generated by burning synthetic insulation
    B. gasoline vapors from a leaking underground tank
    C. replacement of oxygen by carbon dioxide
    D. natural gas entering the vault

24. It is sometimes necessary to make a simple field test to determine the flammability of decorative materials.
    Of the following, the one that generally produces the LEAST reliable results when tested by exposure to a small flame is

    A. all-glass fabric
    B. untreated cotton cloth
    C. flame-retardant treated paper
    D. flexible plastic film

25. The one of the following substances with the LEAST tendency to spontaneous heating is

    A. fish meal          B. lamp black
    C. scrap rubber       D. soap powder

## KEY (CORRECT ANSWERS)

1. B
2. C
3. B
4. A
5. A

6. C
7. C
8. B
9. C
10. C

11. D
12. E
13. B
14. D
15. C

16. B
17. A
18. C
19. C
20. C

21. C
22. B
23. D
24. D
25. B

# TEST 4

DIRECTIONS: Each question or incomplete statement is followed by several suggested answers or completions. Select the one that BEST answers the question or completes the statement. *PRINT THE LETTER OF THE CORRECT ANSWER IN THE SPACE AT THE RIGHT.*

1. Every applicant for a certificate of license to install underground gasoline storage tanks is required to      1.____

    A. be a resident of the city and maintain a place of business in the city
    B. file a bond and evidence of liability insurance
    C. be a resident of the city or maintain a place of business in the city
    D. pass a written examination given by the fire department

2. After firing a blast, the licensed blaster at a construction site discovered that one charge had not detonated and the exact direction of the drill hole could not be determined. The licensed blaster under the supervision and orders of the walking boss used a metal scraper to remove the tamping, after which the hole was reloaded and fired. This action      2.____

    A. complies with the Fire Prevention Code
    B. violates the Code because a metal scraper was used
    C. violates the Code because the Fire Commissioner's approval is required before charges are removed
    D. violates the Code because no notification was given to the Division of Fire Prevention concerning the incident

3. The Fire Prevention Code specifies that a special permit is required for each of the following EXCEPT      3.____

    A. refining petroleum collected from oil separators or manufacturing plants
    B. loading of small arms ammunition by hand in a retail store selling ammunition
    C. operating a wholesale drug or chemical house
    D. generating acetylene gas

4. The one of the following that is the MOST acceptable statement concerning the fire protection for the truck loading rack in a bulk oil terminal is that the rack must be equipped with a      4.____

    A. water spray system, automatically controlled
    B. foam system, remote manually controlled
    C. water spray system, remote manually controlled
    D. foam system, automatically controlled

5. A fire insurance inspector suggested to the manager of a fireproof warehouse that bags of flour be stacked on skids (wooden platforms 6" high, 6x6 feet in area).
Of the following, the BEST justification for this suggestion is that, in the event of a fire, the bags on skids are LESS likely to      5.____

    A. topple
    B. be damaged by water used in extinguishment
    C. catch fire
    D. be ripped by fire equipment

27

6. Permitting piles of scrap paper cuttings to accumulate in a factory building is a bad practice CHIEFLY because they may

   A. ignite spontaneously
   B. interfere with fire extinguishment operations
   C. catch fire from a spark
   D. interfere with escape of occupants if a fire occurs

7. Firefighters are inspecting a furniture factory. During the inspection, they find employees smoking cigarettes in various areas.
   In which area does smoking pose the GREATEST danger of causing a fire?

   A. Employee lounge        B. Woodworking shop
   C. A private office       D. A rest room

8. The MAXIMUM quantity of paints which may be manufactured or stored without a permit, according to the Fire Prevention Code, is _____ gallons.

   A. 20    B. 25    C. 30    D. 50

9. Oil separators are required by the Administrative Code before issuance of a permit to a garage for the storage of volatile inflammable oil if the garage accommodates _____ or more motor vehicles.

   A. four    B. five    C. six    D. ten

10. *The term cellar, as used in the Building Code, shall mean a story having _____ of its height, measured from finished floor to finished ceiling, below the curb level at the center of the street front.*
    The one of the following which, when filled in the blank space, BEST completes the sentence is

    A. more than one-half
    B. no more than one-half
    C. more than three-quarters
    D. no more than three-quarters

11. The Oil Burner Rules of the Board of Standards and Appeals state, *No movable combustible materials shall be stored or maintained within _____ feet of heating apparatus, except where same is protected by fire-retarding material.*
    The one of the following numbers which, when inserted in the blank space above, MOST accurately completes the sentence is

    A. 2    B. 3    C. 4    D. 5

12. As used in the Building Code, the term *horizontal exit* refers to a(n)

    A. exit door on the ground floor which is at the same level as the street grade
    B. corridor or hallway leading to the exit stairs
    C. fire escape with the balcony at the same level as the floor
    D. connection between two floor areas through a fire wall

13. According to the Building Code, a required exit stairway enclosure in a public building MUST have a fire resistance rating of _____ hour(s).

    A. 1    B. 2    C. 3    D. 4

14. A recently enacted section of the Fire Prevention Code places limitations on the use of kerosene-burning equipment.
    When all the provisions of this section of the Code are in full effect, the one of the following uses of kerosene-burning equipment which will NOT be permitted is equipment used exclusively for

    A. cooking purposes
    B. lighting purposes
    C. demonstration and sales purposes
    D. heating purposes in any building in an area not supplied with permanent piped gas

14.____

15. The provisions of the Building Code require that in a building more than two stories high, the required stairways must all continue to the roof EXCEPT in a(n)

    A. office building          B. school building
    C. theater                  D. storage warehouse

15.____

16. The definition of *non-combustible* in the Building Code was recently amended with regard to acoustical and thermal insulation.
    Which one of the following would be *non-combustible* according to the Code?
    Insulation with a flame-spread rating not greater than _____, smoke-developed rating not greater than _____.

    A. 25; 50      B. 50; 50      C. 50; 75      D. 75; 100

16.____

17. A new school dormitory is two stories and less than thirty feet in height. Inspection reveals that there is only one stairway from the second floor and the maximum travel distance to the stair enclosure is 80 feet. The stair enclosure and corridors are provided with automatic sprinkler protection.
    With respect to the provisions of the Building Code as it applies to this situation, it would be MOST appropriate to state that this building

    A. complies with the Code
    B. does not comply with the Code because the maximum travel distance is excessive
    C. does not comply with the Code because two exits remote from each other on each story are lacking
    D. does not comply with the Code because the sprinkler system was not extended into the rooms

17.____

18. Of the following statements, the one that is LEAST in accord with the material and equipment requirements for oil spill control at bulk storage plants and petroleum product pipelines is that

    A. all material and equipment must be of a type acceptable to the Fire Commissioner
    B. dispersants should be used only when directed by the fire department, Coast Guard, or Corps of Engineers
    C. pipeline operators shall provide at least one vacuum truck
    D. the minimum amount of absorbent material at any plant shall be 2,000 pounds

18.____

19. In a high-rise office building over 100 feet in height, the doors opening into interior stair enclosures may NOT be locked from either side at intervals of four stories or less EXCEPT where

    A. the building is equipped with an approved automatic sprinkler system
    B. the doors are equipped with an automatic fail-safe system for opening doors
    C. the second means of egress is a standard fire tower
    D. every floor of the building has a fire warden on duty

20. The Rules of the Board of Standards and Appeals require that combustible materials used for decorative purposes within special occupancy structures be made flameproof. Approval of flameproof materials is

    A. valid for an indefinite period
    B. limited to a period of 6 months
    C. limited to a period of 1 year
    D. limited to a period of 2 years

21. *A multiple dwelling, according to the Multiple Dwelling Law, is a dwelling occupied as the residence of _____ or more families living independently of each other.*
    The one of the following numbers which, when inserted in the blank space above, MOST accurately completes the sentence is

    A. 2   B. 3   C. 4   D. 5

22. The one of the following statements that is MOST accurate is that in multiple dwellings, windows at grade levels at sidewalks, yards, or courts may

    A. not have bars
    B. have bars provided that they are easily removed from the inside of the window
    C. have bars but at least one window in each room must be without bars
    D. have bars but at least one window in each apartment must be without bars

23. The number of extra sprinkler heads which must be kept in the premises of a building with an automatic sprinkler system, according to the Building Code, is

    A. 10
    B. 10 percent of the number of sprinkler heads in the entire system
    C. 6
    D. 6 percent of the number of sprinkler heads in the entire system

24. The Building Code requires that standpipe systems be equipped with pressure reducing valves where the normal hydrostatic pressure at a 2 1/2" hose outlet valve exceeds _____ lbs. per square inch.

    A. 50   B. 55   C. 60   D. 65

25. Walls of structures used for public entertainment may be covered with combustible wall coverings, according to the Building Code, provided that the

    A. wall covering is pasted or cemented directly to the plaster surfaces of the wall
    B. wall covering does not extend more than six feet in height
    C. building is a Class 1 fireproof structure
    D. building has a seating capacity of 600 people or less

## KEY (CORRECT ANSWERS)

1. C
2. A
3. D
4. C
5. B

6. C
7. B
8. A
9. B
10. A

11. D
12. D
13. C
14. D
15. B

16. A
17. A
18. B
19. B
20. C

21. B
22. D
23. C
24. B
25. A

# EXAMINATION SECTION
# TEST 1

DIRECTIONS: Each question or incomplete statement is followed by several suggested answers or completions. Select the one that BEST answers the question or completes the statement. *PRINT THE LETTER OF THE CORRECT ANSWER IN THE SPACE AT THE RIGHT.*

1. Of the following materials, the one which has the HIGHEST tendency to spontaneous heating is

    A. lanolin
    B. linseed oil
    C. coconut oil
    D. turpentine

    1._____

2. The one of the following fabrics used in the manufacture of clothing that is MOST flammable is

    A. wool
    B. acetate
    C. cotton
    D. linen

    2._____

3. Which of the following substances has the LOWEST boiling point?

    A. Turpentine
    B. Benzene
    C. Mineral spirits
    D. Cellosolve

    3._____

4. Which of the following non-solid fuels has the HIGHEST ignition temperature?

    A. Acetone
    B. Carbon monoxide
    C. Ethylene
    D. Methyl alcohol

    4._____

5. Assume that the cellar of a building is 100 feet long, 100 feet wide, and 10 feet high. If natural gas were distributed evenly throughout the cellar, and all openings from the cellar are closed, which one of the following volumes of natural gas would create an explosive atmosphere if suddenly released into this cellar?
    _____ cubic feet.

    A. 2,500
    B. 7,500
    C. 17,500
    D. 25,000

    5._____

6. A lighted cigarette is LEAST likely to start a fire if dropped and left

    A. on a kapok pillow
    B. on cotton bed clothes
    C. in an explosive vapor-air mixture
    D. on dry grass

    6._____

7. A fire marshal inspecting a number of buildings where explosions are suspected as having been caused by dynamite would find that the scene of the dynamite explosion is MOST likely the one where

    A. a large section of wall has toppled, with its mortar remaining intact
    B. there are fragments of shattered cast iron
    C. a window frame has been pushed out from the wall surface, with some or all of the windows remaining intact
    D. the light bulbs in the building have remained unbroken

    7._____

8. During apparatus field inspection of a restaurant located in a building erected in 1972, a fireman finds that the filters for the cooking equipment exhaust system are cleaned every three months and the entire system is cleaned once a year.
This maintenance procedure is

   A. correct
   B. incorrect, because the filters should be discarded at least every three months and the system cleaned at least once a year
   C. incorrect, because the filters should be discarded at least once a year and the system cleaned at least once a year
   D. incorrect, because both the filters and the entire system should be cleaned at least every three months

9. A group home is a facility for the care and maintenance of not less than three nor more than twelve children and is classified by the building code in the same occupancy group as a one-family dwelling.
This much of the definition of a group home GENERALLY is

   A. correct
   B. incorrect, because a group home may not have less than seven children
   C. incorrect, because a group home is for adults, not children
   D. incorrect, because a group home is classified in the same occupancy group as a rooming house

10. A fifty-foot high, five-story multiple dwelling built in 1974 has a floor area of 7,000 square feet on each floor. It is equipped with a non-automatic dry standpipe system. During apparatus field inspection duty, a member discovers that a control valve on the standpipe is in closed position with no placard indicating that this was the normal position of the valve. Further investigation reveals that there is no one in the building who has a certificate of fitness to maintain the standpipe system. Of the following statements concerning the above situation, the one that is CORRECT is that the situation as described is

    A. legal
    B. illegal, because an individual with a certificate of fitness must be on the premises
    C. illegal, because an automatic system is required
    D. illegal, because the control valve must be in the open position

11. A tank truck with a capacity of 4,400 gallons is delivering #4 fuel oil to a multiple dwelling. According to the specifications for tank trucks, the person in control of the truck and supervising this delivery

    A. *does not* require a certificate of fitness because the capacity of the tank is less than 5,000 gallons
    B. *does not* require a certificate of fitness because the tank has light oil
    C. *does not* require a certificate of fitness because the delivery is being made to a non-commercial occupancy
    D. *requires* a certificate of fitness because a fire department permit is needed for all tank trucks delivering #4 fuel oil

12. The multiple dwelling law states that sprinkler systems in lodging houses shall have a supervisory and maintenance service satisfactory to the fire department. The fire department requires a valid inspection of the sprinkler control valve AT LEAST once

A. daily B. semi-weekly
C. weekly D. monthly

13. Anhydrous ammonia is being used in a duplicating machine located in a school office. There is no one in the school with a certificate of fitness for the storage and use of ammonia or for the servicing of the duplicating machine. In this situation, a certificate of fitness is GENERALLY

    A. *not* required because the machine is considered office equipment
    B. *not* required unless the quantity of anhydrous ammonia being stored on the premises is more than two 150-lb. cylinders
    C. *not* required because schools, with regular supervised fire drills, are exempt from certain requirements of the fire prevention code
    D. *required* whether or not a permit is needed under the fire prevention code

14. According to the labor law, fire drills are required to be conducted in certain factory buildings.
    Which of the following statements is CORRECT with respect to such fire drills?

    A. Fire drills are required to be conducted in every factory building in which there are more than 75 persons above or below the street floor.
    B. Fire drills are not required to be conducted in factory buildings less than 100 feet in height.
    C. Fire drills are required to be conducted in every factory building over two stories in height in which more than twenty-five persons are employed above the ground floor unless the sprinkler system and number of occupants of the building are in accordance with the other provisions of the labor law.
    D. The sprinklering of a factory building is not a factor in determining whether or not a building is required to conduct fire drills.

15. An officer tells members during a drill that a red light and a placard should serve to locate the Siamese hose connection of a temporary standpipe system in a building under construction.
    The officer's instructions are

    A. *correct,* because both the red light and a placard are required
    B. *incorrect,* because only the red light is required
    C. *incorrect,* because only a placard is required
    D. *incorrect,* because neither the red light nor a placard is required

16. During apparatus field inspection duty, a fireman inspecting a 40-story office building occupied by 1,000 people is unable to find a fire safety director or deputy fire safety director in the building. The manager of the building states that the fire safety director is out to lunch, that there is no deputy fire safety director, and that he, the manager, is acting as the fire safety director pending the return of the fire safety director. Because the manager does not have a fire safety director certificate of fitness, the fireman issues a violation to him.
    The fireman's action in this situation is

A. *correct,* because local law requires a fire safety director with a certificate of fitness in a building this high to be on duty whenever the building is occupied by more than 500 people
B. *incorrect,* because local law permits the fire safety director to be temporarily relieved, for short intervals, by responsible individuals who do not have the required certificate of fitness
C. *correct,* because local law requires a fire safety director with a certificate of fitness to be on duty in a building this high, regardless of the occupancy of the building
D. *incorrect,* because whenever local law is not complied with, a referral report should be forwarded, and no violation issued

17. A commercial vehicle without a fire department permit is transporting 500 pounds of dynamite from a neighboring outside county through the city to another out-of-town county without stopping to make any deliveries enroute. There is no department pumping engine escort. The situation as described is

   A. *legal,* because the shipment contains less than 1,000 pounds of dynamite
   B. *illegal,* because a pumping engine escort is required whenever explosives are transported without a fire department permit through the city
   C. *legal,* even though a fire department permit has not been issued, because the shipment does not contain any blasting caps
   D. *illegal,* because dynamite may not be transported through the city from one out-of-town location to another

18. Of the following exit doors in buildings erected in 1976, the one that does NOT have to swing outward is a(n)

   A. corridor door from a room used for office purposes with an occupancy of 80 persons
   B. corridor door from a lecture room in a school building where the room has an occupancy of 80 persons
   C. exterior street-floor exit door from a space 2,000 square feet in area in a business building, where the space is occupied by fewer than 50 persons and the maximum travel distance to the door is 50 feet
   D. exterior street-floor exit door from a lobby in a hotel, where the lobby will not be occupied by more than 50 persons and the maximum travel distance to the door is 50 feet

19. During apparatus field inspection duty, a fireman inspecting a 90-foot high apartment house erected in 1972 finds that the standpipe hose is missing from every hose rack in the building. Of the following statements concerning this situation, the one that is CORRECT is that

   A. the situation as described may be legal but the fire-man needs additional information to make a final decision
   B. all such buildings, regardless of when erected, must have the standpipe hose racks equipped with hose
   C. all such buildings, if erected under the new building code, must have their standpipe hose racks equipped with hose
   D. the situation as described would be acceptable for an office building but not for an apartment house

20. A permit is required to store empty combustible packing boxes in a building whenever the    20.____

    A. boxes occupy more than two thousand cubic feet
    B. storage space is less than 50 feet from the nearest wall of a building occupied as a hospital, school, or theater
    C. boxes are of cardboard or similarly combustible material
    D. building is of non-fireproof construction

21. An inspector, taking some clothing to a dry cleaner in his neighborhood, noticed that    21.____
inflammable cleaning fluid was stored in a way which created a fire hazard. The fireman called this to the attention of the proprietor, explaining the danger involved.
This method of handling the situation was

    A. *bad;* the fireman should not have interfered in a matter which was not his responsibility
    B. *good;* the proprietor would probably remove the hazard and be more careful in the future
    C. *bad;* the fireman should have reported the situation to the fire inspector's office without saying anything to the proprietor
    D. *good;* since the fireman was a customer, he should treat the proprietor more leniently than he would treat other violators

22. According to the Building Code, a vertical iron ladder to an escape manhole opening in    22.____
the sidewalk is required from a cellar room when the room is being used as a

    A. coal storage room         B. restaurant kitchen
    C. boiler room               D. factory

23. In a building of public assembly, the provisions of the Fire Prevention Code prohibit the    23.____
use of decorations, drapes, or scenery made of combustible material which have not been rendered fireproof.
Of the following types of occupancies, the one that is exempt from the provisions of this section is a

    A. school       B. hospital       C. church       D. museum

24. As used in the Building Code, a *4-hour fire rating* of a wall means that in a standard fire    24.____
test of four hours duration, the

    A. wall will not collapse
    B. unexposed side of the wall will not char or smolder
    C. temperature on the unexposed side of the wall will not rise
    D. temperature on the unexposed side of the wall will not rise more than a predetermined amount

25. The prohibition against smoking in retail stores applies    25.____

    A. to all stores
    B. only to stores employing more than 25 persons
    C. only to stores accommodating more than 300 persons
    D. only to stores employing more than 25 persons or accommodating more than 300 persons

## KEY (CORRECT ANSWERS)

1. C
2. D
3. B
4. D
5. C

6. C
7. A
8. D
9. B
10. D

11. D
12. C
13. D
14. C
15. A

16. D
17. B
18. C
19. A
20. A

21. B
22. C
23. C
24. D
25. A

———

# TEST 2

DIRECTIONS: Each question or incomplete statement is followed by several suggested answers or completions. Select the one that BEST answers the question or completes the statement. *PRINT THE LETTER OF THE CORRECT ANSWER IN THE SPACE AT THE RIGHT.*

1. The one of the following which is NOT required by the Code for the protection of openings into public halls in old-law tenements less than four stories high is that every  1.____

   A. door opening into the public hall shall be fireproof, having a fire-resisting rating of at least one hour
   B. door opening into the public hall shall be self-closing
   C. glazed panel in a door opening into a public hall shall be glazed with wire glass
   D. transom opening upon any public hall shall be glazed with wire glass and firmly secured in a closed position

2. Firestopping of the space above a hung ceiling into areas not exceeding 3,000 square feet is REQUIRED when the  2.____

   A. structural members within the concealed space are individually protected with materials having the required fire resistance
   B. concealed space is sprinklered
   C. ceiling contributes to the required fire resistance of the floor or roof assembly
   D. ceiling is not an essential part of the fire-resistive assembly

3. When a deluge sprinkler system is provided around the perimeter of a theater stage, manual operating devices as well as automatic controls are required by the Building Code.  3.____
   The MOST complete and accurate statement concerning these manual operating devices is that they should be located

   A. at the emergency control station
   B. adjacent to one exit from the stage
   C. at the emergency control station and adjacent to one exit from the stage
   D. at the emergency control station, adjacent to one exit from the stage, and at the deluge valve

4. Yellow painted Siamese caps on office buildings will indicate that the Siamese serves ONLY  4.____

   A. the standpipe in pressurized stairs
   B. the sprinklers in sub-basement locations
   C. a combination standpipe and sprinkler system
   D. as a supply line to the fire pump for the upper level standpipe outlets

5. Of the following buildings, the one that MUST have emergency smoke-venting equipment is a  5.____

   A. new office building, 275 feet high, equipped throughout with automatic sprinklers
   B. new office building, 175 feet high, without an air conditioning system

39

C. new office building, 75 feet high, without sprinklers and with a central air conditioning system serving more than the floor on which the equipment is located
D. one-story building, classified in occupancy group B-1, greater in depth than 100 feet from a frontage space

6. A factory building was erected in 1912 and was occupied continuously as such until 1950 when it became completely vacant. After many years, it was reoccupied with factory occupancies.
This structure

   A. must comply with the State Labor Law affecting factory buildings erected after October 1, 1913
   B. may be reoccupied as a factory building without changing its classification as one erected before October 1, 1913
   C. may be reoccupied as a factory building erected before October 1, 1913 provided an automatic sprinkler system is installed
   D. cannot be reoccupied as a factory unless it is of fireproof construction

7. A five-story fireproof factory building erected in 1909 has the following occupancies:
      First floor - dress manufacturing
      Second floor - tannery
      Third floor - artificial flower manufacturing
      Fourth floor - machine shop
      Fifth floor - vacant
   Under the State Labor Law, an automatic extinguishing system is

   A. *not required* because the building is classed as fireproof
   B. *required* for the artificial flower factory and all floors above
   C. *not required* if the tannery is moved to the fifth floor
   D. *required* throughout

8. Which one of the following statements does NOT correctly describe the protection requirements for vertical separation of openings?
In buildings classified in occupancy group

   A. E exceeding three stories or 40 feet in height, openings located vertically above one another in exterior walls except in stairway enclosures required to have a fire resistance rating of one hour or more shall be separated by a spandrel wall at least three feet high between the top of one opening and the bottom of the opening immediately above
   B. D exceeding three stories or 40 feet in height, openings located vertically above one another in exterior walls except in stairway enclosures shall have each such opening above the lower one protected against fire by an opening protective
   C. C exceeding three stories or 40 feet in height, openings located vertically above one another in exterior walls except in stairway enclosures shall be protected by a fire canopy of non-combustible materials extending out at least two feet horizontally from the wall and at least as long as the width of the lower opening
   D. B, spandrels and fire canopies shall be constructed to provide at least the fire-resistance rating required for the exterior wall, but in no event less than one hour

9. It is MOST complete and accurate to state that, according to the Manual of Fire Communications, in the event the officer in command of a fire or emergency operation requires additional manpower, in lieu of transmitting additional alarms or special calls, he may

    A. telephone the Office of the Chief of Department, specifying the kind of aid required and when it should be sent
    B. notify the dispatcher by radio of the assistance required, specifying the number of officers and fire-men, and the location to which they shall report
    C. telephone the dispatcher specifying the assistance required, including the number of officers and fire-men needed, location to which they shall report, and the expected time additional manpower will be released
    D. notify the Office of the Chief of Department, specifying the assistance required, the location to which they shall report, the reason for calling additional manpower, and the amount of time they can be expected to be detained

10. While inspecting a sprinklered building, a fire officer is asked by the building manager for his opinion about painting the wooden water tank on the roof. The manager explains it is his understanding that painting the tank will extend its useful life.
    Of the following, it would probably be MOST appropriate for the fire officer to indicate that

    A. painting the interior of the tank below water level will prolong the life of the tank, but painting the exterior may tend to hide structural defects
    B. painting a wooden tank may be desirable from the standpoint of appearance, but it is of questionable value in increasing the life of the tank
    C. the use of paint is undesirable for any purpose on either the exterior or interior of the tank
    D. the manager should consult a painting contractor to find out what his experience and recommendations are

11. In a large warehouse facility, the GREATEST fire hazard potential will result if rubber automotive tires are stored on the

    A. side in stacked piles        B. tread in racks
    C. side on pallets              D. tread in stacked piles

12. During a fire prevention inspection, a firefighter may find a condition which could be the immediate cause of death in the event of a fire.
    Which one of the following conditions in a restaurant is the MOST dangerous?

    A. Blocked exit doors
    B. A crack in the front door
    C. A window that does not open
    D. A broken air conditioning system

13. Firefighters must regularly inspect office buildings to determine whether fire prevention laws have been obeyed. Some of these fire prevention laws are as follows: DOORS: Doors should be locked as follows:
    I. Doors on the ground floor may be locked on the street side to prevent entry into the stairway.
    II. Doors in office buildings that are less than 100 feet in height may be locked on the stairway side on each floor above the ground floor.
    III. Doors in office buildings that are 100 feet or more in height may be locked on the stairway side except for every fourth floor.

    The doors in an office building which is less than 100 feet in height may be locked on the stairway side

    A. on all floors including the ground floor
    B. on all floors above the ground floor
    C. except for every fourth floor
    D. on all floors above the fourth floor

14. SIGNS: Signs concerning stairways should be posted in the following manner:
    I. A sign shall be posted near the elevator on each floor, stating, *IN CASE OF FIRE, USE STAIRS UNLESS OTHERWISE INSTRUCTED.* The sign shall contain a diagram showing the location of the stairs and the letter identification of the stairs.
    II. Each stairway shall be identified by an alphabetical letter on a sign posted on the hallway side of the stair door.
    III. Signs indicating the floor number shall be attached to the stairway side of each door.
    IV. Signs indicating whether re-entry can be made into the building, and the floors where re-entry can be made, shall be posted on the stairway side of each door.

    Which one of the following CORRECTLY lists the information which should be posted on the stairway side of a door?

    A sign will indicate the
    A. floor number, whether re-entry can be made into the building, and the floors where re-entry can be made
    B. alphabetical letter of the stairway, whether re-entry can be made into the building, and the floors where re-entry can be made
    C. alphabetical letter of the stairway and the floor number
    D. alphabetical letter of the stairway, the floor number, whether re-entry can be made into the building, and the floors where re-entry can be made

15. The Fire Department now uses companies on fire duty, with their apparatus, for fire prevention inspection in commercial buildings.
    The one of the following changes which was MOST important in making this inspection procedure practicable was the

    A. reduction of hours of work of firemen
    B. use of two-way radio equipment
    C. use of enclosed cabs on fire apparatus
    D. increase in property values during the post-war period

16. The MAXIMUM length of unlined linen hose which shall be permitted at any standpipe hose outlet valve is

   A. 50'  B. 75'  C. 100'  D. 125'

17. The State Labor Law requires that fire drills be conducted monthly in factory buildings over two stories in height in which more than 25 persons are employed above the ground floor.
   The one of the following statements that is MOST complete and accurate is that the law provides for automatic exemption from this requirement to factory buildings which are

   A. completely sprinklered
   B. completely sprinklered by a system having two adequate sources of water supply
   C. completely sprinklered by a system having two adequate sources of water supply and a maximum number of occupants of any one floor not more than 50 percent above the capacity of the exits required for the same building if unsprinklered
   D. completely sprinklered by a system having two adequate sources of water supply, a maximum number of occupants of any one floor not more than 50 percent above the capacity of the exits required for the same building if unsprinklered and an interior fire alarm system

18. Automatic sprinkler systems installed in the public halls of converted multiple dwellings with a required Siamese are subjected to a hydrostatic pressure test before acceptance. The test pressure for such systems is to be NOT less than

   A. 30 pounds per square inch
   B. 30 pounds per square inch in excess of the normal pressure required for such systems when in service
   C. 200 pounds per square inch
   D. 200 pounds per square inch in excess of the normal pressure required for such systems when in service

19. According to the rules of the Board of Standards and Appeals, when flameproofed materials are subjected to prescribed tests, they shall meet established standards for each of the following properties EXCEPT

   A. flashing              B. duration of flame
   C. duration of glow      D. temperature of flame

20. Each year many children die in fires which they have started while playing with matches. Of the following measures, the one that would be MOST effective in preventing such tragedies is to

   A. warn the children of the dangers involved
   B. punish parents who are found guilty of neglecting their children
   C. keep matches out of the reach of children
   D. use only safety matches

21. Sparks given off by welding torches are a serious fire hazard.
The BEST of the following methods of dealing with this hazard is to conduct welding operations

   A. only in fireproof buildings protected by sprinkler systems
   B. only out-of-doors on a day with little wind blowing
   C. only on materials certified to be non-combustible by recognized testing laboratories
   D. only after loose combustible materials have been cleared from the area and with a man standing by with a hose line

22. A two-story, Class 3, non-fireproof building was originally occupied as a store on the first floor and one apartment on the second floor. Upon inspection, you find that the second floor is now being used for offices. The building is 20' x 50'. There is one stairway made of wood, enclosed with fire-retarded stud partitions, leading directly to the street from the second floor.
The one of the following statements that is MOST complete and accurate is that the situation as described

   A. complies with applicable laws
   B. is illegal because the stair should be of incombustible material
   C. is illegal because there should be two means of egress
   D. is illegal because there should be two means of egress and the stair should be of incombustible material

Questions 23-25.

DIRECTIONS: Questions 23 through 25 are to be answered SOLELY on the basis of the following passage.

Automatic sprinkler systems are installed in many buildings. They extinguish or keep from spreading 96% of all fires in areas they protect. Sprinkler systems are made up of pipes which hang below the ceiling of each protected area and sprinkler heads which are placed along the pipes. The pipes are usually filled with water, and each sprinkler head has a heat sensitive part. When the heat from the fire reaches the sensitive part of the sprinkler head, the head opens and showers water upon the fire in the form of spray. The heads are spaced so that the fire is covered by overlapping showers of water from the open heads.

23. Automatic sprinkler systems are installed in buildings to

   A. prevent the build-up of dangerous gases
   B. eliminate the need for fire insurance
   C. extinguish fires or keep them from spreading
   D. protect 96% of the floor space

24. If more than one sprinkler head opens, the area sprayed will be

   A. flooded with hot water
   B. overlapped by showers of water
   C. subject to less water damage
   D. about 1 foot per sprinkler head

25. A sprinkler head will open and shower water when        25._____

    A. it is reached by heat from a fire
    B. water pressure in the pipes gets too high
    C. it is reached by sounds from a fire alarm
    D. water temperature in the pipes gets too low

---

# KEY (CORRECT ANSWERS)

| | | | |
|---|---|---|---|
| 1. | A | 11. | B |
| 2. | C | 12. | A |
| 3. | C | 13. | B |
| 4. | C | 14. | A |
| 5. | D | 15. | B |
| 6. | B | 16. | D |
| 7. | D | 17. | C |
| 8. | A | 18. | C |
| 9. | B | 19. | D |
| 10. | B | 20. | C |

| | |
|---|---|
| 21. | D |
| 22. | A |
| 23. | C |
| 24. | B |
| 25. | A |

---

# TEST 3

DIRECTIONS: Each question or incomplete statement is followed by several suggested answers or completions. Select the one that BEST answers the question or completes the statement. *PRINT THE LETTER OF THE CORRECT ANSWER IN THE SPACE AT THE RIGHT.*

1. The one of the following which is the MOST valid statement in the Fire Prevention Code regarding height restrictions on combustible fiber storage is that

   A. a clearance of at least 18 inches shall be maintained below the sprinkler head
   B. storage shall be no higher than 20 feet above the floor
   C. storage shall be no higher than 2/3 of the distance from floor to ceiling
   D. storage shall be piled to a height not greater than 6 inches below the top of the enclosing wall

   1.____

2. The one of the following which is NOT among the Fire Prevention Code protection requirements for the storage of television special effects is that

   A. partitions in the storage room shall have at least a one-hour fire resistive rating
   B. the roof of the storage room shall have at least a 1 1/2 hour fire resistive rating
   C. there shall be one sprinkler head for each 80 square feet of floor space in the storage room
   D. there shall be mechanical ventilation providing at least four air changes per hour

   2.____

3. According to the Fire Prevention Code, of the following containers, the ones which are NOT legal for the transportation of gasoline are

   A. 5-gallon cans with metal seals
   B. glass bottles not exceeding 4 ounces each
   C. 55-gallon steel barrels or drums
   D. 10-gallon safety cans

   3.____

4. The following conditions have been found during an inspection:
   I. 10,000 small arms cartridges in a store authorized to sell gunpowder
   II. 500 small arms cartridges in a pawn shop
   III. 200 small arms cartridges in a liquor store
   IV. 100 small arms cartridges in a drug store

   Which of the following choices lists ONLY those of the above conditions that comply with the Fire Prevention Code either because a permit may be issued or because a pernit is not required?

   A. I, II, III  B. I, II, IV
   C. I, III, IV  D. II, III, IV

   4.____

5. While inspecting a building, an officer notices that a standard enclosure having a three-hour fire resistance rating has been constructed above ground on the lowest floor of the building.
   According to the Building Code, the MAXIMUM size fuel oil storage tank that can be placed in this enclosure is one with a capacity of _____ gallons.

   A. 1,100   B. 2,500   C. 10,000   D. 20,000

   5.____

46

6. The one of the following which is NOT a Class B multiple dwelling is a

   A. hotel
   B. boarding school
   C. clubhouse
   D. hospital

7. When inspecting an industrial plant, an officer discovers a conveyor passing through a fire wall with no fire shutter for the opening.
   The MOST valid of the following statements concerning alternate forms of protection is that

   A. no alternate is acceptable; a shutter having fire resistance equal to the wall fire resistance is required
   B. a sprinkler head located in the opening to provide at least 3 gallons per square foot per minute is acceptable
   C. two sprinkler heads to provide a water curtain for the entire opening is acceptable
   D. four water spray nozzles on each side of the opening controlled by an automatic valve actuated by a heat detector is acceptable

8. A new restaurant in a multiple-story building of Class I construction has a false front on the outside of the building representing an English castle.
   The one of the following which meets the Building Code requirement for this condition to be legal is that the false front is of

   A. fire retardant treated wood not over 40 feet high
   B. fire retardant treated wood covering less than 2,000 square feet of surface
   C. slow burning plastic, not over 25 feet high, covering not over 1,000 square feet of surface
   D. slow burning plastic, not over 40 feet high, covering less than 5% of the building surface

9. At a recent fire on the third floor of a building, firemen could not open the locked windows nor could they break the plastic glazing.
   For such conditions, the Building Code requires that

   A. keys to the windows be available in the lobby
   B. one window for each 50 feet of street front be openable from the inside or outside
   C. all plastic glazing be replaced by glass
   D. all locks be removed and replaced with spring latches

10. Showroom spaces located in office buildings over 100 feet high are required to be sprinklered when the

    A. building air conditioning system serves more than the floor in which the equipment is located, and the showroom space exceeds 7,500 square feet in area and is located more than 40 feet above curb level
    B. showroom space is over 1,000 square feet in area and is located more than 40 feet above curb level
    C. showroom space is over 7,500 square feet in area, is not equipped with an approved smoke detection alarm system, and is served by a one-floor mechanical ventilation system
    D. showroom space exceeds 2,500 square feet in area and is located more than 75 feet above curb level

11. In a building classified as occupancy group E, occupied or arranged to be occupied for an occupant load of more than one hundred persons above or below the street level or more than a total of five hundred persons in the entire building, a building evacuation supervisor performs his training activities under the direction of

    A. the battalion chief on duty
    B. the building fire safety director
    C. the building fire brigade supervisor
    D. someone other than any of the above

11._____

12. The one of the following which BEST identifies where a Class E fire alarm signal system will sound continuously upon operation of a manual station is only on the floor where

    A. actuated
    B. actuated and the floor above
    C. actuated and the next two floors above
    D. actuated, the floor above, and the floor below

12._____

13. The ONLY one of the following occupancies in which portable kerosene space heaters approved by the Board of Standards and Appeals may be used in the event of failure of the central heating unit is in

    A. private dwellings
    B. multiple dwellings
    C. places of public assembly
    D. schools

13._____

14. The one of the following which is NOT a requirement relating to oxygen and acetylene torch operations in a building under demolition is that there be

    A. one fire guard in the area of torch operation equipped with a 2 1/2" hose line
    B. one fire guard for each torch operator and an addi-tional fire guard on the floor or level below
    C. fire guards to make an inspection of the exposed area one half hour after completion of torch operations
    D. fire guards to make an inspection of the exposed area one hour after completion of torch operations

14._____

15. Upon responding to an alarm of fire in a building, an officer notes that the Siamese connections are painted yellow.
    This color coding indicates that

    A. the sprinkler system protects only showrooms located not over 40 feet above the curb line
    B. the standpipe riser is only four inches in size
    C. a floor control valve is provided for the sprinkler system on each floor
    D. the Siamese connection supplies a high-expansion foam system

15._____

16. The one of the following which does NOT correctly describe what can happen during manual operation of an elevator with the keyed switch in the *Fireman Service* position is that the

    A. doors will open on all floors but the fire floor
    B. direction of travel can be changed after a floor selection has been made

16._____

C. doors will open only in response to the *Door Open* button in the car
D. doors can be automatically reclosed while in the process of opening

17. The Building Code places restrictions on the suspension of new ceilings below existing suspended ceilings in construction group II in order to restrict the travel of fire in hidden spaces.
The one of the following requirements which BEST describes the nature of this restriction is that the

    A. concealed space shall be provided with firestops to divide the space into sections not exceeding 3,000 square feet each
    B. new ceiling shall be supported directly from the ceiling carrying channels and shall have no openings from the concealed space to the area below
    C. new ceiling shall be of non-combustible construction or have a flame spread rating of 25 or less, and a smoke developed rating of 50 or less
    D. existing ceiling shall be completely removed before the new ceiling is suspended

17.____

18. While inspecting a 125-foot-high factory building constructed in 1912 within 20 feet of an adjacent one-story fireproof garage 12 feet in height, an officer notices that the fire windows in the factory wall facing the garage are glazed with wireglass only to the fourth floor or 65-foot level. Windows above that level are 60 feet higher vertically than the roof of the garage and are glazed with inch plate glass lights 400 square inches in area.
The one of the following which is the PROPER conclusion for the officer to draw is that

    A. such windows comply with the State Labor Law
    B. a violation exists since all fire windows in the wall of a factory building facing any building within 30 feet must be glazed with wireglass
    C. a violation exists since the fire windows in all factory buildings erected before 1913 must have wireglass
    D. none of the fire windows in the factory wall need be wireglass if there are no openings in the garage wall facing it

18.____

19. An officer submits for review a referral report containing statements about the exterior screened stairway of a factory building he has recently inspected which he considers to be in violation of the State Labor Law.
Of the officer's observations listed below, the one that is NOT a violation of the State Labor Law is:

    A. No balcony connecting with the stairs at the fourth floor
    B. Door connecting with the balcony at the third floor opens inward
    C. Stair terminates in rear yard not communicating to a street
    D. Access to balcony at second floor via sliding door

19.____

20. A five story non-fireproof factory building erected in 1908 has an area on all floors of 900 square feet with two exits remote from each other on all floors, except for the fourth floor which is used entirely as a raw material storeroom. No one is regularly employed on that floor. For security reasons, the fourth floor has only one exit.
It would be CORRECT to say that, according to the State Labor Law,

    A. this arrangement is expressly forbidden, as every floor must have two exits
    B. one exit from the fourth floor would be acceptable provided it is protected by an automatic sprinkler system

20.____

C. the one exit from the fourth floor is acceptable provided it conforms to the criteria for a factory exit
D. one exit from the fourth floor is acceptable provided the longest distance to the exit from any point on the floor does not exceed 75 feet

21. Buildings which have been vacated by order of the fire department are kept under surveillance.
When such buildings have been boarded up, surveillance may, with approval, be reduced to once each

    A. week
    B. month
    C. quarter-year
    D. half-year

22. Overly detailed fire prevention inspections are to be avoided CHIEFLY because they

    A. unduly interfere with the normal activities of the occupancy, causing public resentment
    B. require excessive time which could be used to better advantage inspecting other occupancies
    C. tend to result in oversight of some fundamental hazards
    D. are beyond the capabilities of many firemen who are not specifically trained in inspectional techniques

23. Requests for sprinkler re-evaluation are accepted by the fire department, and a re-inspection made, if the petitioner states that substantial changes have been made in the sprinkler system.
The one of the following statements that is MOST accurate and complete is that such re-inspections are made by the division commander

    A. in all instances
    B. except when he has endorsed the original sprinkler order
    C. except when he has endorsed the original sprinkler order or when his workload is excessive
    D. except when he has endorsed the original sprinkler order, his workload is excessive, or the re-evaluation is extremely complex

24. Department regulations require the forwarding of reports to the Fire Commissioner relating to demolition work adjacent to or adjoining company quarters.
The one of the following statements that is MOST accurate and complete is that such reports should be forwarded when notice of the proposed demolition is

    A. received
    B. received and when the work is completed
    C. received, when the work actually starts, and when the work is completed
    D. received, when the work actually starts, when any interruption of work occurs, and when the work is completed

25. The one of the following statements that is MOST complete and accurate is that when a building inspector issues a Violation Order, the time allowed for compliance

    A. must be the specific number of days indicated on the Standard Form of Orders
    B. may be less than the specific number of days indicated on the Standard Form of Orders

C. may be more than the specific number of days indicated on the Standard Form of Orders
D. may be more or less than the specific number of days indicated on the Standard Form of Orders, depending upon the circumstances

## KEY (CORRECT ANSWERS)

1. C
2. D
3. D
4. C
5. D

6. D
7. D
8. C
9. B
10. A

11. B
12. B
13. D
14. A
15. C

16. A
17. D
18. A
19. D
20. C

21. C
22. B
23. D
24. A
25. B

#  TEST 4

DIRECTIONS: Each question or incomplete statement is followed by several suggested answers or completions. Select the one that BEST answers the question or completes the statement. *PRINT THE LETTER OF THE CORRECT ANSWER IN THE SPACE AT THE RIGHT.*

1. Of the following substances, the one that would MOST appropriately be protected with a sprinkler installation is

    A. cellulose acetate
    B. quicklime
    C. magnesium powder
    D. calcium carbide

    1.____

2. Providing clearance around unprotected steel columns in storage occupancies is a practice which is GENERALLY

    A. *desirable,* chiefly because the quantity of combustibles stored is reduced
    B. *undesirable,* chiefly because flue-like conditions will prevail
    C. *desirable,* chiefly because it will allow water from sprinklers to keep the column wet
    D. *undesirable,* chiefly because stock can topple if not supported

    2.____

3. National fire records indicate that over the years restaurant fires have increased in number and in total dollar loss despite technological improvements.
   The large increase in the number of restaurant fires is PRIMARILY attributable to

    A. fires of incendiary origin
    B. duct fires
    C. the use of open flames for cooking
    D. careless handling of smoking materials

    3.____

4. When serving a summons for a violation of the Building Code, it is most important that proper procedure be followed.
   Of the following statements, the one that is MOST acceptable is that a summons may be

    A. mailed to the residence of the building's owner if he is not on the premises
    B. given to a superintendent to be forwarded to the owner if he is not on the premises
    C. placed on the desk or in the immediate vicinity of the owner if he refuses to accept it
    D. made out with the initials of the owner if the full name is not known

    4.____

5. A dry-pipe sprinkler system is generally not considered acceptable protection for an occupancy utilizing flammable liquids MAINLY because

    A. corrosion tends to weaken these systems
    B. water is a poor extinguishing agent for flammable liquids
    C. the systems are too expensive for the purpose
    D. a fast spreading fire may be out of control by the time water arrives

    5.____

6. In order to enforce the fire safety laws, firefighters must inspect buildings and stores.
   It is NOT a good idea for firefighters to let owners of buildings and stores know when they are coming because

    6.____

A. firefighters will waste valuable time if the owner breaks the appointment
B. owners might try to hide fire hazards from the fire-fighters
C. firefighters can make the inspection faster without an appointment
D. owners would be angry if the firefighters were unable to keep the appointment

7. Many older buildings are modernized to give a blank wall appearance by being *wrapped*. 7.____
It is INACCURATE to state, with reference to *wrapped* buildings, that

   A. the use of expanded metal panels reduces the hazard from exposure fires
   B. they are essentially windowless buildings
   C. solid metal panels may be blown loose and scale a considerable distance
   D. expanded metal panels may be hung or mounted a foot or more from the original exterior wall

8. According to the Administrative Code, it is unlawful to manufacture within the city all of 8.____
the following EXCEPT

   A. blank cartridges              B. railroad track torpedoes
   C. flashlight compositions       D. ship signal rockets

9. A newly appointed firefighter is assigned to go with an experienced firefighter to inspect a 9.____
paint store. The paint store owner refuses to allow the inspection, saying that he is closing the store early that day and going on vacation. The new firefighter demands rudely that the inspection be allowed, even though it would be permissible to delay it.
Of the following, it would be BEST for the experienced firefighter to

   A. repeat the demand that the inspection be allowed and quote the law to the store owner
   B. tell the new firefighter that it would be best to schedule the inspection after the store owner's vacation
   C. tell the store owner to step aside, and instruct the new firefighter to enter the store and begin the inspection
   D. tell the new firefighter to forget about the inspection because the store owner is uncooperative

10. One person shall be permitted to supervise more than one interior fire alarm system. 10.____
The one of the following that is NOT in accord with the restrictions placed on this permission is that

   A. the buildings in which the interior fire alarm systems are located must be within an area whose diameter does not exceed six hundred feet
   B. the interior fire alarms in all buildings in the group can be tested within thirty minutes of commencing work daily
   C. the addresses of all buildings shall be listed on the one certificate of fitness
   D. records and logbooks must be kept on each premises

11. The one of the following which is NOT in accord with the Regulations for Use of Halon 11.____
1301, Extinguishing Agent, is that

   A. maximum concentration shall not exceed 10 percent where human habitation is present in the volume to be flooded
   B. minimum concentration of FE 1301 used shall not be less than 10 percent

C. a discharge rate which results in attaining the design concentration in 8 seconds is acceptable
D. a central office connection must be provided for fire detection or systems operation where human habitation is present in the volume to be flooded

12. According to the Fire Prevention Code, a person who holds a permit for the manufacture of inflammable mixtures and who wishes to manufacture combustible mixtures is

A. *required* to obtain another permit
B. *not required* to obtain another permit
C. *not required* to obtain another permit unless the mixtures include stove polishes or insecticides
D. *not required* to obtain another permit unless the mixtures include medicinal and toilet preparations

12.____

13. The one of the following statements which is MOST accurate and complete is that the Fire Prevention Code permits the hanging of fresh-cut decorative greens in places of public assembly only if they do not contain

A. pitch
B. pitch and are hung by means of non-combustible material
C. pitch, are hung by means of non-combustible material, and do not remain for a period in excess of 24 hours
D. pitch, are hung by means of non-combustible material, have been treated with an approved evaporation-retarding product, and do not remain for a period in excess of 48 hours

13.____

14. In any automatic wet-pipe sprinkler system which has standard one-half inch sprinkler heads exposed to cold and subject to freezing, shut-off valves may be provided and the water supply discontinued

A. under no circumstances
B. from November 15 to March 15 when there are five or less such exposed heads
C. from November 1 to April 1 when there are ten or less such exposed heads
D. from November 15 to April 15 when there are fifteen or less such exposed heads

14.____

15. At an inspection of a building, one floor of which is used for combustible fiber storage, the following facts are revealed:
   I. The safe bearing capacity of the floor, as certified by the Department of Buildings, is 250 lbs./sq.ft. The weight of the combustible fiber is 75 lbs./sq.ft.
   II. The floor is 10,000 sq.ft. in area, of which 6,000 sq.ft. is occupied by the fiber bales.
   III. The height from floor to ceiling is 16', and the stacked bales stand 10' high.
In this situation, _____ of the Fire Prevention Code.

A. Item I is in
B. Item II is in
C. Item III is in
D. there is no

15.____

16. Carelessness in smoking is a very common cause of fire.
A lighted cigarette placed on top of most upholstery will GENERALLY

A. cause no damage
B. burn to the end without starting a fire

16.____

C. cause a gradually increasing fire
D. start a fire rapidly

17. The one of the following that is the type of automatic sprinkler system MOST commonly found in museums, art galleries, and storage places for records or valuable merchandise is the _____ system.

    A. deluge
    B. pre-action
    C. dry pipe
    D. sypho-chemical

17.____

18. The Fire Prevention Code requires that a permit be obtained for the storage of more than the equivalent of five barrels of oils and fats.
    The one of the following which is excluded from this requirement is

    A. lubricating oils
    B. grease
    C. edible oils
    D. soap stock

18.____

19. The Fire Prevention Code requires that rooms in dry cleaning establishments in which washing tanks are located be equipped with

    A. asbestos cloths or blankets
    B. carbon dioxide or dry chemical extinguishers
    C. buckets of sand
    D. automatic fire alarm device

19.____

20. The one of the following occupancies which is required to have a two-source water supply for its sprinkler system is one containing

    A. combustible fiber storage
    B. a motion picture film studio
    C. oils and fats storage
    D. a theater

20.____

21. The one of the following statements that is MOST accurate is that the Fire Prevention Code prohibits the storage of distilled liquors and alcohols in

    A. quantities aggregating more than 50 gallons, without a permit
    B. any building of wooden construction
    C. excess of one barrel for each five square feet of floor space
    D. barrels stacked more than one high

21.____

22. A special permit issued by the Fire Commissioner is required for the operation of certain businesses. Concerning parking lots, technical establishments, retail drug stores, and dry cleaning establishments, it is MOST accurate to say that special permits are required for all

    A. four of them
    B. of the above except parking lots
    C. of the above except technical establishments
    D. of the above except retail drug stores

22.____

23. The one of the following chemicals which may NOT be manufactured or stored in a drug and chemical supply house in any quantity is

   A. acetone
   B. benzole
   C. chloride of nitrogen
   D. metallic magnesium

24. A permit is required for the storage of empty wooden packing boxes in buildings if the quantity stored exceeds

   A. one ton
   B. 2,000 square feet of area
   C. 2,000 cubic feet of space
   D. one ton or 2,000 square feet of area, whichever is the smaller amount

25. The MAXIMUM number of excess liquefied petroleum gas cylinders that may be stored in a single structure protected by an approved dry sprinkler system is

   A. 25    B. 50    C. 75    D. 100

## KEY (CORRECT ANSWERS)

1. A
2. C
3. A
4. C
5. D

6. B
7. A
8. D
9. B
10. C

11. B
12. B
13. C
14. C
15. D

16. B
17. B
18. C
19. A
20. B

21. B
22. A
23. C
24. C
25. B

# EXAMINATION SECTION
# TEST 1

DIRECTIONS: Each question or incomplete statement is followed by several suggested answers or completions. Select the one that BEST answers the question or completes the statement. *PRINT THE LETTER OF THE CORRECT ANSWER IN THE SPACE AT THE RIGHT.*

1. During an inspection of a plant which manufactures paper products, the officer observes completed work being placed in paper cartons. The cartons are then stacked on wooden skids in a separate storage area awaiting shipment.
   The one of the following which is generally the MOST appropriate evaluation of the practice described in this situation is that skids

   A. are highly combustible, adding much fuel to the fire
   B. permit excess air flow to fires
   C. minimize water damage losses by raising stock off the floor
   D. provide space under the stock, thus permitting fire to be more readily extinguished

   1.____

2. Assume that a three-story, Class 3 non-fireproof building has been converted to two-family use. There is one stairway to the street, 2'8" wide. The doors to the apartments all swing in. There are no fire escapes.
   The one of the following statements that is MOST accurate is that the situation as described

   A. complies with all applicable laws
   B. is illegal because the stairs are too narrow
   C. is illegal because two means of egress are required
   D. is illegal because the doors do not swing in the direction of egress

   2.____

3. The flammability limits of aviation fuels are of little significance in understanding their fire hazard properties CHIEFLY because the fuels

   A. have practically the same limits
   B. form flammable vapor-air mixtures at all temperatures
   C. ignite readily under tank failure conditions
   D. resist flashing to vapor when in the gelled form

   3.____

4. An inspector enters a luncheonette and discovers that the owner, the only person on duty, apparently does not understand English.
   The one of the following which would be the BEST action for the inspector to take in this situation is to attempt to

   A. make the owner understand by speaking English in a loud, clear voice
   B. make the owner understand by using sign language
   C. find a customer or passerby who can act as an interpreter
   D. question the owner closely to determine whether he really does not understand English

   4.____

5. For proper protection of low flash point flammable liquid processes, automatic sprinkler protection with a strong water supply is essential.
   The BEST justification of this statement is that

   5.____

A. a sprinkler system with a strong water supply will extinguish most fires involving such processes
B. water from sprinklers will reduce the intensity of burning of the liquid and the danger to exposures
C. although the sprinklers are ineffective on flammable liquid fires, they provide protection in the event of other types of fires
D. water from the sprinklers will dilute the flammable liquid and make extinguishment easier

6. According to the regulations, company commanders shall cause a thorough inspection of all schools within their administrative district.
Such inspections shall be made

   A. annually
   B. semi-annually
   C. at the beginning of each school term
   D. within 60 days after school opens for the fall term

7. While inspecting a garage, a fire inspector notices that a garage license has not been issued for the premises by the Department of Licenses.
The inspector should

   A. discontinue his inspection pending a determination by the Department of Licenses of the allowable motor vehicle occupancy
   B. complete his inspection and forward it (including a statement of the allowable motor vehicle occupancy) with a request that a copy be sent to the Department of Licenses
   C. discontinue his inspection and request that a communication (inquiry form) be sent to the Department of Licenses asking for an explanation
   D. complete his inspection and forward it with a request that the Department of Licenses be asked to determine the allowable motor vehicle occupancy

Questions 8-11.

DIRECTIONS: Questions 8 through 11 are to be answered on the basis of the information given in the following paragraph.

The principal value of inspection work is in the knowledge obtained relating to the various structural features of the building and the protective features provided. Knowledge of the location of stairways and elevators, the obstruction provided by merchandise, the danger from absorption of water by baled stock, the potential hazard of rupture of containers such as drums or cylinders, and the location of protective equipment, all are essential features to be noted and later discussed in company school and officer's college.

8. According to the above paragraph, the CHIEF value of inspection work is to gather information which will aid in

   A. fixing responsibility for fires
   B. planning firefighting operations
   C. training new firemen
   D. obtaining compliance with the Building Code

9. The one of the following objects which would be the MOST help in accomplishing the objective of the inspection as stated in the above paragraph is a

   A. copy of the Building Code
   B. chemical analysis kit
   C. plan of the building
   D. list of the building's tenants

10. An example of a *structural feature* contained in the above paragraph is the

    A. location of stairways and elevators
    B. obstruction provided by merchandise
    C. danger of absorption of water by baled stock
    D. hazard of rupture of containers such as drums or cylinders

11. Of the following, the BEST example of what is meant by a *protective feature,* as used in the above paragraph, is

    A. a fire extinguisher
    B. a burglar alarm
    C. fire insurance
    D. a medical first-aid kit

12. When a violation order is to be served and the owner or person in charge of the premises cannot readily be located, every effort shall be made to serve such order. Of the following statements concerning the attempts to serve such an order, the one that is NOT correct is:

    A. Attempt to ascertain from occupants or people in the area the name and address of the owner or management
    B. Send a member to effect service if the owner or management is located in the city but out of the company district
    C. Make an appointment by telephone for service of the order
    D. Post the violation notice prominently in or on the premises and mail a copy to the owner or management

13. Every applicant for a certificate of license to install underground gasoline storage tanks is required to

    A. be a resident of the city and maintain a place of business in the city
    B. file a bond and evidence of liability insurance
    C. be a resident of the city or maintain a place of business in the city
    D. pass a written examination given by the fire department

14. The Fire Prevention Code specifies that a special permit is required for each of the following EXCEPT

    A. refining petroleum collected from oil separators or manufacturing plants
    B. loading of small arms ammunition by hand in a retail store selling ammunition
    C. operating a wholesale drug or chemical house
    D. generating acetylene gas

15. The one of the following that is the MOST acceptable statement concerning the fire protection for the truck loading rack in a bulk oil terminal is that the rack must be equipped with a

A. water spray system, automatically controlled
B. foam system, remote manually controlled
C. water spray system, remote manually controlled
D. foam system, automatically controlled

16. The one of the following which is NOT in accord with the regulations for the use of Halon 1301, extinguishing agent, is that

    A. maximum concentration shall not exceed 10 percent where human habitation is present in the volume to be flooded
    B. minimum concentration of FE 1301 used shall not be less than 10 percent
    C. a discharge rate which results in attaining the design concentration in 8 seconds is acceptable
    D. a central office connection must be provided for fire detection or systems operating where human habitation is present in the volume to be flooded

16.____

17. Members of the uniformed force are authorized to issue summonses where fire perils exist, although it is generally preferable to first issue a violation order to correct the illegal condition.
    However, members must issue a summons immediately in a licensed place of public assembly upon noting

    A. an obstructed revolving exit door in a crowded cabaret
    B. the absence of a certified standpipe system operator in a theatre
    C. an inoperative fire extinguishing system in a restaurant cooking duct
    D. standees in a motion picture theatre

17.____

18. During the course of an inspection at a blasting site, an officer notes that the magazine has been provided with electrical security devices, and that it contains eight 10-pound cartons of explosives which are to be stored overnight, overhead wires run from the magazine to the watchman's shanty, and the driller, without a C. of F., loads holes under the direct supervision of the blaster. The condition as described is generally ILLEGAL because

    A. explosives must be in original and unbroken packages of 50 or 25 pound capacity only
    B. storage of explosives between the hours of 10 P.M. and 6 A.M. is prohibited
    C. all electrical wiring must be protected by heavy wall conduit and be buried at least 12 inches deep
    D. no person may load holes in blasting operations unless they hold a certificate of fitness

18.____

19. The one of the following that is LEAST in accord with the regulations for the use of Halon 1301 extinguishing agent systems is that

    A. these systems are limited to applications as automatic total flooding systems for interior Class B and C fires and Class A fires that are not deep-seated
    B. abort systems are permitted for smoke detector activated systems which provide the manual capacity to *dump* the Halon 1301 immediately
    C. actuation of only one products-of-combustion device will fail to initiate the *dump* of Halon 1301 but will actuate the local and central office company alarms
    D. concentrations used shall not exceed 10 percent in areas where human habitation is present in the volume to be flooded

19.____

20. Interstate transportation of petroleum products into and through the city in tank trucks which do NOT conform to fire department requirements is GENERALLY    20._____

    A. *not permitted* even when the pickups are all made outside the city and no pickups are made in the city
    B. *permitted* without restriction if the vehicles comply with United States Department of Transportation regulations governing interstate commerce
    C. *not permitted* where deliveries are to be made in the city
    D. *permitted* during non-business hours, along regularly established commercial routes

21. Of the following occupancies constructed and occupied in 1962, each of which accommodates less than 300 persons, the one that CANNOT be described as a *place of assembly,* according to the applicable building code, is a    21._____

    A. college assembly hall           B. motion picture theatre
    C. courtroom                       D. legitimate theatre

22. According to the labor law, the one of the following conditions that is generally considered to be LEGAL in a 5-story building constructed and occupied as a factory since 1911 is that    22._____

    A. a single means of egress is provided from a floor of 2500 sq.ft. or less where no person is regularly employed
    B. no point on the upper floor which is equipped with an approved sprinkler system is more than 200 feet distant from an exit
    C. one of the two required stairways extends to the roof from which there is egress to an adjacent building
    D. there are double swinging doors leading to an exit on an upper floor where more than 5 persons are employed

23. Certain old factory buildings may be found to have some fire escapes which are not in accordance with the requirements of the labor law.
    It is generally CORRECT to state of these substandard factory exits that they    23._____

    A. may be used in computing occupancy exit requirements if maintained in good repair and the building is equipped with an automatic sprinkler
    B. must be provided with a counterbalanced stairway in lieu of the former drop ladder in guides
    C. shall be kept clear of all obstructions and periodically used during required fire drills
    D. may not be equipped with any exit or directional sign at the openings leading thereto

24. According to the labor law, the use of plate glass in fire windows in fireproof buildings is    24._____

    A. *prohibited,* except in buildings less than 75 feet in height
    B. *permitted,* if the fire windows are located more than 30 feet horizontally from the nearest opening in the wall of another building
    C. *prohibited* for use in all fire windows in fireproof buildings
    D. *permitted* if the fire windows are more than 30 feet above the roof of a building within a horizontal distance of 25 feet

25. Under certain conditions, a newsstand may be located in a street floor lobby which serves as an exit passageway for a building constructed after 1976.
The one of the following which is NOT one of these conditions is that the newsstand must

    A. occupy no more than 100 square feet or 5 percent of the net floor area of the lobby, whichever is greater
    B. not reduce the clear width of the lobby at any point
    C. be located at least 30 feet from an exit door
    D. be protected by at least 2 automatic sprinkler heads if constructed of combustible material

25.___

---

# KEY (CORRECT ANSWERS)

| | | | |
|---|---|---|---|
| 1. | C | 11. | A |
| 2. | A | 12. | D |
| 3. | C | 13. | C |
| 4. | C | 14. | D |
| 5. | B | 15. | C |
| 6. | A | 16. | B |
| 7. | D | 17. | C |
| 8. | B | 18. | D |
| 9. | C | 19. | D |
| 10. | A | 20. | D |

| | |
|---|---|
| 21. | C |
| 22. | B |
| 23. | A |
| 24. | B |
| 25. | B |

# TEST 2

DIRECTIONS: Each question or incomplete statement is followed by several suggested answers or completions. Select the one that BEST answers the question or completes the statement. *PRINT THE LETTER OF THE CORRECT ANSWER IN THE SPACE AT THE RIGHT.*

1. Suppose that a factory has stored within it a number of substances. 1.____
 If the owner asked you which of the following is MOST likely to constitute a fire hazard, you would reply

    A. sodium chloride
    B. calcium chloride
    C. chromium
    D. silicon dioxide

2. Vertical openings, such as dumbwaiters, elevators, and chutes, are the bane of a fire- 2.____
 fighting force.
 This condition arises MAINLY because the existence of such openings in a burning building facilitates

    A. accidental falls
    B. generation of gases
    C. spread of the fire
    D. the perpetration of arson

3. Suppose that a neighbor were to ask you whether there is more hazard in the use of ker- 3.____
 osene than gasoline at ordinary room temperature.
 You should reply that there is MORE hazard in the use of

    A. *kerosene,* because it gives off dangerous quantities of explosive vapors which are lighter than air
    B. *gasoline,* because gasoline vapor may flow along the floor and be ignited at a long distance from its point of origin
    C. *kerosene,* because its flash point is very low
    D. *gasoline,* particularly because when ignited it burns

4. Steel supporting beams in buildings often are surrounded by a thin layer of concrete to 4.____
 keep the beams from becoming hot and collapsing during a fire.
 The one of the following statements which BEST explains how collapse is prevented by this arrangement is that concrete

    A. becomes stronger as its temperature is increased
    B. acts as an insulating material
    C. protects the beam from rust and corrosion
    D. reacts chemically with steel at high temperatures

5. It has been suggested that property owners should be charged a fee each time the Fire 5.____
 Department is called to extinguish a fire on their property.
 Of the following, the BEST reason for *rejecting* this proposal is that

    A. delay in calling the Fire Department may result
    B. many property owners don't occupy the property they own
    C. property owners may resent such a charge as they pay real estate taxes
    D. it may be difficult to determine on whose property a fire started

6. An officer inspecting buildings in a commercial area came to one whose outside surface appeared to be of natural stone. The owner told the officer that it was not necessary to inspect his building as it was *fireproof*. The officer, however, completed his inspection of the building.
Of the following, the BEST reason for continuing the inspection is that

   A. stone buildings catch fire as readily as wooden buildings
   B. the Fire Department cannot make exceptions in its inspection procedures
   C. the building may have been built of imitation stone
   D. interiors and contents of stone buildings can catch fire

7. From the viewpoint of fire safety, the CHIEF advantage of a foam rubber mattress compared to a cotton mattress is that the foam rubber mattress

   A. is slower burning
   B. generates less heat when burning
   C. does not smolder
   D. is less subject to water damage

8. At a social gathering, a fire chief hears a man who describes himself as the owner of the XYZ factory state that he *pays off* fire department inspectors who visit his establishment. When the chief asks the man whether he will repeat his statement under oath, the man refuses with the remark, *I am not looking for trouble.*
In this situation, the chief should

   A. forget the incident since the factory owner is not willing to give evidence
   B. investigate the background and reputation of the man to determine whether he really owns the factory and has any reason for making false statements about the fire department
   C. report the incident to police authorities
   D. report the incident to higher authorities in the fire department

9. The one of the following methods of storing large piles of coal which is undesirable because it increases the danger of spontaneous heating is

   A. making the pile compact by use of a roller
   B. storing the coal on smooth, solid ground
   C. covering the sides and top of the pile with road tar
   D. mixing coal of various sizes in one pile

10. The one of the following materials which has the LEAST tendency to spontaneous heating is

    A. baled hides
    B. bagged charcoal
    C. bulk fish scrap
    D. boxed mineral wool

11. In most buildings in which lighting is provided by artificial means and an auxiliary system for emergency exit lighting is not provided, phosphorescent exit and directional signs are required.
Of the following occupancies, the one which is generally EXCLUDED from this requirement is a

    A. warehouse
    B. school dormitory
    C. hospital
    D. library

12. In determining overcrowding or adequacy of means of egress, a fire officer must be aware that the minimum number of persons to be provided for in any floor area shall be the number which can be accommodated within the net floor area at a given occupancy and area per person.
Accordingly, the GREATEST concentration of persons to be provided for will be generally found in a

    A. basement sales area
    B. high school classroom
    C. dance hall
    D. work room

13. Of the following statements, the one that is generally ACCURATE concerning the installation of combustible luminous suspended ceilings is that they may

    A. not be installed below an existing suspended ceiling
    B. be installed below existing sprinkler heads
    C. not be used in any room in occupancy group F (assembly)
    D. be installed in corridors not exceeding 100 sq.ft.

14. The building code exempts from the sprinkler requirements those floors which are generally unventilated but are equipped with a given openable area.
A fixed window will be considered openable if it is

    A. equipped with an interior heat sensitive device to actuate the automatic fire shutters
    B. of frangible glass panels and located 15 feet below grade
    C. within 8 feet of an openable window of at least 3 feet x 3 feet dimension
    D. readily broken and not more than 110 feet above grade

15. Of the following, the MOST complete and accurate statement about exit requirements is that there shall be at least two door openings, remote from each other and leading to exits from every room or enclosed space, in a business occupancy (E) in which the total occupant load *exceeds*

    A. 25    B. 50    C. 75    D. 100

16. On October 23, 1976, 25 persons died and many were injured as a result of an arson fire in an illegal social club in the Bronx.
Of the following, the MOST probable contributory cause of this multiple loss of life was the

    A. door to the club was not self-closing and was opened in the direction of egress when the fire occurred
    B. front windows had been bricked-up and prevented access by department ladders
    C. confusing layout caused many patrons to bypass the secondary means of egress and become trapped in the toilet rooms
    D. original lath and plaster had been replaced by combustible wood paneling and there had been an extensive use of highly flammable decorations

17. It is INCORRECT for a fire officer giving training on the protection of electronic data processing (EDP) units and ancillary equipment against fire damage to state that

A. the design features of EDP units make them relatively resistant to damage by temperatures under 600° F
B. smoke and acids produced by fire can adversely affect the operation of computer equipment and magnetic components
C. the heat and steam produced by a fire and its extinguishment that would not normally damage ordinary paper records may easily damage magnetic tapes
D. in cases where fire can spread throughout or beyond the computer's housing, a fixed $CO_2$ system may be required

18. Of the following exit and access requirements relating to dead-end corridors in various occupancy group buildings, it is generally MOST accurate to state that

    A. no more than one classroom shall be permitted on a dead-end corridor in an educational occupancy
    B. storage of combustible materials in non-combustible lockers is permitted in dead-end corridors in an institutional occupancy
    C. dead-end corridors are not permitted in an assembly occupancy
    D. no more than one patient bedroom is permitted in a dead-end corridor in an institutional occupancy

19. In the past, building marquee collapses have resulted in the injury or death of firefighters. According to the new building code, marquees are generally

    A. not permitted
    B. permitted if supported by incombustible piers at the curb line
    C. not permitted to project beyond the street line
    D. permitted on buildings of a public nature but may have to be removed if the building occupancy is changed

20. When a standpipe system is altered, extended, or extensively repaired, it must undergo certain inspections and tests.
    Of the following, it is generally MOST accurate to state that the

    A. entire system shall be subjected to the hydrostatic test pressure
    B. altered, new or repaired section shall be subjected to the pressure test and the entire system subjected to the flow test
    C. flow test shall be confined to a determination that water is available at the top outlet of each riser
    D. pressure test in buildings not exceeding 3 stories or 40 feet in height need only sustain 150 percent of the normal hydrostatic pressure at the topmost hose outlet

21. A substance which is subject to *spontaneous combustion* is one that

    A. is explosive when heated
    B. is capable of catching fire without an external source of heat
    C. acts to speed up the burning of material
    D. liberates oxygen when heated

Questions 22-25.

DIRECTIONS: Questions 22 through 25 are to be answered on the basis of the following paragraph.

5 (#2)

For the five-year period 2006-2010, inclusive, the average annual fire loss in the United States amounted to approximately $1,354,830,000. Included in this estimate is $1,072,666,000 damage to buildings and contents, and $282,164,000 average annual loss in aircraft, motor vehicles, forest and other miscellaneous fires not involving buildings. Preliminary estimates indicate that the total United States fire loss in 2011 was $1,615,000,000. These are property damage fire losses only and do not include indirect losses resulting from fires which are just as real and sometimes far more serious than property damage losses. But because evaluation of indirect monetary losses is usually very difficult, their importance in the national fire waste picture is often overlooked.

22. According to the data in the above paragraph, the BEST of the following estimates of the total direct fire loss in the United States for the six-year period 2006-2011, inclusive, is

    A. $1,400,000,000     B. $2,700,000,000
    C. $7,000,000,000     D. $8,400,000,000

23. The BEST example of an indirect fire loss, as that term is used in the above paragraph, is monetary loss due to

    A. smoke or water damage to exposures
    B. condemnation of foodstuffs following a fire
    C. interruption of business following a fire
    D. forcible entry by firemen operating at a fire

24. Suppose that during the period 2011-2015 the average annual fire loss to buildings and contents increases 10 percent, and the average annual loss due to fires not involving buildings decreases 10 percent. The MOST valid of the following conclusions is that the average annual fire loss for the 2011-2015 period, compared to the losses for the 2006-2011 period,

    A. will increase
    B. will decrease
    C. will be unchanged
    D. cannot be calculated from the information given

25. If a comparison is made between total annual direct and indirect fire losses on the basis of the information given in the above paragraph, the MOST valid of the following conclusions is that

    A. generally, direct losses are higher
    B. generally, indirect losses are higher
    C. generally, direct and indirect losses are approximately equal
    D. there is not sufficient information to determine which is higher or if they are approximately equal

## KEY (CORRECT ANSWERS)

| | | | |
|---|---|---|---|
| 1. | D | 11. | D |
| 2. | C | 12. | A |
| 3. | B | 13. | C |
| 4. | B | 14. | A |
| 5. | A | 15. | D |
| 6. | D | 16. | A |
| 7. | C | 17. | C |
| 8. | D | 18. | A |
| 9. | D | 19. | D |
| 10. | D | 20. | C |

21. B
22. D
23. C
24. A
25. D

# TEST 3

DIRECTIONS: Each question or incomplete statement is followed by several suggested answers or completions. Select the one that BEST answers the question or completes the statement. *PRINT THE LETTER OF THE CORRECT ANSWER IN THE SPACE AT THE RIGHT.*

1. It has been suggested that companies be given additional Apparatus Field Inspection Duty and other inspectional duties as punishment for poor performance of evolutions, poor condition of equipment or quarters, etc.
   Of the following, the MOST valid objection to this proposal is that

   A. the punishment does not directly improve the skills or functions which are found to be deficient
   B. inspectional activities would be degraded by making such assignments a form of punishment
   C. the punishment is imposed on a group rather than on an individual basis
   D. scheduling of regular inspectional activities would be disrupted

   1.____

2. The Administrative Code authorizes members to issue summonses in cases arising under laws relating to fires and to fire peril.
   Departmental regulations require that such summonses be returnable in the appropriate court _____ than 14 calendar days, _____ Sundays and holidays.

   A. not less; including        B. not less; excluding
   C. not more; including        D. not more; excluding

   2.____

3. When conducting an Apparatus Field Inspection of an occupancy with a required and approved sprinkler system, it is MOST important, of the following, for firemen to make certain that

   A. feeder lines are adequate to supply the number of sprinkler heads
   B. sprinkler heads are sufficient and properly spaced
   C. stock does not interfere with the proper distribution of water from sprinkler heads
   D. records of monthly hydrostatic pressure tests are properly kept and are up to date

   3.____

4. While inspecting an above-ground storage tank installation, an inspector notices leakage of the contents through *weep* holes in a tank.
   This is a sign that the

   A. tank contents are under excessive pressure
   B. strength of the entire tank may be endangered by corrosion
   C. volumetric capacity of the tank has been exceeded
   D. tank is *breathing* as intended

   4.____

5. A member on inspectional duty came across, in a building under construction, a propane gas heater with its safety valve negated by means of wire and tape across the buttons at the top of the safety assembly.
   Of the following actions taken by the member in this situation, the one that is NOT in accord with departmental orders is the

   5.____

A. serving of a violation order to discontinue use of devices to negate safety features on propane gas heaters on premises
B. picking up of the permits for storage and use of propane
C. notification of the Battalion Chief of the administrative district concerned
D. impounding of the propane heater

6. Of the following, the PRIMARY purpose of holding fire tests at a high-rise office building is to

   A. determine the hazard of polyurethane insulation
   B. evaluate the effectiveness of sprinklers with a limited water supply
   C. test the effectiveness of stair pressurization
   D. develop procedures for venting the fire floor by window vents

7. At the first sign of a fire, the manager of a motion picture theatre had the lights turned on and made the following announcement: *Ladies and gentlemen, the management has found it necessary to dismiss the audience. Please remain seated until it is time for your aisle to file out. In leaving the theatre, follow the directions of the ushers. There is no danger involved.*
The manager's action in this situation was

   A. *proper*
   B. *improper,* chiefly because he did not tell the audience the reason for the dismissal
   C. *improper,* chiefly because he did not permit all members of the audience to leave at once
   D. *improper,* chiefly because he misled the audience by saying that there was no danger

8. Generally, sprinkler heads must be replaced each time they are used.
The BEST explanation of why this is necessary is that the sprinkler heads

   A. are subject to rusting after discharging water
   B. may become clogged after discharging water
   C. have a distorted pattern of discharge of water after use
   D. are set off by the effect of heat on metal and cannot be reset

9. A fire insurance inspector suggested to the manager of a fireproof warehouse that bags of flour be stacked on skids (wooden platforms 6" high, 6x6 feet in area). Of the following, the BEST justification for this suggestion is that in the event of a fire, the bags on skids are less likely to

   A. topple
   B. be damaged by water used in extinguishment
   C. catch fire
   D. be ripped by fire equipment

10. Permitting piles of scrap paper cuttings to accumulate in a factory building is a bad practice CHIEFLY because they may

    A. ignite spontaneously
    B. interfere with fire extinguishment operations
    C. catch fire from a spark or smoldering match
    D. interfere with escape of occupants if a fire occurs

3 (#3)

11. High grass and weeds should not be permitted to grow near a building CHIEFLY because, in the event of a grass fire, the weeds and grass may

    A. give off toxic fumes
    B. limit maneuverability of firemen
    C. interfere with the escape of occupants from the building
    D. bring the fire to the building and set it on fire

11.____

12. Visitors near patients in *oxygen tents* are not permitted to smoke.
    The BEST of the following reasons for this prohibition is that

    A. the flame of the cigarette or cigar may flare dangerously
    B. smoking tobacco is irritating to persons with respiratory disease
    C. smoking in bed is one of the major causes of fires
    D. diseases may be transmitted by means of tobacco smoke

12.____

13. A MAJOR difference between the building code currently in effect and the one in effect prior to it is that in the current code

    A. doors to the outside grade must be the same size as corridor doors
    B. sprinklering of a building will permit a reduction in total door width
    C. the width of an exit door is based on the width of the corridor leading to it
    D. the width of exit doors is based on both the number of persons and the type of occupancy

13.____

14. While inspecting a one-story factory building erected in 1962, you notice that an exit door has been relocated. The size, location, and lighting of all exits in the building comply with the old building code in effect before.
    To determine whether the relocated exit is a legal one, it is necessary to check the provisions of

    A. the State Labor Law and the new building code for the relocated exit *only*
    B. the State Labor Law *only*
    C. the new building code for the relocated exit *only*
    D. none of the foregoing since checking the old building code is sufficient

14.____

15. The new building code divides the construction clauses into two major construction groups.
    These two groups are called

    A. fireproof and non-fireproof
    B. rigid frame and flexible frame
    C. commercial and residential
    D. combustible and noncombustible

15.____

16. The State Labor Law requires that the balconies and stairways of outside fire escapes be able to safely sustain a live load, in pounds per square foot, of _____ with a safety factor of _____.

    A. 75; two   B. 90; four   C. 105; two   D. 120; four

16.____

17. A plant manufacturing nitro-cellulose products has 100 employees. The Fire Prevention Code requires that these premises be equipped with fire pails filled with water. The required MINIMUM number of such pails must be

    A. 25    B. 50    C. 75    D. 100

18. The MAIN purpose of an oil separator is to

    A. separate volatile inflammable oils from other oils
    B. provide a fireproof block between a spark or flame device and an oil storage tank
    C. prevent volatile inflammable oils from flowing into a sewer
    D. make it impossible for the wrong kind of oil to be delivered from a bulk storage plant

19. The MAXIMUM quantity of fuel oil permitted to be stored in an exposed tank in the cellar of a two-family dwelling is _____ gallons.

    A. 225    B. 550    C. 750    D. 875

20. According to the Fire Prevention Code, the MAXIMUM quantity of paint (other than water base) that may be stored without a permit is _____ gallons.

    A. 10    B. 15    C. 20    D. 25

21. Of the following licenses, certificates of qualification, or certificates of fitness, the Fire Department does NOT issue the one authorizing the holder to

    A. operate refrigerating machines (unlimited capacity)
    B. install underground storage tanks for gasoline
    C. operate low pressure boilers using #6 oil
    D. install oil burning equipment

22. In the course of your work in a residential area, you see a wood frame, brick veneer dwelling, two-stories and attic in height, erected in 1965. The building is occupied by two families, with a living room in the attic.
    Without special approval by the Board of Standards and Appeals, this condition could

    A. not be legal
    B. be legal provided that there is a fire escape from the attic
    C. be legal provided the stair enclosure is properly fire retarded
    D. be legal provided that the attic living room is not used as a bedroom

23. A typical occupancy falling into the Assembly occupancy group as used in the building code would be a

    A. radio station         B. library
    C. nursing home          D. tavern

24. Of the following situations, the one in which a fire escape may NOT be considered a legal means of egress is in a three-story

    A. factory building erected in 1912
    B. mixed occupancy building with a store on the first floor and one family on each of the floors above, erected in 1965
    C. multiple dwelling erected in 1971
    D. office building erected in 1950 and altered in 1972

25. A storage garage is one that has 25._____
    A. a stock room for repair parts for vehicles
    B. an area for vehicles that are not used on a daily basis
    C. a gasoline tank to supply gasoline to the vehicles
    D. room only for vehicles that are to be sold

---

## KEY (CORRECT ANSWERS)

| | | | |
|---|---|---|---|
| 1. | B | 11. | D |
| 2. | A | 12. | A |
| 3. | C | 13. | D |
| 4. | B | 14. | B |
| 5. | A | 15. | D |
| 6. | C | 16. | B |
| 7. | A | 17. | B |
| 8. | D | 18. | C |
| 9. | B | 19. | B |
| 10. | C | 20. | C |

| | |
|---|---|
| 21. | D |
| 22. | A |
| 23. | D |
| 24. | C |
| 25. | C |

---

# TEST 4

DIRECTIONS: Each question or incomplete statement is followed by several suggested answers or completions. Select the one that BEST answers the question or completes the statement. *PRINT THE LETTER OF THE CORRECT ANSWER IN THE SPACE AT THE RIGHT.*

1. A violation order is to be served requiring the immediate removal of liquefied petroleum gas cylinders when such cylinders are found on construction sites without a permit issued by the Fire Department.
Pending removal of such cylinders,

   A. vacate procedures are to be instituted
   B. a fireman is to be detailed to the site to safeguard the illegally stored gas cylinders
   C. the contractor is to be ordered to provide a watchman to safeguard the illegally stored gas cylinders
   D. the Police Department is to be notified so that a patrolman can be assigned to the site to safeguard the illegally stored gas cylinders

1.____

2. A four-story loft building is now occupied as follows: Street level - furniture repair and refinishing shop; 2nd story - one apartment occupied by an artist-in-residence, wife, and 5 young children; 3rd story - two apartments each occupied by an artist-in-residence and his wife; 4th story - one apartment occupied by an artist-in-residence, his wife, and his mother-in-law. The building is non-fireproof construction, 40' x 70', is 50' in height, and has an automatic wet sprinkler system protecting the furniture shop. The occupancy as described is

   A. legal
   B. illegal, because the sprinkler system does not extend throughout the building
   C. illegal, because the number of occupants exceeds the permissible limits
   D. illegal, because of the presence of the furniture repair and refinishing shop

2.____

3. Some organizations have adopted the National Fire Protection Association diamond-shaped coding system for identifying characteristics of hazardous materials. The diamond shown in the diagram at the right has its boxes labeled W, X, Y, and Z.
Under the National Fire Protection Association coding system, the lettered boxes represent, respectively,

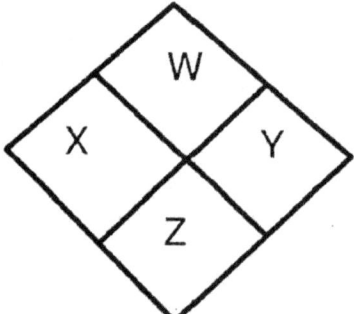

   A. X - Health, Y - Reactive, W - Flammable
   B. X - Reactive, Y - Flammable, W - Health
   C. X - Health, Y - Reactive, Z - Flammable
   D. X - Flammable, Y - Health, Z - Reactive

3.____

4. The shut sprinkler control valve is one of industry's greatest fire hazards. When it is necessary to shut down a system for repairs or other reasons, certain precautions should be taken.
   Of the following statements regarding such precautions, the LEAST acceptable is to

   A. have the system shut down during non-working hours
   B. have the system shut down during working hours while normal operations are going on
   C. notify the Fire Department of the intended shutdown
   D. prepare to supply the system through the two-inch drain in the event of an emergency or fire

Questions 5-8.

DIRECTIONS: Questions 5 through 8 are to be answered on the basis of the information given in the following paragraph.

A mixture of a combustible vapor and air will burn only when the proportion of fuel to air lies within a certain range, i.e., between the upper and lower limits of flammability. If a third, non-combustible gas is now added to the mixture, the limits will be narrowed. As increasing amounts of diluent are added, the limits come closer until, at a certain critical concentration, they will converge. This is the peak concentration. It is the minimum amount of diluent that will inhibit the combustion of any fuel-air mixture.

5. If additional diluent is added beyond the peak concentration, the flammable limits of the mixture will

   A. converge rapidly
   B. diverge slowly
   C. diverge rapidly
   D. not be affected

6. If the four numbers listed below were peak concentration values obtained in a test of four diluents, then the MOST efficient diluent would have the value of

   A. 7.5    B. 10    C. 12.5    D. 15

7. The word *inhibit,* as used in the last sentence of the above paragraph, means MOST NEARLY

   A. slow the rate of
   B. prevent entirely the occurrence of
   C. reduce the intensity of
   D. retard to an appreciable extent the manifestation of

8. The one of the graphs shown below which BEST represents the process described in the paragraph is

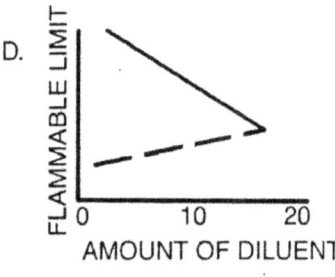

——————— UPPER FLAMMABLE LIMITS

— — — — — — LOWER FLAMMABLE LIMITS

9. Of the following metals, the one which is LEAST acceptable as a non-sparking metal for tools is

   A. hardened copper
   B. bronze
   C. brass
   D. copper alloys

10. Of the heating defects responsible for hotel fires, the MAJOR defect is

    A. defective flues
    B. overheated appliances
    C. defective appliances
    D. inadequate clearance

11. Community relations and fire prevention education efforts must be concentrated in residential neighborhoods, particularly in the depressed areas of the city.
    The one of the following which does NOT provide support for this point of view is that

    A. residential occupants are exposed to more serious occupancy hazards than industrial workers
    B. open hydrants, excessive false alarms, and hostile acts are concentrated in depressed areas
    C. rubbish fires and vacant building fires are most frequent in these areas
    D. the primary incidence of fire takes place in residential areas

12. The State Multiple Dwelling Law allows a *family* to have four boarders, and the City Multiple Dwelling Law allows a *family* to have only two boarders.
    In the city, a *family* is allowed

A. two boarders because the Multiple Dwelling Code is the more restrictive requirement
B. four boarders because the State law takes precedence over the city code
C. two or four boarders, depending upon whether the Law or Code applies to a given situation
D. two or four boarders, at the discretion of the Fire Commissioner

13. Fire Department regulations governing the issuance of city-wide permits for the use of combustible gases during temporary torch operations require fire guards to make inspections after completion of torch operations for the purpose of detecting fire. Signed inspection reports are to be filed and available for examination by the Fire Department.
The one of the following which is MOST accurate and complete is that such inspections are to be made _____ after completion of operations.

13._____

A. every 15 minutes, for a period of one hour,
B. one-half hour and one hour
C. every half hour, for a period of two hours,
D. one half hour, one hour, and two hours,

14. On an A.F.I.D., a company comes upon the following garages:
   I. Adjacent to a dwelling occupied by one family, storing two cars, one owned by the family and the other by the next door neighbor who pays a monthly rental
   II. In a dwelling outside the fire limits, occupied by one family storing three cars owned by the family
   III. In a fireproof dwelling occupied by three families in two stories above the garage, with two means of egress and no entrances to any apartment through the garage, storing two cars owned by tenants

14._____

A Fire Department permit is required for

A. none of these garages
B. garages I and III
C. garages II and III
D. all three garages

15. If a building is altered under the provisions of the building code, and the building is not provided with sprinkler protection, the one of the following actions that the company officer should take is to

15._____

A. transmit an A-8 report for referral to the Department of Buildings
B. issue a summons to the owner of the building
C. prepare a report on Department letterhead and send it to the Division of Fire Prevention
D. call the Department of Buildings and notify them about the violation

16. The one of the following fibers that can be made into fabric which can be effectively treated with common water-soluble-salt flame-retardant solutions is

16._____

A. dacron   B. nylon   C. rayon   D. nomex

17. The inspection of public assembly occupancies classified as theatres in company administrative districts should be scheduled so that each such premises is inspected AT LEAST once every

17._____

A. 30 days, approximately one half hour before scheduled performances
B. 30 days, at irregular time periods when premises are open to the public

C. three months, approximately one half hour before scheduled performances
D. three months, at irregular time periods when premises are open to the public

18. The one of the following automatic fire alarm detectors that works on the principle of uneven expansion of bi-metallic strips is the _____ device.

    A. rate compensation
    B. ionization type
    C. rate of rise type
    D. fixed temperature

19. The one of the following which is probably the MOST frequent source of ignition of flammable vapors in hospital operating rooms is

    A. static electricity
    B. x-ray equipment
    C. sterilizing machinery
    D. electric cauterizing devices

20. At an open demonstration, polyurethane foam, widely used in furniture, was exposed to fire.
    In this demonstration, it was shown that the foam

    A. was self-extinguishing
    B. flamed and gave off acrid smoke
    C. could not be ignited
    D. melted but would not flame

Questions 21-23.

DIRECTIONS: Questions 21 through 23 are to be answered on the basis of the following paragraph.

Shafts extending into the top story, except those stair shafts where the stairs do not continue to the roof, shall be carried through and at least two feet above the roof. Every shaft extending above the roof, except open shafts and elevator shafts, shall be enclosed at the top with a roof of materials having a fire resistive rating of one hour and a metal skylight covering at least three-quarters of the area of the shaft in the top story, except that skylights over stair shafts shall have an area not less than one-tenth the area of the shaft in the top story, but shall be not less than fifteen square feet in area. Any shaft terminating below the top story of a structure and those stair shafts not required to extend through the roof shall have the top enclosed with materials having the same fire resistive rating as required for the shaft enclosure.

21. The above paragraph states that the elevator shafts which extend into the top story are

    A. not required to have a skylight but are required to extend at least two feet above the roof
    B. neither required to have a skylight nor to extend above the roof
    C. required to have a skylight covering at least three-quarters of the area of the shaft in the top story and to extend at least two feet above the roof
    D. required to have a skylight covering at least three-quarters of the area of the shaft in the top story but are not required to extend above the roof

22. The one of the following skylights which meets the requirements of the above paragraph is a skylight measuring

   A. 4' x 4' over a stair shaft which, on the top story, measures 20' x 9'
   B. 4 1/2' x 3 1/2' over a pipe shaft which, on the top story, measures 5' x 4'
   C. 2 1/2' x 1 1/2' over a dumbwaiter shaft which, on the top story, measures 2 1/2' x 2 1/2'
   D. 4' x 3' over a stair shaft which, on the top story, measures 15' x 6'

23. Suppose that in a Class I building, a shaft which does not go to the roof is required to have a three-hour fire resistive rating.
   In regard to the material enclosing the top of this shaft, the above paragraph

   A. states that a one-hour fire resistive rating is required
   B. states that a three-hour fire resistive rating is required
   C. implies that no fire resistive rating is required
   D. neither states nor implies anything about the fire resistive rating

Questions 24-25.

DIRECTIONS: Questions 24 and 25 are to be answered SOLELY on the basis of the following passage.

The four different types of building collapses are as follows:

1. <u>Building Wall Collapse</u> - An outside wall of the building collapses but the floors maintain their positions.

2. <u>Lean-to Collapse</u> - One end of a floor collapses onto the floor below it. This leaves a sheltered area on the floor below.

3. <u>Floor Collapse</u> - An entire floor falls to the floor below it but large pieces of machinery in the floor below provide spaces which can provide shelter.

4. <u>Pancake Collapse</u> - A floor collapses completely onto the floor below it, leaving no spaces. In some cases, the force of this collapse causes successive lower floors to collapse.

24. The MOST serious injuries are likely to occur at _____ collapses.

   A. pancake         B. lean-to
   C. floor           D. building wall

25. Of the following, a floor collapse is MOST likely to occur in a(n)

   A. apartment building    B. private home
   C. factory building      D. hotel

26. When using a standardized survey report during AFID, it generally is NOT advisable to make an inspection of the facilities in the strict sequence of the items on the form PRIMARILY because the

   A. sequence of the items in the form may not correspond to the physical arrangement of the occupancy or structure
   B. members performing inspection duty will be more likely to make errors of omission rather than commission on the forms

C. occupancy or structure may require a multi-inspector, multi-page form inspectional approach
D. procedure does not permit distribution of tasks among all the members participating in the inspection

27. Sparks given off by welding torches are a serious fire hazard.
The BEST of the following methods of dealing with this hazard is to conduct welding operations only

A. in fireproof buildings protected by sprinkler systems
B. out-of-doors on a day with little wind blowing
C. on materials certified to be non-combustible by recognized testing laboratories
D. after loose combustible materials have been cleared from the area and with a man standing by with a hose line

28. Two types of steel hoops are commonly found on older wooden gravity tanks - round hoops and flat ones.
The one of the following statements concerning such hoops that is MOST accurate is that hidden corrosion is a serious problem with _____ hoops.

A. the round hoops but not with the flat
B. the flat hoops but not with the round
C. both types of
D. neither type of

29. While on AFID, you come across a clothing factory which shows evidence of poor housekeeping practices.
For you to imply to the owner that the Fire Department will conduct frequent inspections of his premises until satisfactory conditions are maintained is

A. *proper,* mainly because the owner may be persuaded by it to maintain satisfactory conditions
B. *improper,* mainly because the owner may feel that he is being harassed
C. *proper,* mainly because any means which result in the elimination of hazardous conditions are permissible
D. *improper,* mainly because threats which may not be carried out should not be made

30. Generally, officers on fire prevention inspection duty do not inspect the living quarters of private dwellings unless the occupants agree to the inspection.
The BEST of the following explanations of why private dwellings are excluded from compulsory inspections is that

A. private dwellings seldom catch fire
B. fires in private dwellings are more easily extinguished than other types of fires
C. people may resent such inspections as an invasion of privacy
D. the monetary value of private dwellings is lower than that of other types of occupancies

## KEY (CORRECT ANSWERS)

| | | | | | |
|---|---|---|---|---|---|
| 1. | C | 11. | A | 21. | A |
| 2. | D | 12. | A | 22. | B |
| 3. | A | 13. | B | 23. | B |
| 4. | B | 14. | B | 24. | A |
| 5. | D | 15. | A | 25. | C |
| 6. | A | 16. | C | 26. | A |
| 7. | B | 17. | A | 27. | D |
| 8. | D | 18. | D | 28. | B |
| 9. | C | 19. | A | 29. | A |
| 10. | A | 20. | B | 30. | C |

# EXAMINATION SECTION
# TEST 1

DIRECTIONS: Each question or incomplete statement is followed by several suggested answers or completions. Select the one that BEST answers the question or completes the statement. *PRINT THE LETTER OF THE CORRECT ANSWER IN THE SPACE AT THE RIGHT.*

1. A television receiver has a GREATER inherent fire hazard than a conventional radio receiver because

    A. of greater electrical leakage
    B. cabinets are inadequately ventilated
    C. higher voltage is used in the system
    D. they are operated for longer periods of time
    E. the coaxial cable lead-in is covered with a highly flammable coating

2. Of the following, the MOST frequent factor contributing to conflagrations in the United States and Canada in the last 25 years has been

    A. high winds
    B. lack of exposure protection
    C. delayed alarms
    D. congestion of hazardous occupancies
    E. inadequate water distribution system

3. If, upon reinspection of a plant which has 30 days to comply with a previous order, you find that the order has not been completely obeyed but that some work has taken place, you SHOULD

    A. report to proper authorities to obtain legal action
    B. assume the delay is unavoidable and check again in 30 days
    C. inform the person in charge that a 10-day extension will be granted and that legal action will be taken if the order has not been followed
    D. issue a summons for failure to comply
    E. none of the above

4. An analysis of loss records in one city showed that one-third of the total loss in building fires was in residence buildings and that, of the total loss in such buildings, in the year under study, nearly 80 percent was in multiple dwelling buildings.
The one of the following courses of action for the Fire Department which should be taken IMMEDIATELY on the basis of this report is to

    A. relocate companies
    B. recommend sprinkler protection for multiple dwellings
    C. institute special training fighting multiple dwelling fires
    D. reduce the protection given to other than multiple dwelling residences
    E. inspect multiple dwellings more thoroughly

5. It is good practice to so install heating devices that under conditions of maximum heat (long-continued exposure) they will not cause the temperature of exposed woodwork to exceed 160° F. This practice is

A. *correct*, because of the possibility that wood and other combustible materials, after long-continued exposure to relatively moderate heat, may ignite at temperatures far below their usual ignition temperatures
B. *not correct*, because no wood in ordinary use will ignite at a temperature of less than 400°F and, consequently, the requirement is needlessly severe
C. *correct*, because oxidation proceeds much more rapidly at higher temperatures
D. *not correct*, because oxidation proceeds much more slowly at higher temperatures
E. *correct*, because under prolonged heating the temperature of the air in the room will build up until the ignition point is reached unless the applied temperature is kept sufficiently low

6. Analysis of the causes of fires is important, as only by knowing the causes of fires is it possible to effectively prevent fire.
An analysis of fires in rooms used for spraying flammable paints and finishes has shown that the MOST important of the following causes is

   A. smoking by employees
   B. defective electrical equipment
   C. spontaneous ignition of paint deposits, rubbish, and wiping rags
   D. static electricity resulting from friction
   E. cutting and welding operations

6.____

7. The flammability or combustibility of radioactive materials has little or no direct effect on the fire hazard of a laboratory PRIMARILY because

   A. the unusual structural characteristics of such a laboratory serve to limit possible fire spread from such hazards
   B. water or water spray are effective on most radioactive substances
   C. the quantities of such material in any one laboratory are usually small
   D. laboratory fire prevention and firefighting facilities usually exceed maximum fire hazards
   E. such materials are inherently of a low order of combustibility

7.____

8. Comparison of the burning qualities of foam rubber and cotton mattresses shows that GENERALLY

   A. a cotton mattress burns faster but cooler
   B. a foam rubber mattress burns slower but hotter
   C. a foam rubber mattress burns faster and hotter
   D. a cotton mattress burns faster and hotter
   E. the potential fire hazard of a foam rubber mattress is higher

8.____

9. During Christmas and other holiday shopping seasons, it is required that frequent inspections shall be made of department stores at irregular intervals. Of the following, the MOST important reason for this inspection procedure is to

   A. prevent unnecessary interference with store operations
   B. check characteristic holiday operations
   C. permit more frequent and thorough coverage of the stores in question
   D. avoid delay in urgent fire operations
   E. permit more flexible scheduling of inspection

9.____

10. The fire load computation of a building indicates, for the most part, the    10.____

    A. risk of a fire breaking out
    B. rate at which a fire is likely to grow
    C. combustibility of the various parts of the building rather than its contents
    D. amount of combustibles and the method of protection
    E. maximum fire stress to which the building might be subjected

11. It is far more important that escape routes from multistory buildings should be protected    11.____
    against smoke and hot gases than from direct flame or heat.
    This statement is

    A. *not correct;* resistive construction is likely to be smoke-resistive as well
    B. *correct;* adequate means for ventilation is essential to prevent cutting off escape routes
    C. *not correct;* unless corridors and escape stairs are constructed of fire resistive materials, progress of fire cannot be blocked
    D. *correct;* unless properly protected from smoke and hot gases, escape stairs would be unusable by occupants
    E. *not correct;* unless properly protected against direct flame or heat, escape routes cannot resist smoke or hot gases

12. The MINIMUM width of exit usually required for a single file of persons is MOST NEARLY    12.____
    _____ inches.

    A. 15-17        B. 18-20        C. 21-23
    D. 24-27        E. 27-30

13. The MOST pronounced method of reducing the fire and life hazards in public buildings is    13.____
    by

    A. ample exits of any type
    B. ample stairways inside the buildings
    C. the use of exit signs and panic locks
    D. fire-resisting construction suitable for the occupancy
    E. installing fire extinguishers in every hallway

14. From all viewpoints, the MOST hazardous materials that could be stored, constituting a    14.____
    life as well as a fire hazard, would be

    A. second-hand niter bags
    B. used motor vehicles
    C. loose or baled vegetable fibers
    D. pyroxylin and pyroxylin plastic products
    E. foam rubber mattresses

15. The CHIEF fire hazard of welding and cutting operations is    15.____

    A. flames of the torch igniting nearby material
    B. broken hose line
    C. flying sparks
    D. backfiring of torch
    E. tank explosion

16. Of the following items associated with motion picture theatres, the PRIMARY hazard is  16.____

    A. misuse of electricity
    B. heating defects
    C. smoking and matches
    D. projection booth fires
    E. improperly lit exits

17. The MOST hazardous method of fumigation is by the use of  17.____

    A. heat (125° F)
    B. carbon tetrachloride mixture with flammable fumigant
    C. carbon dioxide mixture with flammable fumigant
    D. carbon bisulphide
    E. carbon monoxide

18. The combined use of inspections, periodic reports of activities, follow-up procedures, special reports from subordinates, and a rating system comprise a system of  18.____

    A. coordination
    B. command
    C. control
    D. representation
    E. on-the-job training

19. What should be provided in air conditioning ducts to PREVENT the spread of fire and smoke through a property?  19.____

    A. Automatic dampers
    B. Intake screens
    C. Steel wool air filters
    D. Heat actuated devices
    E. Halon extinguishers

20. The OUTSTANDING fire hazard of boarding and rooming houses is  20.____

    A. misuse of electricity
    B. smoking and matches
    C. heating defects
    D. incendiary
    E. kitchen fires

21. The SIMPLEST and MOST feasible method of avoiding the overheating of woodwork near any high temperature heating appliance is by  21.____

    A. filling the intervening space with insulating material
    B. covering the woodwork with sheet metal
    C. providing an air space between the woodwork and the appliance
    D. covering the woodwork with asbestos sheets
    E. painting the woodwork with varnish

22. The PRINCIPLE source of fire hazard in connection with heating equipment in mercantile buildings comes from  22.____

    A. defective wiring
    B. insufficient clearance from combustible materials
    C. the storage and handling of fuel
    D. defective motors
    E. none of the above

23. More ink has been spilled on the item of smoking as a cause of fire than on any other, but the total result has been negligible.
    This situation is BEST accounted for by the fact that  23.____

A. smoking is generally an automatic act performed unthinkingly
B. truly effective facilities for elimination of smoking hazards are exceedingly cumbersome or expensive
C. most people regard smoking as a personal prerogative and resent control measures
D. smoking is practiced by many individuals with defective intelligence and social attitudes
E. individual behavior cannot be controlled

24. There are two basic factors in assessing building construction from the fire prevention standpoint. One is the combustibility of materials.
The other is

    A. extinguishment facilities
    B. excess structural strength
    C. ventilation control
    D. limitation of fire spread
    E. means of access and egress

25. The LEAST accurate statement concerning the protection of openings in walls and partitions is:

    A. Protection of wall openings may prevent either the horizontal or the vertical spread of fire
    B. The general features of a building have no bearing on the extent to which such protection is necessary
    C. The protection secured by fire doors and fire windows cannot be better than the fire resistant value of the walls
    D. Good solid walls are preferable to those with fire doors in restricting the spread of fire
    E. Sprinkler systems may provide adequate protection

26. The one of the following which is NOT included among the six categories in which all structures are classified by the Administrative Code with respect to type of construction is _____ structures.

    A. heavy timber    B. metal    C. wood frame
    D. fire-resistant  E. fireproof

27. All storage tanks, comprising or forming a part of an oil storage plant, shall be buried so that the tops thereof shall be a distance below the grade level of AT LEAST

    A. 1'    B. 2'    C. 3'    D. 4'    E. 6'

28. According to the Administrative Code, a Class B refrigeration system is one

    A. capable of less than 15 tons capacity
    B. containing not more than 20 lbs. of refrigerant
    C. capable of less than 30 tons capacity
    D. containing 1000 pounds or over of refrigerant
    E. capable of 40 tons capacity or over

29. According to the Administrative Code, it shall be unlawful to transport or store guncotton EXCEPT in

   A. strong wooden cases lined with liquid-proof paper
   B. strong wooden cases
   C. carboys so tinted as to exclude light
   D. water-tight metal vessels
   E. aluminum or other non-tarnishing metal

30. One purpose of building inspections is to enable the Fire Department to plan its operations before a fire starts.
    This statement is

   A. *incorrect;* no two fires are alike
   B. *correct;* many firefighting problems can be anticipated
   C. *incorrect;* fires should be prevented, not extinguished
   D. *correct;* the Fire Department should have detailed plans for every possible emergency
   E. *incorrect;* fires are not predictable

## KEY (CORRECT ANSWERS)

| | | |
|---|---|---|
| 1. C | 11. D | 21. C |
| 2. A | 12. C | 22. B |
| 3. A | 13. D | 23. A |
| 4. E | 14. D | 24. D |
| 5. A | 15. C | 25. B |
| 6. C | 16. D | 26. D |
| 7. C | 17. D | 27. B |
| 8. C | 18. C | 28. C |
| 9. B | 19. A | 29. D |
| 10. E | 20. C | 30. B |

# TEST 2

DIRECTIONS: Each question or incomplete statement is followed by several suggested answers or completions. Select the one that BEST answers the question or completes the statement. *PRINT THE LETTER OF THE CORRECT ANSWER IN THE SPACE AT THE RIGHT.*

1. According to the Fire Prevention Code, an essential oil is defined as an oil     1.____

    A. needed to provide the viscosity of a given grade of oil
    B. derived from animal life and not from mineral sources
    C. which has low volatility at room temperature
    D. used for flavoring or perfuming purposes
    E. required as the base of lubricating compounds

2. According to the Fire Prevention Code, it shall be UNLAWFUL to sell or deliver for use     2.____

    A. sticks or cartridges of explosives which are packed so as to lie on their sides
    B. any explosive except in original and unbroken packages
    C. dynamite in cases of 25 and 50 lbs.
    D. nitroglycerine in liquid form under any circumstances
    E. any explosives packed in quantities in excess of 50 lbs.

3. The Fire Prevention Code requires that a storage garage containing more than four motor vehicles shall be continuously under the supervision of one or more persons, each holding a certificate of fitness.     3.____
   The MAXIMUM number of such certificated persons required for any garage shall be

    A. 7    B. 6    C. 5    D. 4    E. 3

4. According to the annual report statistics for the last years, the floor of multiple dwellings where fires started MOST frequently was the     4.____

    A. cellar        B. 1st floor      C. 2nd floor
    D. 3rd floor     E. roof

5. You are assigned to inspect buildings for fire hazards. The one of the following MOST appropriately used for fire-retardant coating of wood is     5.____

    A. varnish       B. shellac        C. wood stain
    D. lacquer       E. white wash

6. An officer taking some clothing to a dry cleaner in his neighborhood noticed that inflammable cleaning fluid was stored in a way which created a fire hazard. The officer called this to the attention of the proprietor, explaining the danger involved.     6.____
   This method of handling the situation was

    A. *bad;* the officer should not have interfered in a matter which was not his responsibility
    B. *good;* the proprietor would probably remove the hazard and be more careful in the future
    C. *bad;* the officer should have reported the situation to the fire inspector's office without saying anything to the proprietor

89

D. *good;* since the officer was a customer, he should treat the proprietor more leniently than he would treat other violators
E. *bad;* the officer should have ordered the proprietor to remove the violation immediately and issued a summons

7. Automobile fires are caused MOST frequently by   7.____

   A. overheating of the motor
   B. gasoline explosion
   C. defective carburetor
   D. defective or overheated brakes
   E. faulty ignition wiring

8. The PRINCIPAL fire hazard in connection with heating equipment in mercantile buildings comes from   8.____

   A. failure to operate and clean equipment properly
   B. insufficient clearance from combustible material
   C. use of improper types or grades of fuel
   D. defective flues
   E. exposed wiring in heating controls

9. Supermarket fires have in common the fact that MOST fires occur in the   9.____

   A. utility area
   B. sales area
   C. basement storage area
   D. check-out and packaging area
   E. shelves containing paper products

10. Of the following, the LEAST accurate statement concerning Field Violation Cards is that   10.____

    A. when all the violations listed on a Field Violation Card have been complied with, such card shall be placed in the Occupancy Folder
    B. not more than two Minor Violation Orders shall be recorded on any one card
    C. not more than two Major Violation Orders shall be recorded on any one card
    D. when the space on both sides is completely used for entries, such card is placed on file in the Occupancy Folder
    E. when subsequent violations are found for a building which previously complied with violations found, the additional entries shall be made on the same Field Violation Card

11. Of the following statements concerning coal storage, the one that is ACCEPTABLE is:   11.____

    A. Coal for storage should preferably be deposited in horizontal layers
    B. Alternate wetting and drying will prevent development of heat in the pile
    C. The desirable height of a properly stored coal pile is 25 to 30 feet
    D. Storage of mixed sizes of coal together will reduce spontaneous ignition to a minimum
    E. Standing timbers should be placed in coal piles to provide air access and circulation

12. The Multiple Dwelling Law provides that, in every multiple dwelling erected after April 18, 1929, every stair, fire stair, and fire tower beyond a specified width shall be provided with a handrail on each side.

    This specified width is

    A. 3'2"   B. 3'8"   C. 4'2"   D. 4'10"   E. 5'6"

13. The one of the following for which the Official Action Guide provides that a permit is required for storage, regardless of quantity and purpose, is

    A. shale oil
    B. heavy lubricating oil
    C. machine oil
    D. kerosene
    E. illuminating oil

Questions 14-16.

DIRECTIONS: Questions 14 through 16, inclusive, are to be answered on the basis of the following paragraph.

A flameproof fabric is defined as one which, when exposed to small sources of ignition, such as sparks or smoldering cigarettes, does not burn beyond the vicinity of the source of ignition. Cotton fabrics are the materials commonly used that are considered most hazardous. Other materials, such as acetate rayons and linens, are somewhat less hazardous, and woolens and some natural silk fabrics, even when untreated, are about equal to the average treated cotton fabric insofar as flame spread and ease of ignition are concerned. The method of application is to immerse the fabric in a flame-proofing solution. The container used must be large enough so that all the fabric is thoroughly wet and there are no folds which the solution does not penetrate.

14. According to the above paragraph, a flameproof fabric is one which

    A. is unaffected by heat and smoke
    B. resists the spread of flames when ignited
    C. burns with a cold flame
    D. cannot be ignited by sparks or cigarettes
    E. may smolder but cannot burn

15. According to the above paragraph, woolen fabrics which have not been flameproofed are as likely to catch fire as _____ fabrics.

    A. treated silk
    B. treated acetate rayon
    C. untreated linen
    D. untreated synthetic
    E. treated cotton

16. In the method described above, the flameproofing solution is BEST applied to the fabric by _____ the fabric.

    A. sponging   B. spraying   C. dipping
    D. brushing   E. sprinkling

17. The daily peak time for the number of fires in the city, in general,

    A. varies from day to day
    B. is about 9 A.M.

C. is at about 5 P.M.
D. is at about 1 A.M.
E. varies from season to season

18. According to the Multiple Dwelling Law, a part of a building is *fire-retarded* if it is protected against fire in an approved manner with materials of fire-resistive ratings of AT LEAST _____ hour(s).

    A. one    B. two    C. three    D. four    E. five

19. The Multiple Dwelling Law permits the conduct of business in any multiple dwelling EXCEPT that

    A. no space in a non-fireproof multiple dwelling may be used for a bakery or business where fat is boiled under any condition
    B. the number of persons employed in manufacturing enterprises in multiple dwellings shall be limited to a maximum of seven persons
    C. exits of the dwelling portion and the business space may be common if the number of persons employed is limited to ten persons or less
    D. when the ground story of any non-fireproof multiple dwelling is extended for business purposes, the underside of the roof of such extension shall be fire-retarded if there are fire escapes above such extension
    E. there shall be no manufacturing business conducted above the second floor of any non-fireproof multiple dwelling

20. According to the Building Code, a sprinkler system is NOT required in

    A. garages in cellars of multiple dwellings if area is less than 5,000 square feet
    B. dressing rooms and stage of auditoriums of large public high schools where seating capacity is less than 1,500
    C. furnished rooms of converted non-fireproof multiple dwellings if the public hall has sprinkler protection
    D. non-fireproof lodging houses if equipped with an automatic, closed-circuit fire alarm system
    E. department stores if each floor does not exceed 10,000 square feet

21. The Building Code requires that in all newly constructed loft buildings used for mercantile purposes,

    A. 8 inch standpipe risers shall be installed in buildings 150 feet or more in height
    B. standpipes be installed if 75 feet in height or over
    C. the minimum size of standpipe riser in a building 100 feet high be at least 3 inches
    D. when a standpipe is required, no point on a floor be more than 75 feet from a riser
    E. multiple standpipe risers may not be cross-connected

22. The proscenium of a theatre is MOST closely associated with the

    A. stage
    B. special entrance for scenery
    C. street entrance and exit
    D. passageways to boxes
    E. balcony arch over the orchestra section

23. The MAXIMUM quantity of kerosene fuel oil that may be stored for heating and cooking use without a permit from the Fire Commissioner is _____ gallons.   23._____

    A. 10      B. 25      C. 50      D. 100      E. 150

24. An ACCEPTABLE method of absorbing waste oils in a dry cleaning establishment is, according to the Fire Prevention Code,   24._____

    A. a quantity of sand spread on the floor
    B. use of thin asbestos fibre flooring
    C. non-combustible cloth on the floor
    D. diatomaceous earth or equivalent absorbent material spread on the floor
    E. woven glass fibre mats

25. Suppose you are making an inspection of a factory. During the inspection, the factory manager asks you a technical question which you cannot answer.   25._____
Of the following, the BEST procedure for you to follow is to

    A. tell him you are not there to answer his questions but to make an inspection
    B. guess at the answer so that he won't doubt your competency
    C. tell him you don't know the answer but that you will look it up and notify him
    D. give him the title of a textbook that probably would contain the information
    E. change the subject by asking him a question

26. While performing building inspections, a fireman finds a janitor in the basement checking for a gas leak by holding a lighted match to the gas pipes.   26._____
Of the following, the fireman's FIRST action should be to

    A. reprimand the janitor for endangering life and property
    B. explain the hazards of this action to the janitor
    C. report the janitor to his superior as incompetent
    D. tell the janitor to put out the match
    E. issue a summons for this action

27. According to the Administrative Code, a refrigerant is defined as the chemical agent used to produce refrigeration other than   27._____

    A. brine
    B. a chemical of the hydrocarbon clan
    C. the compressor
    D. methyl bromide
    E. ammonia

28. The Administrative Code defines as a combustible mixture any substance which, when tested in a Tagliabue open cup tester, emits an inflammable vapor at temperatures   28._____

    A. below 100° F            B. above 300° F
    C. between 100° F and 300° F    D. below 125° F
    E. above 125° F

29. A partially filled gasoline drum is a more dangerous fire hazard than a full one.   29.____
Of the following, the BEST justification for this statement is that

   A. a partially filled gasoline drum contains relatively little air
   B. gasoline is difficult to ignite
   C. when a gasoline drum is full, the gasoline is more explosive
   D. gasoline vapors are more explosive than gasoline itself
   E. air is not combustible

30. The tendency of this substance to spontaneous heating is very slight. It is usually   30.____
shipped in bulk. This substance should be kept dry, and storing or loading in hot wet piles should be avoided.
This description applies MOST closely to

   A. metal powder    B. soft coal    C. charcoal
   D. scrap film      E. jute

---

## KEY (CORRECT ANSWERS)

| | | | |
|---|---|---|---|
| 1. D | 11. A | 21. B | |
| 2. B | 12. B | 22. A | |
| 3. E | 13. A | 23. A | |
| 4. A | 14. B | 24. A | |
| 5. E | 15. E | 25. C | |
| 6. B | 16. C | 26. D | |
| 7. E | 17. C | 27. A | |
| 8. B | 18. A | 28. C | |
| 9. A | 19. E | 29. D | |
| 10. E | 20. E | 30. E | |

---

# TEST 3

DIRECTIONS: Each question or incomplete statement is followed by several suggested answers or completions. Select the one that BEST answers the question or completes the statement. *PRINT THE LETTER OF THE CORRECT ANSWER IN THE SPACE AT THE RIGHT.*

1. An inspector is denied access to a building by the building manager after presenting his identification. Of the following actions, it would be MOST appropriate for the captain to

   A. post an official notice of inspection on the premises
   B. notify the enforcement unit of the division of fire prevention
   C. give orders to have three routine inspections of premises made before taking special measures to gain access
   D. contact the building owner by telephone to request access

1.____

Questions 2-5.

DIRECTIONS: Questions 2 through 5 are to be answered on the basis of the information given in the following paragraph.

Old buildings are liable to possess a special degree of fire risk merely because they are old. Outmoded electrical wiring systems and installation of new heating appliances for which the building was not designed may contribute to the increased hazard. Old buildings have often been altered many times; parts of the structure may antedate building codes; dangerous defects may have been covered up. On the average, old buildings contain more lumber than comparable new buildings which, in itself, makes old buildings more susceptible to fire. It is not true, though, that sound lumber in old buildings is drier than new lumber. Moisture content of lumber varies with that of the atmosphere to which it is exposed.

2. According to the above paragraph, old buildings present a special fire hazard CHIEFLY because of the

   A. poor planning of the buildings when first designed
   B. haphazard alteration of the buildings
   C. failure to replace worn out equipment
   D. inadequate enforcement of the building codes

2.____

3. We may conclude from the above paragraph that lumber

   A. should not be used in buildings unless absolutely necessary
   B. should not be used near electrical equipment
   C. is more inflammable than newer types of building materials
   D. tends to lose its moisture at a constant rate

3.____

4. According to the above paragraph, the amount of moisture in the wooden parts of a building depends upon the

   A. age of the building
   B. moisture in the surrounding air

4.____

95

C. type of heating equipment used in the building
D. quality of lumber used

5. In regard to building codes, the above paragraph implies that

   A. old buildings are exempt from the provisions of building codes
   B. some buildings now in use were built before building codes were adopted
   C. building codes usually don't cover electrical wiring systems
   D. building codes generally are inadequate

6. According to Department Regulations, the *Monthly Statistical Report - Field Inspection Activity* should include company field inspection duty of all

   A. types
   B. types except re-inspection duty on violation orders
   C. types except surveillance inspection duty
   D. types except inspectional duty relative to complaints

7. During field inspection of a building containing an automatic sprinkler system, you note that the shut-off valves are located where they are not readily accessible. The one of the following procedures to follow in this situation, according to department regulations, is to

   A. write an order to the owner or occupant requiring correction of the physical defect
   B. require no action by the owner or occupant but make special note of the valve location in the building record file
   C. bring to the attention of the owner or occupant the potential water damage hazard inherent in this situation
   D. write an order to the owner or occupant for a sign indicating valve location

8. The difficulties encountered in fighting fire in the cellar of a pool supply occupancy were compounded by bulk storage of calcium hypochlorite.
   This bleaching and sanitizing agent is LEAST likely to

   A. be unstable and highly combustible when finely divided
   B. form a mixture that spontaneously bursts into flame on contact with oxidizable material
   C. decompose when involved in fire, by liberating oxygen and intensifying the fire
   D. have an increased fire and explosion potential when pre-mixed with algaecides and fungicides as an all-purpose water treatment

9. Acetylene is a particularly hazardous flammable gas because, in addition to its flammability, it is reactive and unstable. Consequently, its storage and handling in some respects differs from other flammable gases. The following statements may be pertinent to acetylene and its storage:
   I. Acetylene is not toxic but can have an anesthetic effect
   II. Copper must be avoided in most acetylene piping and equipment
   III. Acetylene gas can explode if subjected to more than 15 psi
   Which one of the following choices lists only those of the abovementioned statements that are generally CORRECT?

   A. I, II        B. II, III        C. I, III        D. I, II, III

10. Before leaving quarters to perform apparatus field inspection duty (AFID) at a hospital, a company officer holds a drill on institutional fire safety.
    It would be MOST appropriate for the officer to tell the members that the MAJORITY of fires in hospitals generally occur in

    A. storage rooms
    B. lounges
    C. patients' rooms
    D. corridors

11. Special fire hazards in industry are sometimes diminished by automatic carbon dioxide fixed-pipe extinguishing systems. While difficult to check an existing system for compliance with design and installation standards, certain of the following conditions can be noted during a building inspection to determine whether it is apparently operative and in good order:
    I. Have cylinders been weighed within the past five years and is there a visible record of such weighing?
    II. Are automatic-closing doors and shutters unobstructed and free to close upon actuation?
    III. Are there means accessible during a fire of manually actuating the system?
    Which of the following choices contains only those of the above conditions that are generally VALID?

    A. I, II   B. II, III   C. I, III   D. I, II, III

12. A considerable number of serious burn injuries and fatalities result from fires involving clothing being worn. The following may or may not be correct statements concerning Fire Department experience gained from such fires:
    I. Cotton and rayon have proved to be relatively nonflammable fibers
    II. Nylon and acetate melt and liquefy under fire exposure, thereby tending to aggravate the severity of burn injuries
    III. Victims of clothing fires are more likely to be persons over 60 years of age than children under 10
    Which of the following choices contains only those of the above-mentioned statements that are generally CORRECT?

    A. I, II   B. I, III   C. II, III   D. I, II, III

13. Some communities have a program for inspecting dwellings, conducted as a courtesy and service to householders.
    The USUAL effect of a dwelling-house inspection campaign is

    A. annoyance on the part of homeowners and their refusal to admit firemen
    B. anticipation of firemen's visits by cleaning up before their arrival
    C. avoidance of major problems found by firemen and their stressing instead the easily corrected conditions
    D. embarrassment of both firemen and homeowners by the procedure and their seeking premature termination of the visit

14. Of the following agents for transferring flammable and combustible liquids, the BEST one is

    A. air pressure
    B. hydraulic or inert gas
    C. straight gravity discharge systems
    D. positive displacement pumps

15. The effect of applying wallpaper to a new interior finish surface on the flame propagation characteristics of that surface is GENERALLY considered

    A. minimal
    B. moderate
    C. considerable
    D. severe

16. While you are on apparatus field inspection duty, one of your members reports that he has issued an order to a building owner to remedy a violation forthwith. The member states that the owner seems agitated and hostile and refuses to correct the condition. You decide to speak to the owner yourself.
    In discussing this situation with the owner, it is MOST advisable for you to

    A. inform the owner firmly but bluntly that he is incorrect in insisting the condition does not require correction
    B. try to convince the owner that you are an expert in this area and that your knowledge should not be questioned
    C. express an appropriate degree of anger at the owner's refusal to correct an unsafe condition
    D. stick to discussion of the specific violation and avoid trying to convince the owner of the importance of correcting all fire hazards

17. Experience with the city fire prevention program GENERALLY demonstrates that

    A. fires have increased in the public areas of ghetto multiple dwellings despite intensive inspections
    B. inspections are ineffective in both loft buildings and ghetto multiple dwellings
    C. the extensive educational program in the schools in the 1950's resulted in decreases in the number of fires and false alarms when the children reached adulthood
    D. fires have increased in the living areas of ghetto multiple dwellings

18. It is common to find self-closing doors kept open with wooden wedges or other fastenings. To eliminate such unsafe hazards, hooks, fitted with fusible links, have been designed to hold the doors open.
    GENERALLY, these hooks are

    A. *desirable,* if placed low enough for convenient use
    B. *undesirable,* unless placed behind doors, where they would not be subject to damage
    C. *desirable,* if used only on stair and corridor doors
    D. *undesirable* under practically all conditions

19. While supervising an inspection of a commercial building, an officer notices some wooden packing cases resting against a steam riser. He advises the owner to move the stock at least 12 inches away from the riser to permit air to circulate.
    This advice GENERALLY is

    A. *proper;* however, a clearance of 36 inches should have been suggested
    B. *improper;* steam risers do not reach the ignition temperature of wood
    C. *proper;* standard practice uses a rise of 90F above room temperature as the maximum permissible temperature on surrounding woodwork
    D. *improper;* the air space suggested may permit hidden fire to travel behind the stock

20. Realistic fire tests to determine the actual burning characteristics of several rigid foam plastic wall and roof assemblies have been conducted within recent years. Of the following conclusions, the one BEST supported by this research is that

   A. low flame spread, rigid polystyrene foam, encased in aluminum skins, required automatic sprinkler protection for satisfactory performance under fire conditions
   B. low flame spread, rigid polyurethane foam, encased in aluminum skins, required automatic sprinkler protection for satisfactory performance under fire conditions
   C. rigid, foamed polyurethane products produce minimum fire contribution when sprayed on walls
   D. materials with a small-scale flame spread rating of 25 are practically self-extinguishing

20.____

21. At a neighborhood community organization meeting and discussion on *Fire Safety in the Home,* a woman asked the officer representing the Fire Department where spot-type heat detectors should be placed in a room to give an alarm properly if fire should occur. The officer responded that the center of the ceiling was the best location. He added that any point on the ceiling was the next best, and, if it were necessary to mount the detector on a side wall, it should be placed at least 6 inches but no more than 12 inches from the ceiling. The officer's instructions to the citizen were

   A. *correct*
   B. *incorrect* in his statement of *any point on the ceiling;* spot-type detectors should not be placed on ceilings in the corner of rooms
   C. *incorrect* in his statement *at least 6 inches from the ceiling*
   D. *incorrect;* side wall locations for spot-type detectors are preferable to ceiling locations

21.____

22. Safety cans for indoor handling of small quantities of flammable liquids are approved when equipped with pouring outlets that have tight-fitting caps or valves which are normally kept closed by springs, except when manual pressure is applied to keep them open. During apparatus field inspection, a company officer finds that small unsafe containers are being utilized at a certain location. Wishing to use this discovery to convince the occupants of the premises of the superiority of the authorized container, the officer decides to explain the advantages of the approved type.
Of the following, the MOST complete and accurate explanation he could give is that the approved container

   A. prevents spillage if accidentally tipped over
   B. is self-venting if exposed to fire and prevents spillage if accidentally tipped over
   C. provides relief venting in case of explosion, is self-venting if exposed to fire, and prevents spillage if accidentally tipped over
   D. prevents a static charge from building up during pouring operations, provides relief venting in case of explosion, is self-venting if exposed to fire, and prevents spillage if accidentally tipped over

22.____

23. While inspecting a cylindrical gravity tank for an automatic sprinkler system, a chief observes that the water in the tank is 10 feet deep and that the tank has a diameter of 9 feet. He asks the building manager how many gallons are in the tank and receives the reply, *About 10,000.*
Based on his own observation and calculations, the chief should

23.____

A. *agree* that the manager's answer is probably correct
B. *disagree* with the manager's answer; the answer is more nearly 20,000 gallons
C. *disagree* with the manager's answer; the answer is more nearly 15,000 gallons
D. *disagree* with the manager's answer; the answer is more nearly 5,000 gallons

24. The one of the following that is NOT an accurate statement with respect to the findings of a survey conducted by a member of the National Commission on Fire Prevention and Control concerning the public's knowledge of fire safety is that

    A. many youngsters indicated that they were likely to do something dangerous if a frying pan caught fire
    B. many adults and most youngsters did not know that a 15-ampere fuse is the safest for ordinary household lighting circuits
    C. most youngsters and adults indicated they would make the mistake of opening a hot door
    D. most youngsters and adults did not know that carbon monoxide can rob them of their judgment and coordination

25. You are inspecting a building for violations. You must perform the following steps in the order given:
    I. Find the manager of the building and introduce yourself.
    II. Have the manager accompany you during the inspection.
    III. Start the inspection by checking the Fire Department permits which have been issued to the building. The permits are located in the office of the building.
    IV. Inspect the building for violations of the Fire Prevention Laws. Begin at the roof and work down to the basement or cellar.
    V. As you inspect, write on a piece of paper any violations you find and explain them to the building manager.

    You are inspecting a supermarket. After entering the building, you identify yourself to the store manager and ask him to come along during the inspection. Which one of the following actions should you take NEXT?

    A. Start inspecting the supermarket, beginning at the basement.
    B. Start inspecting the supermarket, beginning at the roof.
    C. Ask to see the Fire Department permits which have been issued to the supermarket.
    D. Write down any violations which are seen while introducing yourself to the manager.

26. Many fires are caused by improper use of oxyacetylene torches.
    The MAIN cause of such fires is the

    A. high pressure under which the gases are stored
    B. failure to control or extinguish sparks
    C. high temperatures generated by the equipment
    D. explosive nature of the gases used

Questions 27-29.

DIRECTIONS: Questions 27 through 29 are to be answered on the basis of the following paragraph.

The only openings permitted in fire partitions except openings for ventilating ducts shall be those required for doors. There shall be but one such door opening unless the provision of additional openings would not exceed in total width of all doorways 25 percent of the length of the wall. The minimum distance between openings shall be three feet. The maximum area for such a door opening shall be 80 square feet, except that such openings for the passage of motor trucks may be a maximum of 140 square feet.

27. According to the above paragraph, openings in fire partitions are permitted only for

    A. doors
    B. doors and windows
    C. doors and ventilation ducts
    D. doors, windows, and ventilation ducts

27._____

28. In a fire partition 22 feet long and 10 feet high, the MAXIMUM number of doors 3 feet wide and 7 feet high is

    A. 1    B. 2    C. 3    D. 4

28._____

29.

The one of the following statements about the layout shown on the preceding page that is MOST accurate is that the

    A. total width of the openings is too large
    B. truck opening is too large
    C. truck and door openings are too close together
    D. layout is acceptable

29._____

30. The Rules of the Board of Standards and Appeals provide that in a coin-operated dry-cleaning establishment spotting and sponging may be done by

    A. the general public or a qualified operator if water only is used
    B. a qualified operator if water only is used
    C. the general public if water only is used or by a qualified operator if inflammable liquids are used
    D. neither the general public nor a qualified operator

30._____

## KEY (CORRECT ANSWERS)

| | | |
|---|---|---|
| 1. B | 11. B | 21. B |
| 2. B | 12. C | 22. B |
| 3. C | 13. B | 23. D |
| 4. B | 14. D | 24. C |
| 5. B | 15. A | 25. C |
| 6. A | 16. D | 26. B |
| 7. D | 17. D | 27. C |
| 8. A | 18. D | 28. A |
| 9. D | 19. C | 29. B |
| 10. C | 20. A | 30. B |

# TEST 4

DIRECTIONS: Each question or incomplete statement is followed by several suggested answers or completions. Select the one that BEST answers the question or completes the statement. *PRINT THE LETTER OF THE CORRECT ANSWER IN THE SPACE AT THE RIGHT.*

1. An officer is performing a routine quarterly inspection in a large motion picture theatre. Which one of the following actions taken by the officer during his inspection would generally be CORRECT?

    A. His first action is to proceed to the box office to review the theatre inspection log book.
    B. He informs the theatre owner that daily entries made by the owner in the log book should contain the name of the person designated to prevent any undue excitement or possible panic and indicate the location of the nearest street fire alarm box.
    C. Upon finding that the theatre owner has failed to maintain the log in the prescribed manner, the officer serves him with a summons.
    D. He examines the entries made since the previous inspection by an officer and records the results of this examination.

2. The owner of a building which comes under the jurisdiction of the Housing Maintenance Code would be in compliance with the Code if he

    A. installs, in a dwelling unit, a gas-fired refrigerator which is equipped with a flue assembly composed of non-metallic material
    B. obtains combustion air for the gas-fueled water heater in a bedroom in his new law tenement directly from the outer air
    C. connects each gas-fueled heater to the rigid gas piping supply line by means of a metallic flexible gas connection
    D. arranges to have the gas appliance in his old law tenement inspected by a licensed plumber on a biennial basis

3. Of the following activities, the one the code specifically permits bulk or waste oil recovery plants to do is

    A. refine waste oil for resale without a permit
    B. mix waste oil with No. 6 fuel oil for use in approved fuel oil burners
    C. transport waste oil in the vendor's container in 220 gallon quantities without a permit
    D. store waste oil in premises other than storage plants or buried tank systems in quantities greater than those restricting other combustible oils

4. A chief, visiting a company performing apparatus field inspection, is informed by the lieutenant in command of a hazardous situation just encountered in a fur processing plant. In the presence of the factory manager, the two officers discussed various sections of the Administrative Code which might be relevant and several approaches to the problem that could be taken by the fire department to abate the hazard. Finally, the chief directed the lieutenant to issue certain orders to the manager. Discussing this problem in the presence of the manager was

1.____

2.____

3.____

4.____

103

A. *proper,* mainly because he probably would realize that the fire department was not acting arbitrarily or unreasonably
B. *improper,* mainly because he might prefer one of the approaches which was suggested and rejected
C. *proper,* mainly because the activities of the fire department should, whenever possible, be open to the public
D. *improper,* mainly because inaccurate statements may have been made during the preliminary discussion

5. A chief supervising apparatus field inspection duty activities comes upon a company just as it is completing inspection of a clothing manufacturing plant. The lieutenant in command reports that the company has issued minor violation orders for five conditions which they discovered. The chief considers four of the conditions cited clear violations of the Administrative Code. The fifth condition he considers a borderline case which he, himself, would not have handled by issuing a violation order.
In this situation, the BEST of the following courses for the chief to take is to

A. direct the lieutenant to cancel the violation order for the borderline situation
B. say nothing to the lieutenant at this time but later warn him against unduly strict interpretation of the Administrative Code
C. accept the lieutenant's findings without any comment at this time or later
D. question the lieutenant closely about various sections of the Administrative Code to determine whether he has a proper understanding of its requirements

Questions 6-7.

DIRECTIONS: Questions 6 and 7 are to be answered SOLELY on the basis of the following passage.

Following is a list of rules for fire extinguishers which are required in different types of public buildings in the city:

Rule 1: Hospitals, nursing homes, hotels, and motels must have one 2 1/2 gallon water extinguisher for every 2,500 square feet, or part thereof, of floor area on each floor.

Rule 2: Stores with floor areas of 1,500 square feet or less must have one 2 1/2 gallon water extinguisher. Stores with floor areas of over 1,500 square feet must have one 2 1/2 gallon water extinguisher for every 2,500 square feet, or part thereof, of floor area on each floor.

Rule 3: Kitchens must have one 2 1/2 gallon foam extinguisher or one 5 pound dry chemical extinguisher for every 1,250 square feet, or part thereof, of floor area on each floor. For kitchen areas, this rule is in addition to Rules 1 and 2.

6. An inspector is inspecting a one-story nursing home which has a total of 3,000 square feet of floor area. This includes a kitchen, which is 1,500 square feet in area, in the rear of the floor.
Of the following, the inspector should conclude that the nursing home should be equipped with _____ extinguisher(s) and _____ extinguisher(s).

A. 1 water; 1 foam
B. 1 water; 1 dry chemical
C. 2 water; 2 foam
D. 2 foam; 1 dry chemical

7. An inspector is inspecting a store which has two floors. The first floor has 2,600 square feet. The second floor has 1,450 square feet.
The store should be equipped with AT LEAST

   A. two 2 1/2 gallon water extinguishers, one for each floor
   B. three 2 1/2 gallon water extinguishers, two for the first floor and one for the second floor
   C. two 2 1/2 gallon foam extinguishers, one for each floor
   D. two 2 1/2 gallon extinguishers, either foam or water, one for each floor

7.____

8. A recycling sprinkler head called *The Aquamatic* has been developed that will turn itself off after the fire is extinguished and turn itself on again if the fire should rekindle.
Of the following, it would generally be INACCURATE to state that this recycling sprinkler head

   A. has been approved by the Underwriters' Laboratories for installation where there is high risk of flash fires
   B. is capable of discharging 30 gpm and is approved by the Underwriters' Laboratories for use in systems engineered to make maximum use of available water
   C. eliminates the need to turn off the main valve to replace Aquamatic elements
   D. has a 165° temperature rating, the usual 1/2 inch national pipe thread, is mounted in the pendant position and is approved for installation in any sprinkler system, new or old

8.____

9. Assume that you are supervising a scheduled inspection of auxiliary fire protection equipment in a tunnel in the absence of a deputy chief.
In supervising the inspection, it would be appropriate for you to do all of the following EXCEPT

   A. utilize the members of the Rescue Company in carrying out specific inspectional duties
   B. notify the dispatcher of the units participating, the designated radio contact, and the units which are not available for response to their assigned alarms
   C. make a written recommendation suggesting a corrective procedure to upgrade a particular piece of inadequate equipment
   D. forward referrals and recommendations through official channels to the division of fire prevention for transmittal to the various agencies concerned and for necessary follow-up

9.____

10. What was formerly known as the *spray sprinkler* is now designated as the *standard sprinkler* and is generally similar in appearance to the old type head.
Of the following, the MOST NEARLY accurate statement about the modern one-half inch sprinkler head is that

    A. a larger area of coverage is secured by directing all the water downward and horizontally
    B. the present upright spray sprinkler operates on the direct spray principle

10.____

C. major changes in deflector design have reduced discharge capacities, but have increased particle division
D. there is increased exposure to the ceiling, but more direct discharge on the burning materials

11. The one of the following which is generally a CORRECT statement about automatic deluge sprinkler systems is that they are

   A. installed in properties when there is a danger of serious water damage due to accidental functioning
   B. equipped with quartzoid bulb type activators in lieu of fusible links
   C. controlled by a quick-opening valve known as the deluge valve
   D. ineffective where ceilings are unusually high and heads would not open quickly enough

12. An inspection of the private class 3 box cards of the computerized alarm assignment system should reveal that the cards PROPERLY list the

   A. company numbers of those engine and ladder companies responding to each terminal under the *Response Policy* column
   B. battalion number of the battalion chief assigned to respond to each terminal under the *B.C.* column
   C. company numbers of the engine and ladder companies assigned to the associated street box
   D. address of the alarm service company

13. The General Accounting Office in Washington publicized the fact that there is a possible defect in some models of a certain smoke detector.
The one of the following which BEST describes this defect is that these detectors

   A. failed to signal an alarm under heavy smoke conditions
   B. expected battery life is only three months or less
   C. have smoke entry vents which are too narrow so that dust tends to render the detectors ineffective
   D. are overheating and, in time, tend to self-ignite

14. Assume that you are a fire officer who has been asked to address a local community group on the relative merits of smoke and heat detectors and the proper placement, operation, and maintenance of the various types of detectors. During this meeting, it would be MOST appropriate for you to point out that

   A. it is more advisable to install a smoke detector than a heat detector in the kitchen
   B. placement of a smoke detector in a room below an insulated attic should be on the ceiling towards the center of the room
   C. placing a smoke detector in the hallway near each sleeping area and on every floor level not containing a sleeping area will provide minimal protection
   D. a smoke detector installed on the ceiling near a doorway should be placed closer to the wall above the doorway than the distance from the ceiling to the top of the door

15. The basic multiple-death fire safety problem in nursing home facilities is GENERALLY considered to be the failure to   15._____

   A. confine the fire's resultant products of combustion to the room of origin
   B. conduct and properly supervise comprehensive fire exit and evacuation drills
   C. adequately service and maintain existing smoke-detection and smoke-control systems
   D. reduce the combustible contents of patients' rooms and enforcement of the no-smoking restrictions by a trained staff

16. The basic assumption of fire prevention educational programs is that people frequently   16._____

   A. must be forced into obeying fire laws
   B. are unaware of the dangers involved in some of their actions
   C. don't care whether or not their actions are dangerous
   D. assume that fire insurance protects them against all fire loss

Questions 17-19.

DIRECTIONS: Questions 17 through 19 are to be answered on the basis of the following paragraph.

Unlined linen hose is essentially a fabric tube made of closely woven linen yarn. Due to the natural characteristics of linen, very shortly after water is introduced, the threads swell after being wet, closing the minute spaces between them making the tube practically watertight. This type of hose tends to deteriorate rapidly if not thoroughly dried after use or if installed where it will be exposed to dampness or the weather. It is not ordinarily built to withstand frequent service or for use where the fabric will be subjected to chafing from rough or sharp surfaces.

17. Seepage of water through an unlined linen hose is observed when the water is first turned on.   17._____
   From the above paragraph, we may conclude that the seepage

   A. indicates that the hose is defective
   B. does not indicate that the hose is defective provided that the seepage is proportionate to the water pressure
   C. does not indicate that the hose is defective provided that the seepage is greatly reduced when the hose becomes thoroughly wet
   D. does not indicate that the hose is defective provided that the seepage takes place only at the surface of the hose

18. Unlined linen hose is MOST suitable for use   18._____

   A. as a garden hose
   B. on fire department apparatus
   C. as emergency fire equipment in buildings
   D. in fire department training schools

19. The use of unlined linen hose would be LEAST appropriate in a(n)   19._____

   A. outdoor lumber yard
   B. non-fireproof office building

C. department store
D. cosmetic manufacturing plant

20. Doors in theatres and other places of public assembly usually open outwardly. The MAIN reason for this requirement is, in the event of fire, to

   A. provide the widest possible passageway for escape of the audience
   B. prevent panic-stricken audience from jamming the doors in a closed position
   C. indicate to the audience the safe direction of travel
   D. prevent unauthorized persons from entering the building

21. Fire prevention inspections should be conducted at irregular hours or intervals. The BEST justification for this *irregularity* is that it permits the firemen to

   A. make inspections when they have free time
   B. see the inspected establishments in their normal condition and not in their *dressed-up* condition
   C. avoid making inspections at times which would be inconvenient for the inspected establishments
   D. concentrate their inspectional activities on those establishments which present the greatest fire hazard

22. Static electricity is a hazard in industry CHIEFLY because it may cause

   A. dangerous or painful burns
   B. chemical decomposition of toxic elements
   C. sparks which can start an explosion
   D. overheating of electrical equipment

Questions 23-25.

DIRECTIONS: Questions 23 through 25 are to be answered on the basis of the following paragraph.

   A plastic does not consist of a single substance, but is a blended combination of several. In addition to the resin, it may contain various fillers, plasticizers, lubricants, and coloring material. Depending upon the type and quantity of substances added to the binder, the properties, including combustibility, may be altered considerably. The flammability of plastics depends upon the composition and, as with other materials, upon their physical size and condition. Thin sections, sharp edges, or powdered plastics will ignite and burn more readily than the same amount of identical material in heavy sections with smooth surfaces.

23. According to the above paragraph, all plastics contain a

   A. resin
   B. resin and a filler
   C. resin, filler, and plasticizer
   D. resin, filler, plasticizer, lubricant, and coloring material

24. The one of the following conclusions that is BEST supported by the above paragraph is that the flammability of plastics

    A. generally is high
    B. generally is moderate
    C. generally is low
    D. varies considerably

25. According to the above paragraph, *plastics* can BEST be described as

    A. a trade name
    B. the name of a specific product
    C. the name of a group of products which have some similar and some dissimilar properties
    D. the name of any substance which can be shaped or molded during the production process

26. While on inspection duty, an inspector discovers the superintendent of a tenement just starting to remove boxes and other material which are blocking hallways. Apparently, the superintendent started removal as soon as he saw the inspector approach.
    In this situation, it is MOST important that the inspector

    A. warn the superintendent of the penalties for violation of the Fire Prevention Code
    B. help the superintendent remove the material blocking the hallways
    C. commend the superintendent for his efforts to maintain a safe building
    D. check again, after completing the inspection, to see whether the material has been removed completely

27. Persons engaged in certain hazardous activities are required to obtain a Fire Department permit or certificate for which a fee is charged.
    The MAIN reason for requiring permits or certificates is to

    A. obtain revenue for the city government
    B. prevent unqualified persons from engaging in these activities
    C. obtain information about these activities in order to plan for fire emergencies
    D. warn the public of the hazardous nature of these activities

28. An inspector, on his way to work, is stopped by a citizen who complains that the employees of a nearby store frequently pile empty crates and boxes in a doorway, blocking passage.
    The one of the following which would be the MOST appropriate action for the inspector to take is to

    A. assure the citizen that the fire department's inspectional activities will eventually *catch up* with the store
    B. obtain the address of the store and investigate to determine whether the citizen's complaint is justified
    C. obtain the address of the store and report the complaint to his superior officer
    D. ask the citizen for specific dates on which this practice has occurred to determine whether the complaint is justified

29. While inspecting a business building, you discover an oil burner installation with the following features:
    I. Installed on the third story, whose floor is 40' above the street level
    II. Oil delivery lines to the burner are one and one-half inches iron pipe size, and
    III. Pressure in the oil lines to the burner is 25 lbs. per square inch

    The one of the following statements concerning this installation and the applicable sections of the rules of the Board of Standards and Appeals that is MOST accurate is that

    A. feature I is a violation of the rules
    B. feature II is a violation of the rules
    C. feature III is a violation of the rules
    D. the installation complies with the rules

30. The Fire Department now uses companies on fire duty, with their apparatus, for fire prevention inspection in commercial buildings.
    The one of the following changes which was MOST important in making this inspection procedure practicable was the

    A. reduction of hours of work of firemen
    B. use of two-way radio equipment
    C. use of enclosed cabs on fire apparatus
    D. increase in property values during the post-war period

## KEY (CORRECT ANSWERS)

| | | |
|---|---|---|
| 1. C | 11. D | 21. B |
| 2. D | 12. B | 22. C |
| 3. D | 13. B | 23. A |
| 4. D | 14. B | 24. D |
| 5. C | 15. A | 25. C |
| 6. C | 16. B | 26. D |
| 7. B | 17. C | 27. B |
| 8. C | 18. C | 28. C |
| 9. D | 19. A | 29. D |
| 10. A | 20. B | 30. B |

# EXAMINATION SECTION
## TEST 1

DIRECTIONS: Each question or incomplete statement is followed by several suggested answers or completions. Select the one that BEST answers the question or completes the statement. *PRINT THE LETTER OF THE CORRECT ANSWER IN THE SPACE AT THE RIGHT.*

1. When conducting a needs assessment for the purpose of education planning, an agency's FIRST step is to identify or provide
   A. a profile of population characteristics
   B. barriers to participation
   C. existing resources
   D. profiles of competing resources

2. Research has demonstrated that of the following, the MOST effective medium for communicating with external publics is(are)
   A. video news releases
   B. television
   C. radio
   D. newspapers

3. Basic ideas behind the effort to influence the attitudes and behaviors of a constituency include each of the following EXCEPT the idea that
   A. words, rather than actions or events, are most likely to motivate
   B. demands for action are a usual response
   C. self-interest usually figures heavily into public involvement
   D. the reliability of change programs is difficult to assess

4. An agency representative is trying to craft a pithy message to constituents in order to encourage the use of agency program resources.
   Choosing an audience for such messages is easiest when the message
   A. is project- or behavior-based
   B. is combined with other messages
   C. is abstract
   D. has a broad appeal

5. Of the following factors, the MOST important to the success of an agency's external education or communication programs is the
   A. amount of resources used to implement them
   B. public's prior experiences with the agency
   C. real value of the program to the public
   D. commitment of the internal audience

6. A representative for a state agency is being interviewed by a reporter from a local news network. The representative is being asked to defend a program that is extremely unpopular in certain parts of the municipality.
   When a constituency is known to be opposed to a position, the MOST useful communication strategy is to present

A. only the arguments that are consistent with constituents' views
B. only the agency's side of the issue
C. both sides of the argument as clearly as possible
D. both sides of the argument, omitting key information about the opposing position

7. The MOST significant barriers to effective agency community relations include
   I. widespread distrust of communication strategies
   II. the media's "watchdog" stance
   III. public apathy
   IV. statutory opposition

   The CORRECT answer is:
   A. I only   B. I and II   C. II and III   D. III and IV

8. In conducting an education program, many agencies use workshops and seminars in a classroom setting.
   Advantages of classroom-style teaching over other means of educating the public include each of the following, EXCEPT
   A. enabling an instructor to verify learning through testing and interaction with the target audience
   B. enabling hands-on practice and other participatory learning techniques
   C. ability to reach an unlimited number of participants in a given length of time
   D. ability to convey the latest, most up-to-date information

9. The _____ model of community relations is characterized by an attempt to persuade the public to adopt the agency's point of view.
   A. two-way symmetric         B. two-way asymmetric
   C. public information        D. press agency/publicity

10. Important elements of an internal situation analysis include the
    I. list of agency opponents      II. communication audit
    III. updated organizational almanac   IV. stakeholder analysis

    The CORRECT answer is:
    A. I and II   B. I, II, and III   C. II and III   D. I, II, III and IV

11. Government agency information efforts typically involve each of the following objectives, EXCEPT to
    A. implement changes in the policies of government agencies to align with public opinion
    B. communicate the work of agencies
    C. explain agency techniques in a way that invites input from citizens
    D. provide citizen feedback to government administrators

12. Factors that are likely to influence the effectiveness of an educational campaign include the
    I. level of homogeneity among intended participants
    II. number and types of media used
    III. receptivity of the intended participants
    IV. level of specificity in the message or behavior to be taught

    The CORRECT answer is:
    A. I and II   B. I, II, and III   C. II and III   D. I, II, III, and IV

13. An agency representative is writing instructional objectives that will later help to measure the effectiveness of an educational program.
    Which of the following verbs, included in an objective, would be MOST helpful for the purpose of measuring effectiveness?
    A. Know   B. Identify   C. Learn   D. Comprehend

14. A state education agency wants to encourage participation in a program that has just received a boost through new federal legislation. The program is intended to include participants from a wide variety of socioeconomic and other demographic characteristics. The agency wants to launch a broad-based program that will inform virtually every interested party in the state about the program's new circumstances.
    In attempting to deliver this message to such a wide-ranging constituency, the agency's BEST practice would be to
    A. broadcast the same message through as many different media channels as possible
    B. focus on one discrete segment of the public at a time
    C. craft a message whose appeal is as broad as the public itself
    D. let the program's achievements speak for themselves and rely on word-of-mouth

15. Advantages associated with using the World Wide Web as an educational tool include
    I. an appeal to younger generations of the public
    II. visually-oriented, interactive learning
    III. learning that is not confined by space, time, or institutional association
    IV. a variety of methods for verifying use and learning

    The CORRECT answer is:
    A. I only   B. I and II   C. I, II, and III   D. I, II, II, and IV

16. In agencies involved in health care, community relations is a critical function because it
    A. serves as an intermediary between the agency and consumers
    B. generates a clear mission statement for agency goals and priorities
    C. ensures patient privacy while satisfying the media's right to information
    D. helps marketing professionals determine the wants and needs of agency constituents

17. After an extensive campaign to promote its newest program to constituents, an agency learns that most of the audience did not understand the intended message.
    MOST likely, the agency has
    A. chosen words that were intended to inform, rather than persuade
    B. not accurately interpreted what the audience really needed to know
    C. overestimated the ability of the audience to receive and process the message
    D. compensated for noise that may have interrupted the message

17.____

18. The necessary elements that lead to conviction and motivation in the minds of participants in an educational or information program include each of the following, EXCEPT the _____ of the message.
    A. acceptability            B. intensity
    C. single-channel appeal    D. pervasiveness

18.____

19. Printed materials are often at the core of educational programs provided by public agencies.
    The PRIMARY disadvantage associated with print is that it
    A. does not enable comprehensive treatment of a topic
    B. is generally unreliable in term of assessing results
    C. is often the most expensive medium available
    D. is constrained by time

19.____

20. Traditional thinking on public opinion holds that there is about _____ percent of the public who are pivotal to shifting the balance and momentum of opinion—they are concerned about an issue, but not fanatical, and interested enough to pay attention to a reasoned discussion.
    A. 2          B. 10          C. 33          D. 51

20.____

21. One of the most useful guidelines for influencing attitude change among people is to
    A. invite the target audience to come to you, rather than approaching them
    B. use moral appeals as the primary approach
    C. use concrete images to enable people to see the results of behaviors or indifference
    D. offer tangible rewards to people for changes in behavior

21.____

22. An agency is attempting to evaluate the effectiveness of its educational program. For this purpose, it wants to observe several focus groups discussing the same program.
    Which of the following would NOT be a guideline for the use of focus groups?
    A. Focus groups should only include those who have participated in the program.
    B. Be sure to accurately record the discussion.
    C. The same questions should be asked at each focus group meeting.
    D. It is often helpful to have a neutral, non-agency employee facilitate discussions.

22.____

23. Research consistently shows that _____ is the determinant most likely to make a newspaper editor run a news release.
    A. novelty   B. prominence   C. proximity   D. conflict

24. Which of the following is NOT one of the major variables to take into account when considering a population-needs assessment?
    A. State of program development   B. Resources available
    C. Demographics                   D. Community attitudes

25. The FIRST step in any communications audit is to
    A. develop a research instrument
    B. determine how the organization currently communicates
    C. hire a contractor
    D. determine which audience to assess

## KEY (CORRECT ANSWERS)

| | | | |
|---|---|---|---|
| 1. | A | 11. | A |
| 2. | D | 12. | D |
| 3. | A | 13. | B |
| 4. | A | 14. | B |
| 5. | D | 15. | C |
| 6. | C | 16. | A |
| 7. | D | 17. | B |
| 8. | C | 18. | C |
| 9. | B | 19. | B |
| 10. | C | 20. | B |

21. C
22. A
23. C
24. C
25. D

# TEST 2

DIRECTIONS: Each question or incomplete statement is followed by several suggested answers or completions. Select the one that BEST answers the question or completes the statement. *PRINT THE LETTER OF THE CORRECT ANSWER IN THE SPACE AT THE RIGHT.*

1. A public relations practitioner at an agency has just composed a press release highlighting a program's recent accomplishments and success stories.
   In pitching such releases to print outlets, the practitioner should
   I. e-mail, mail, or send them by messenger
   II. address them to "editor" or "news director"
   III. have an assistant call all media contacts by telephone
   IV. ask reporters or editors how they prefer to receive them

   The CORRECT answer is:
   A. I and II   B. I and IV   C. II, III, and IV   D. III only

   1.____

2. The "output goals" of an educational program are MOST likely to include
   A. specified ratings of services by participants on a standardized scale
   B. observable effects on a given community or clientele
   C. the number of instructional hours provided
   D. the number of participants served

   2.____

3. An agency wants to evaluate satisfaction levels among program participants, and mails out questionnaires to everyone who has been enrolled in the last year.
   The PRIMARY problem associated with this method of evaluative research is that it
   A. poses a significant inconvenience for respondents
   B. is inordinately expensive
   C. does not allow for follow-up or clarification questions
   D. usually involves a low response rate

   3.____

4. A communications audit is an important tool for measuring
   A. the depth of penetration of a particular message or program
   B. the cost of the organization's information campaigns
   C. how key audiences perceive an organization
   D. the commitment of internal stakeholders

   4.____

5. The "ABCs" of written learning objectives include each of the following, EXCEPT
   A. Audience   B. Behavior   C. Conditions   D. Delineation

   5.____

6. When attempting to change the behaviors of constituents, it is important to keep in mind that
   I. most people are skeptical of communications that try to get them to change their behaviors
   II. in most cases, a person selects the media to which he exposes himself
   III. people tend to react defensively to messages or programs that rely on fear as a motivating factor
   IV. programs should aim for the broadest appeal possible in order to include as many participants as possible

   The CORRECT answer is:
   A. I and II   B. I, II and III   C. II and III   D. I, II, III, and IV

7. The "laws" of public opinion include the idea that it is
   A. useful for anticipating emergencies
   B. not sensitive to important events
   C. basically determined by self-interest
   D. sustainable through persistent appeals

8. Which of the following types of evaluations is used to measure public attitudes before and after an information/educational program?
   A. Retrieval study
   B. Copy test
   C. Quota sampling
   D. Benchmark study

9. The PRIMARY source for internal communications is(are) usually
   A. flow charts
   B. meetings
   C. voice mail
   D. printed publications

10. An agency representative is putting together informational materials—brochures and a newsletter—outlining changes in one of the state's biggest benefits programs.
    In assembling print materials as a medium for delivering information to the public, the representative should keep in mind each of the following trends:
    I. For various reasons, the reading capabilities of the public are in general decline
    II. Without tables and graphs to help illustrate the changes, it is unlikely that the message will be delivered effectively
    III. Professionals and career-oriented people are highly receptive to information written in the form of a journal article or empirical study
    IV. People tend to be put off by print materials that use itemized and bulleted (●) lists

    The CORRECT answer is:
    A. I and II   B. I, II and III   C. II and III   D. I, II, III, and IV

11. Which of the following steps in a problem-oriented information campaign would typically be implemented FIRST?
    A. Deciding on tactics
    B. Determining a communications strategy
    C. Evaluating the problem's impact
    D. Developing an organizational strategy

12. A common pitfall in conducting an educational program is to
    A. aim it at the wrong target audience
    B. overfund it
    C. leave it in the hands of people who are in the business of education, rather than those with expertise in the business of the organization
    D. ignore the possibility that some other organization is meeting the same educational need for the target audience

13. The key factors that affect the credibility of an agency's educational program include
    A. organization
    B. scope
    C. sophistication
    D. penetration

14. Research on public opinion consistently demonstrates that it is
    A. easy to move people toward a strong opinion on anything, as long as they are approached directly through their emotions
    B. easier to move people away from an opinion they currently hold than to have them form an opinion about something they have not previously cared about
    C. easy to move people toward a strong opinion on anything, as long as the message appeals to their reason and intellect
    D. difficult to move people toward a strong opinion on anything, no matter what the approach

15. In conducting an education program, many agencies use meetings and conferences to educate an audience about the organization and its programs. Advantages associated with this approach include
    I. a captive audience that is known to be interested in the topic
    II. ample opportunities for verifying learning
    III. cost-efficient meeting space
    IV. the ability to provide information on a wider variety of subjects

    The CORRECT answer is:
    A. I and II   B. I, III and IV   C. II and III   D. I, II, III and IV

16. An agency is attempting to evaluate the effectiveness of its educational programs. For this purpose, it wants to observe several focus groups discussing particular programs.
    For this purpose, a focus group should never number more than _____ participants.
    A. 5   B. 10   C. 15   D. 20

17. A _____ speech is written so that several agency members can deliver it to different audiences with only minor variations.
    A. basic  B. printed  C. quota  D. pattern

18. Which of the following statements about public opinion is generally considered to be FALSE?
    A. Opinion is primarily reactive rather than proactive.
    B. People have more opinions about goals than about the means by which to achieve them.
    C. Facts tend to shift opinion in the accepted direction when opinion is not solidly structured.
    D. Public opinion is based more on information than desire.

19. An agency is trying to promote its educational program.
    As a general rule, the agency should NOT assume that
    A. people will only participate if they perceive an individual benefit
    B. promotions need to be aimed at small, discrete groups
    C. if the program is good, the audience will find out about it
    D. a variety of methods, including advertising, special events, and direct mail, should be considered

20. In planning a successful educational program, probably the first and most important question for an agency to ask is:
    A. What will be the content of the program?
    B. Who will be served by the program?
    C. When is the best time to schedule the program?
    D. Why is the program necessary?

21. Media kits are LEAST likely to contain
    A. fact sheets           B. memoranda
    C. photographs with captions   D. news releases

22. The use of pamphlets and booklets as media for communication with the public often involves the disadvantage that
    A. the messages contained within them are frequently nonspecific
    B. it is difficult to measure their effectiveness in delivering the message
    C. there are few opportunities for people to refer to them
    D. color reproduction is poor

23. The MOST important prerequisite of a good educational program is an
    A. abundance of resources to implement it
    B. individual staff unit formed for the purpose of program delivery
    C. accurate needs assessment
    D. uneducated constituency

24. After an education program has been delivered, an agency conducts a program evaluation to determine whether its objectives have been met.
General rules about how to conduct such an education program valuation include each of the following, EXCEPT that it
   A. must be done immediately after the program has been implemented
   B. should be simple and easy to use
   C. should be designed so that tabulation of responses can take place quickly and inexpensively
   D. should solicit mostly subjective, open-ended responses if the audience was large

25. Using electronic media such as television as means of educating the public is typically recommended ONLY for agencies that
   I. have a fairly simple message to begin with
   II. want to reach the masses, rather than a targeted audience
   III. have substantial financial resources
   IV. accept that they will not be able to measure the results of the campaign with much precision

   The CORRECT answer is:
   A. I and II    B. I, II and III    C. II and IV    D. I, II, III and IV

# KEY (CORRECT ANSWERS)

| 1. B | 11. C |
| 2. C | 12. D |
| 3. D | 13. A |
| 4. C | 14. D |
| 5. D | 15. B |
| 6. B | 16. B |
| 7. C | 17. D |
| 8. D | 18. D |
| 9. D | 19. C |
| 10. A | 20. D |

21. B
22. B
23. C
24. D
25. D

# READING COMPREHENSION
## UNDERSTANDING WRITTEN MATERIALS
# EXAMINATION SECTION

DIRECTIONS FOR THIS SECTION:

Each question or incomplete statement is followed by several suggested answers or completions. Select the one that *BEST* answers the question or completes the statement. *THEN, PRINT THE LETTER OF THE CORRECT ANSWER IN THE SPACE AT THE RIGHT.*

Your answers are to be based *ONLY* on the information that is given or that can be assumed from the reading passages.

# TEST 1

Questions 1-5.

DIRECTIONS: Answer Questions 1 through 5 on' the basis of the passage below.

Arsonists are people who set fires deliberately, They don't look like criminals, but they cost the nation millions of dollars in property loss, and sometimes loss of life. Arsonists set fires for many different reasons. Sometimes a shopkeeper sees no way out of losing his business, and sets fire to it so he can collect the insurance. Another type of arsonist wants revenge, and sets fire to the home or shop of someone he feels has treated him unfairly. Some arsonists just like the excitement of seeing the fire burn and watching the firefighters at work; arsonists of this type have even been known to help fight the fire.

1. The writer of the passage feels that arsonists
   A. usually return to the scene of the crime
   B. work at night          C. don't look like criminals
   D. never leave their fingerprints

2. An arsonist is a person who
   A. intentionally sets a fire    B. enjoys watching fires
   C. wants revenge               D. needs money

3. Arsonists have been known to help fight fires because they
   A. felt guilty              B. enjoyed the excitement
   C. wanted to earn money     D. didn't want anyone hurt

4. Shopkeepers sometimes become arsonists in order to
   A. commit suicide           B. collect insurance money
   C. hide a crime             D. raise their prices

5. The *point* of this passage is that arsonists
   A. would make good firefighters   B. are not criminals
   C. are mentally ill               D. are not all alike

Questions 6-11.

DIRECTIONS: Answer Questions 6 through 11 on the basis of the passage below.

Water and ventilation are the keys to fire fighting. Firefighters put out most fires by hosing water on the burning material, and by letting the smoke and gases out. When burning material is soaked with cooling water it can no longer produce gases that burn. In a closed room, hot gases can raise the temperature enough for the room to burst into flame. This can happen even though the room is far away from the fire itself. Therefore, firefighters chop holes in roofs and smash windows in order to empty the house of gases quickly. This is called ventilation.

6. Burning material will stop giving off hot gases when it is
    A. allowed to burn freely    B. exposed to fresh air
    C. cooled with water    D. sprayed with chemicals

6._____

7. Hot gases cause a room to burn by
    A. creating a draft    B. exploding
    C. giving off sparks    D. raising the room temperature

7._____

8. A room can burst into flames even though it is
    A. far from the fire    B. soaked with water
    C. well ventilated    D. cold and damp

8._____

9. Firefighters sometimes smash windows and chop holes in roofs in order to
    A. reach trapped victims    B. remove burning materials
    C. ventilate a building    D. escape from a fire

9._____

10. Ventilation is important in fire fighting because it
    A. releases trapped smoke and gases
    B. puts out flames by cooling them
    C. makes it easier for firefighters to breathe
    D. makes the flames easier to see and reach with a hose

10._____

11. Hot gases are *most* dangerous when they are in a room that is
    A. large    B. closed    C. damp    D. cool

11._____

Questions 12-15.

DIRECTIONS: Answer Questions 12 through 15 on the basis of the passage below.

When there is a large fire in an occupied apartment or tenement, the fire escapes often become overcrowded. To relieve this overcrowding, a portable ladder is often raised to the first level of the fire escape and put opposite to the drop ladder. For added help, an additional ladder can be raised from the ground to the second level. If the fire escape is located in the rear of the building, a "gooseneck" ladder that hooks over the roof can also be used. Then firefighters can help some occupants from the fire escape to the roof instead of to the ground.

Test 1

12. Portable ladders are raised to fire escapes so that
    A. firefighters can reach the roof from outside
    B. occupants can reach a higher level of the fire escape
    C. firefighters can enter windows more easily
    D. occupants can leave fire escapes more rapidly

    12._____

13. If all the ladders described in the passage are used, *how many* ways can the occupants reach the ground directly by ladder from the fire escape at the first level?
    A. 1    B. 2    C. 3    D. 4

    13._____

14. A "gooseneck" ladder is sometimes used
    A. opposite the drop ladder   B. from the top level
    C. from the first level       D. from the second level

    14._____

15. The *main* topic of the paragraph is:
    A. Relieving overcrowding on fire escapes
    B. Setting up and using portable ladders
    C. Rescuing occupants from apartments
    D. Using the roof to escape from fires

    15._____

Questions 16-20.

DIRECTIONS:   Answer Questions 16 through 20 on the basis of the passage below.

   Fire often travels inside the partitions of a burning building. Many partitions contain wooden studs that support the partitions. The studs leave a space for the fire to travel along. Flames may spread from the bottom to the upper floors through the partitions. Sparks from a fire in the upper part of a partition may fall and start a fire at the bottom. Some signs that a fire is spreading inside a partition are: (1) blistering paint, (2) discolored paint or wallpaper, or (3) partitions that feel hot to the touch. If any of these signs is present, the partition must be opened up to look for the fire. Finding cobwebs inside the partition is one sign that fire has not spread through the partition.

16. Fires can spread inside partitions because
    A. there are spaces between studs inside of partitions
    B. fires can burn anywhere
    C. partitions are made out of materials that burn easily
    D. partitions are usually painted or wallpapered

    16._____

17. Cobwebs inside a partition are a sign that the fire has not spread inside the partition because
    A. cobwebs are fire resistant
    B. fire destroys cobwebs easily
    C. spiders don't build cobwebs near fires
    D. cobwebs fill up the spaces between studs

    17._____

18. If a firefighter sees the paint on a partition beginning to blister, he should *first*
    A. wet down the partition
    B. check the partitions in other rooms
    C. chop a hole in the partition
    D. close windows and doors and leave the room

    18._____

19. *One* way to tell if fire is spreading within a partition is the
    A. temperature of the partition   B. color of the smoke
    C. age of the plaster             D. spacing of the studs

20. The *main* point of the passage is:
    A. How fire spreads inside partitions
    B. How cobwebs help firefighters
    C. How partitions are built
    D. How to keep fires from spreading

Questions 21-25.

DIRECTIONS:   Answer Questions 21 through 25 on the basis of the passage below.

There is hardly a city in the country that is not short of fire protection in some areas within its boundaries. These municipalities have spread out and have re-shuffled their residential, business, and industrial districts without readjusting the existing protective fire forces, or creating new protection units. Fire stations are still situated according to the needs of earlier times and have not been altered or improved to house modern fire fighting equipment. They are neither efficient for carrying out their tasks nor livable for the men who must occupy them.

21. Of the following, the title which *BEST* describes the central idea of the above passage is:
    A. The Dynamic Nature of Contemporary Society
    B. The Cost of Fire Protection
    C. The Location and Design of Fire Stations
    D. The Design and Use of Fire Fighting Equipment
    E. The Growth of American Cities

22. According to the above passage, fire protection is inadequate in the United States in
    A. *most* areas of *some* cities
    B. *some* areas of *most* cities
    C. *some* areas in *all* cities
    D. *all* areas in *some* cities
    E. *most* areas in *most* cities

23. The *one* of the following criteria for planning of fire stations which is *NOT* mentioned in the above passage is:
    A. Comfort of firemen       B. Proper location
    C. Design for modern equipment
    D. Efficiency of operation  E. Cost of construction

24. Of the following suggestions for improving the fire service, the *one* which would *BEST* deal with the problem discussed in the passage above would involve
    A. specialized training in the use of modern fire apparatus
    B. replacement of obsolete fire apparatus
    C. revision of zoning laws
    D. longer basic training for probationary firemen
    E. reassignment of fire districts

25. The tone of the author of the passage above may BEST be characterized by which one of the following adjectives:
   A. Hopeful   B. Negative   C. Hopeless   D. Striving   E. Critical

25._____

# TEST 2

Questions 1-6.

DIRECTIONS:  Answer Questions 1 through 6 on the basis of the passage below.

During search operations the first step is usually to rescue victims who can be seen and heard, or those whose exact locations are known. Disorganized or careless search must be avoided since victims may be underneath rubble. Disorganized movement could cause injury or death. The best method is to start from the outer edge and work toward the center of an area. Sometimes a trapped or buried victim may be located by calling out or by tapping on pipes. Rescue workers should first call out, then have a period of silence to listen for sounds from a victim.

1. The *main* point of the paragraph is that
   A. firefighters should call and listen often
   B. trapped victims can usually be heard
   C. searching should be an organized procedure
   D. many victims are buried in fires

1._____

2. Normally, the *first* victims to be rescued during a search are those who are
   A. unconscious       B. trapped under rubble
   C. easy to see and hear   D. injured

2._____

3. When searching for buried victims, it is very important for firefighters to
   A. have periods of silence   B. keep moving constantly
   C. search rubble piles quickly
   D. stay away from rubble piles

3._____

4. The *best* way to search an area is
   A. around the edges       B. from center to edge
   C. from corner to corner   D. from edge to center

4._____

5. Disorganized movement by a rescue worker can cause
   A. panic and confusion   B. property destruction
   C. wasted time           D. death or injury

5._____

6. Tapping on pipes is a good way to locate victims because
   A. firefighters can use Morse code
   B. sound travels through a pipe
   C. firefighters can signal each other this way
   D. pipes usually aren't covered by rubble

6._____

Questions 7-10.

DIRECTIONS: Answer Questions 7 through 10 on the basis of the passage below.

When backing a fire truck into the firehouse, all firefighters should remain outside the building. Firefighters assigned to stop traffic should face traffic so they can alert the driver in case of an emergency. Additional firefighters should stand on the sidewalk in front of the firehouse to guide the driver. The truck should be slowly backed into the firehouse and immediately stopped upon orders of any firefighter. When the truck is completely in the firehouse, then and only then should the officer contact central headquarters for the placement of the company in service. Following this, the officer orders the entrance doors closed.

Use this diagram to help answer Questions 7 through 9. The letters indicate where firefighters are standing.

7. The truck is backing into the firehouse. *Which* firefighter is *NOT* needed according to the regulations?
   A. Firefighter A        B. Firefighter B
   C. Firefighter C        D. Firefighter D

8. *Which* firefighters are responsible for stopping cars? Firefighters
   A. A and C    B. C and E    C. A and B    D. B and E

9. *Which* firefighters can order the truck to stop?
   A. Firefighters A and B only    B. Firefighters C and E only
   C. Firefighter D only           D. Any of them

10. *When* is central headquarters notified that the company is ready to be put in service?
    A. When the truck is returning from a fire
    B. After the truck is parked in the firehouse
    C. After the firehouse doors are closed
    D. When all of the firefighters have entered the firehouse

10._____

Questions 11-15.

DIRECTIONS: Answer Questions 11 through 15 on the basis of the passage below.

Unless they have had a fire, most people are not aware of the things firefighters do. Too often the public thinks of firefighters as lounging around a firehouse between fires. Firefighters can help change this image in small ways by their appearance, by greeting visitors who come to the firehouse, by their behavior on the street at a fire, and by treating the public in a courteous manner. For example, 90 percent of the rescues made by the average fire department take place at relatively small fires, not at spectacular extra alarm fires. The public rarely hears about them because the fire departments seldom let the press know about firefighters who have performed acts of bravery at routine fires.

11. *What* are firefighters doing when not fighting fires?
    A. Lounging around the firehouse
    B. Working on public relations projects
    C. Making repairs to the equipment
    D. The passage doesn't say

11._____

12. The passage places responsibility for improving the fire department's image on the
    A. fire department itself    B. press    C. public
    D. people rescued by firefighters

12._____

13. *Most* of the rescues made by firefighters take place at
    A. extra alarm fires
    B. special emergencies where no fire is involved
    C. relatively small fires    D. spectacularly large fires

13._____

14. The public rarely hears about rescues made by firefighters at routine fires because
    A. information about fires must be kept confidential
    B. fire departments seldom report these rescues to the press
    C. most of these rescues take place late at night
    D. reporters aren't interested in covering routine fires

14._____

15. *What* would be the *BEST* title for this passage?
    A. An Inside Look at the Fire Department
    B. Making the Most of Fire Prevention Week
    C. Improving the Fire Department's Public Image
    D. Brave Acts Performed by Firefighters

15._____

Questions 16-19.

DIRECTIONS: Answer Questions 16 through 19 on the basis of the passage below.

Ventilation, as used in fire-fighting operations, means opening up a building or structure in which a fire is burning to release the accumulated heat, smoke and gases. Lack of knowledge of the principles of ventilation on the part of firemen may result in unnecessary punishment due to ventilation being neglected or improperly handled. While ventilation itself extinguishes no fires, when used in an intelligent manner, it allows firemen to get at the fire more quickly, easily, and with less danger and hardship.

16. According to the above paragraph, the MOST important result of failure to apply the principles of ventilation at a fire may be
    A. loss of public confidence    B. disciplinary action
    C. waste of water    D. excessive use of equipment
    E. injury to firemen

16._____

17. It may be inferred from the above paragraph that the CHIEF advantage of ventilation is that it
    A. eliminates the need for gas masks
    B. reduces smoke damage
    C. permits firemen to work closer to the fire
    D. cools the fire
    E. enables firemen to use shorter hose lines

17._____

18. Knowledge of the principles of ventilation, as defined in the above paragraph, would be LEAST important in a fire in a
    A. tenement house    B. grocery store    C. ship's hold
    D. lumberyard    E. office building

18._____

19. We may conclude from the above paragraph that, for the well-trained and equipped fireman, ventilation is
    A. a simple matter    B. rarely necessary
    C. relatively unimportant    D. a basic tool
    E. sometimes a handicap

19._____

Questions 20-22.

DIRECTIONS: Answer Questions 20 through 22 on the basis of the passage below.

A fire of undetermined origin started in the warehouse shed of a flour mill. Although there was some delay in notifying the fire department, they practically succeeded in bringing the fire under control when a series of dust explosions occurred which caused the fire to spread and the main building was destroyed. The fire department's efforts were considerably handicapped because it was undermanned, and the water pressure in the vicinity was inadequate.

20. From the information contained in the above paragraph, it is MOST accurate to state that the cause of the fire was
    A. suspicious    B. unknown    C. accidental
    D. arson    E. spontaneous combustion

20._____

21. In the fire described above, the MOST important cause of the fire spreading to the main building was the
    A. series of dust explosions
    B. delay in notifying the fire department
    C. inadequate water pressure
    D. lack of manpower
    E. wooden construction of the building

22. In the fire described above, the fire department's efforts were handicapped CHIEFLY by
    A. poor leadership
    B. out-dated apparatus
    C. uncooperative company employees
    D. insufficient water pressure    E. poorly trained men

Questions 23-25.

DIRECTIONS:   Answer Questions 23 through 25 on the basis of the passage below.

    A flameproof fabric is defined as one which, when exposed to small sources of ignition such as sparks or smoldering cigarettes, does not burn beyond the vicinity of the source of the ignition. Cotton fabrics are the materials commonly used that are considered most hazardous. Other materials, such as acetate rayons and linens, are somewhat less hazardous, and woolens and some natural silk fabrics, even when untreated, are about the equal of the average treated cotton fabric insofar as flame-spread and ease of ignition are concerned. The method of application is to immerse the fabric in a flameproofing solution. The container used must be large enough so that all the fabric is thoroughly wet and there are no folds which the solution does not penetrate.

23. According to the above paragraph, a flameproof fabric is one which
    A. is unaffected by heat and smoke
    B. resists the spread of flames when ignited
    C. burns with a cold flame
    D. cannot be ignited by sparks or cigarettes
    E. may smolder but cannot burn

24. According to the above paragraph, woolen fabrics which have not been flameproofed are as likely to catch fire as
    A. treated silk fabrics
    B. treated acetate rayon fabrics
    C. untreated linen fabrics
    D. untreated synthetic fabrics
    E. treated cotton fabrics

25. In the method described above, the flameproofing solution is BEST applied to the fabric by
    A. sponging the fabric       B. spraying the fabric
    C. dipping the fabric        D. brushing the fabric
    E. sprinkling the fabric

# KEYS (CORRECT ANSWER)

## TEST 1

1. C
2. A
3. B
4. B
5. D

6. C
7. D
8. A
9. C
10. A

11. B
12. D
13. B
14. B
15. A

16. A
17. B
18. C
19. A
20. A

21. C
22. B
23. E
24. E
25. E

## TEST 2

1. C
2. C
3. A
4. D
5. D

6. B
7. D
8. C
9. D
10. B

11. D
12. A
13. C
14. B
15. C

16. E
17. C
18. D
19. D
20. B

21. A
22. D
23. B
24. E
25. C

# PREPARING WRITTEN MATERIAL
# EXAMINATION SECTION
# TEST 1

DIRECTIONS: Each question or incomplete statement is followed by several suggested answers or completions. Select the one that BEST answers the question or completes the statement. *PRINT THE LETTER OF THE CORRECT ANSWER IN THE SPACE AT THE RIGHT.*

1. The one of the following sentences which is LEAST acceptable from the viewpoint of correct usage is:
   A. The police thought the fugitive to be him.
   B. The criminals set a trap for whoever would fall into it.
   C. It is ten years ago since the fugitive fled from the city.
   D. The lecturer argued that criminals are usually cowards.
   E. The police removed four bucketfuls of earth from the scene of the crime.

1.____

2. The one of the following sentences which is LEAST acceptable from the viewpoint of correct usage is:
   A. The patrolman scrutinized the report with great care.
   B. Approaching the victim of the assault, two bruises were noticed by the patrolman.
   C. As soon as I had broken down the door, I stepped into the room.
   D. I observed the accused loitering near the building, which was closed at the time.
   E. The storekeeper complained that his neighbor was guilty of violating a local ordinance.

2.____

3. The one of the following sentences which is LEAST acceptable from the viewpoint of correct usage is:
   A. I realized immediately that he intended to assault the woman, so I disarmed him.
   B. It was apparent that Mr. Smith's explanation contained many inconsistencies.
   C. Despite the slippery condition of the street, he managed to stop the vehicle before injuring the child.
   D. Not a single one of them wish, despite the damage to property, to make a formal complaint.
   E. The body was found lying on the floor.

3.____

4. The one of the following sentences which contains NO error in usage is:
   A. After the robbers left, the proprietor stood tied in his chair for about two hours before help arrived.
   B. In the cellar I found the watchman's hat and coat.
   C. The persons living in adjacent apartments stated that they had heard no unusual noises.

4.____

131

D. Neither a knife or any firearms were found in the room.
E. Walking down the street, the shouting of the crowd indicated that something was wrong.

5. The one of the following sentences which contains NO error in usage is:
   A. The policeman lay a firm hand on the suspect's shoulder.
   B. It is true that neither strength nor agility are the most important requirement for a good patrolman.
   C. Good citizens constantly strive to do more than merely comply the restraints imposed by society.
   D. No decision was made as to whom the prize should be awarded.
   E. Twenty years is considered a severe sentence for a felony.

6. Which of the following sentences is NOT expressed in standard English usage?
   A. The victim reached a pay-phone booth and manages to call police headquarters.
   B. By the time the call was received, the assailant had left the scene.
   C. The victim has been a respected member of the community for the past eleven years.
   D. Although the lighting was bad and the shadows were deep, the storekeeper caught sight of the attacker.
   E. Additional street lights have since been installed, and the patrols have been strengthened.

7. Which of the following sentences is NOT expressed in standard English usage?
   A. The judge upheld the attorney's right to question the witness about the missing glove.
   B. To be absolutely fair to all parties is the jury's chief responsibility.
   C. Having finished the report, a loud noise in the next room startled the sergeant.
   D. The witness obviously enjoyed having played a part in the proceedings.
   E. The sergeant planned to assign the case to whoever arrived first.

8. In which of the following sentences is a word misused?
   A. As a matter of principle, the captain insisted that the suspect's partner be brought for questioning.
   B. The principle suspect had been detained at the station house for most of the day.
   C. The principal in the crime had no previous criminal record, but his closest associate had been convicted of felonies on two occasions.
   D. The interest payments had been made promptly, but the firm had been drawing upon the principal for these payments.
   E. The accused insisted that his high school principal would furnish him a character reference.

9. Which of the following statements is ambiguous?   9.____
    A. Mr. Sullivan explained why Mr. Johnson had been dismissed from his job.
    B. The storekeeper told the patrolman he had made a mistake.
    C. After waiting three hours, the patients in the doctor's office were sent home.
    D. The janitor's duties were to maintain the building in good shape and to answer tenants' complaints.
    E. The speed limit should, in my opinion, be raised to sixty miles an hour on that stretch of road.

10. In which of the following is the punctuation or capitalization faulty?   10.____
    A. The accident occurred at an intersection in the Kew Gardens section of Queens, near the bus stop.
    B. The sedan, not the convertible, was struck in the side.
    C. Before any of the patrolmen had left the police car received an important message from headquarters.
    D. The dog that had been stolen was returned to his master, John Dempsey, who lived in East Village.
    E. The letter had been sent to 12 Hillside Terrace, Rutland, Vermont 05702.

Questions 11-25.

DIRECTIONS: Questions 11 through 25 are to be answered in accordance with correct English usage; that is, standard English rather than nonstandard or substandard. Nonstandard and substandard English includes words or expressions usually classified as slang, dialect, illiterate, etc., which are not generally accepted as correct in current written communication. Standard English also requires clarity, proper punctuation and capitalization and appropriate use of words. Write the letter of the sentence NOT expressed in standard English usage in the space at the right.

11. A. There were three witnesses to the accident.   11.____
    B. At least three witnesses were found to testify for the plaintiff.
    C. Three of the witnesses who took the stand was uncertain about the defendant's competence to drive.
    D. Only three witnesses came forward to testify for the plaintiff.
    E. The three witnesses to the accident were pedestrians.

12. A. The driver had obviously drunk too many martinis before leaving for home.   12.____
    B. The boy who drowned had swum in these same waters many times before.
    C. The petty thief had stolen a bicycle from a private driveway before he was apprehended.
    D. The detectives had brung in the heroin shipment they intercepted.
    E. The passengers had never ridden in a converted bus before.

13. A. Between you and me, the new platoon plan sounds like a good idea.
    B. Money from an aunt's estate was left to his wife and he.
    C. He and I were assigned to the same patrol for the first time in two months.
    D. Either you or he should check the front door of that store.
    E. The captain himself was not sure of the witness's reliability.

14. A. The alarm had scarcely begun to ring when the explosion occurred.
    B. Before the firemen arrived at the scene, the second story had been destroyed.
    C. Because of the dense smoke and heat, the firemen could hardly approach the now-blazing structure.
    D. According to the patrolman's report, there wasn't nobody in the store when the explosion occurred.
    E. The sergeant's suggestion was not at all unsound, but no one agreed with him.

15. A. The driver and the passenger they were both found to be intoxicated.
    B. The driver and the passenger talked slowly and not too clearly.
    C. Neither the driver nor his passengers were able to give a coherent account of the accident.
    D. In a corner of the room sat the passenger, quietly dozing.
    E. the driver finally told a strange and unbelievable story, which the passenger contradicted.

16. A. Under the circumstances I decided not to continue my examination of the premises.
    B. There are many difficulties now not comparable with those existing in 1960.
    C. Friends of the accused were heard to announce that the witness had better been away on the day of the trial.
    D. The two criminals escaped in the confusion that followed the explosion.
    E. The aged man was struck by the considerateness of the patrolman's offer.

17. A. An assemblage of miscellaneous weapons lay on the table.
    B. Ample opportunities were given to the defendant to obtain counsel.
    C. The speaker often alluded to his past experience with youthful offenders in the armed forces.
    D. The sudden appearance of the truck aroused my suspicions.
    E. Her studying had a good affect on her grades in high school.

18. A. He sat down in the theater and began to watch the movie.
    B. The girl had ridden horses since she was four years old.
    C. Application was made on behalf of the prosecutor to cite the witness for contempt.
    D. The bank robber, with his two accomplices, were caught in the act.
    E. His story is simply not credible.

19.
A. The angry boy said that he did not like those kind of friends.
B. The merchant's financial condition was so precarious that he felt he must avail himself of any offer of assistance.
C. He is apt to promise more than he can perform.
D. Looking at the messy kitchen, the housewife felt like crying.
E. A clerk was left in charge of the stolen property.

19.____

20.
A. His wounds were aggravated by prolonged exposure to sub-freezing temperatures.
B. The prosecutor remarked that the witness was not averse to changing his story each time he was interviewed.
C. The crime pattern indicated that the burglars were adapt in the handling of explosives.
D. His rigid adherence to a fixed plan brought him into renewed conflict with his subordinates.
E. He had anticipated that the sentence would be delivered by noon.

20.____

21.
A. The whole arraignment procedure is badly in need of revision.
B. After his glasses were broken in the fight, he would of gone to the optometrist if he could.
C. Neither Tom nor Jack brought his lunch to work.
D. He stood aside until the quarrel was over.
E. A statement in the psychiatrist's report disclosed that the probationer vowed to have his revenge.

21.____

22.
A. His fiery and intemperate speech to the striking employees fatally affected any chance of a future reconciliation.
B. The wording of the statute has been variously construed.
C. The defendant's attorney, speaking in the courtroom, called the official a demagogue who contempuously disregarded the judge's orders.
D. The baseball game is likely to be the most exciting one this year.
E. The mother divided the cookies among her two children.

22.____

23.
A. There was only a bed and a dresser in the dingy room.
B. John was one of the few students that have protested the new rule.
C. It cannot be argued that the child's testimony is negligible; it is, on the contrary, of the greatest importance.
D. The basic criterion for clearance was so general that officials resolved any doubts in favor of dismissal.
E. Having just returned from a long vacation, the officer found the city unbearably hot.

23.____

24.
A. The librarian ought to give more help to small children.
B. The small boy was criticized by the teacher because he often wrote careless.
C. It was generally doubted whether the women would permit the use of her apartment for intelligence operations.
D. The probationer acts differently every time the officer visits him.
E. Each of the newly appointed officers has 12 years of service.

24.____

25. A. The North is the most industrialized region in the country.
    B. L. Patrick Gray 3d, the bureau's acting director, stated that, while "rehabilitation is fine" for some convicted criminals, "it is a useless gesture for those who resist every such effort."
    C. Careless driving, faulty mechanism, narrow or badly kept roads all play their part in causing accidents.
    D. The childrens' books were left in the bus.
    E. It was a matter of internal security; consequently, he felt no inclination to rescind his previous order.

25.____

## KEY (CORRECT ANSWERS)

| | | | | |
|---|---|---|---|---|
| 1. | C | | 11. | C |
| 2. | B | | 12. | D |
| 3. | D | | 13. | B |
| 4. | C | | 14. | D |
| 5. | E | | 15. | A |
| 6. | A | | 16. | C |
| 7. | C | | 17. | E |
| 8. | B | | 18. | D |
| 9. | B | | 19. | A |
| 10. | C | | 20. | C |

21. B
22. E
23. B
24. B
25. D

# TEST 2

DIRECTIONS: Each question or incomplete statement is followed by several suggested answers or completions. Select the one that BEST answers the question or completes the statement. *PRINT THE LETTER OF THE CORRECT ANSWER IN THE SPACE AT THE RIGHT.*

Questions 1-6.

DIRECTIONS: Each of Questions 1 through 6 consists of a statement which contains a word (one of those underlined) that is either incorrectly used because it is not in keeping with the meaning the quotation is evidently intended to convey, or is misspelled. There is only one INCORRECT word in each quotation. Of the four underlined words, determine if the first one should be replaced by the word lettered A, the second replaced by the word lettered B, the third replaced by the word lettered C, or the fourth replaced by the word lettered D.

1. Whether one depends on fluorescent or artificial light or both, adequate standards should be maintained by means of systematic tests.
   A. natural   B. safeguards   C. established   D. routine

2. A police officer has to be prepared to assume his knowledge as a social scientist in the community.
   A. forced   B. role   C. philosopher   D. street

3. It is practically impossible to indicate whether a sentence is too long simply by measuring its length.
   A. almost   B. tell   C. very   D. guessing

4. Strong leaders are required to organize a community for delinquency prevention and for dissemination of organized crime and drug addiction.
   A. tactics   B. important   C. control   D. meetings

5. The demonstrators who were taken to the Criminal Courts building in Manhattan (because it was large enough to accommodate them), contended that the arrests were unwarranted.
   A. demonstraters    B. Manhatten
   C. accomodate       D. unwarranted

6. They were guaranteed a calm atmosphere, free from harassment, which would be conducive to quiet consideration of the indictments.
   A. guarenteed    B. atmspher
   C. harassment    D. inditements

Questions 7-11.

DIRECTIONS: Each of Questions 7 through 11 consists of a statement containing four words in capital letters. One of these words in capital letters is not in keeping with the meaning which the statement is evidently intended to carry. The four words in capital letters in each statement are reprinted after the statement. Print the capital letter preceding the one of the four words which does MOST to spoil the true meaning of the statement in the space at the right.

7. Retirement and pension systems are essential not only to provide employees with with a means of support in the future, but also to prevent longevity and CHARITABLE considerations from UPSETTING the PROMOTIONAL opportunities RETIRED members of the career service. 7.____
   A. charitable    B. upsetting    C. promotional    D. retired

8. Within each major DIVISION in a properly set up public or private organization, provision is made so that each NECESSARY activity is CARED for and lines of authority and responsibility are clear-cut and INFINITE. 8.____
   A. division    B. necessary    C. cared    D. infinite

9. In public service, the scale of salaries paid must be INCIDENTAL to the services rendered, with due CONSIDERATION for the attraction of the desired MANPOWER and for the maintenance of a standard of living COMMENSURATE with the work to be performed. 9.____
   A. incidental            B. consideration
   C. manpower            D. commensurate

10. An understanding of the AIMS of an organization by the staff will AID greatly in increasing the DEMAND of the correspondence work of the office, and will to a large extent DETERMINE the nature of the correspondence. 10.____
    A. aims    B. aid    C. demand    D. determine

11. BECAUSE the Civil Service Commission strongly feels that the MERIT system is a key factor in the MAINTENANCE of democratic government, it has adopted as one of its major DEFENSES the progressive democratization of its own procedures in dealing with candidates for positions in the public service. 11.____
    A. Because    B. merit    C. maintenance    D. defenses

Questions 12-14.

DIRECTIONS: Questions 12 through 14 consist of one sentence each. Each sentence contains an incorrectly used word. First, decide which is the incorrectly used word. Then, from among the options given, decide which word, when substituted for the incorrectly used word, makes the meaning of the sentence clear.
EXAMPLE:
The U.S. national income exhibits a pattern of long term deflection.
   A. reflection    B. subjection    C. rejoicing    D. growth

The word *deflection* in the sentence does not convey the meaning the sentence evidently intended to convey. The word *growth* (Answer D), when substituted for the word *deflection*, makes the meaning of the sentence clear. Accordingly, the answer to the question is D.

12. The study commissioned by the joint committee fell compassionately short of the mark and would have to be redone.  12.____
    A. successfully  B. insignificantly
    C. experimentally  D. woefully

13. He will not idly exploit any violation of the provisions of the order.  13.____
    A. tolerate  B. refuse  C. construe  D. guard

14. The defendant refused to be virile and bitterly protested service.  14.____
    A. irked  B. feasible  C. docile  D. credible

Questions 15-25.

DIRECTIONS: Questions 15 through 25 consist of short paragraphs. Each paragraph contains one word which is INCORRECTLY used because it is NOT in keeping with the meaning of the paragraph. Find the word in each paragraph which is INCORRECTLY used and then select as the answer the suggested word which should be substituted for the incorrectly used word.

SAMPLE QUESTION:
In determining who is to do the work in your unit, you will have to decide just who does what from day to day. One of your lowest responsibilities is to assign work so that everybody gets a fair share and that everyone can do his part well.
    A. new  B. old  C. important  D. performance

EXPLANATION:
The word which is NOT in keeping with the meaning of the paragraph is *lowest*. This is the INCORRECTLY used word. The suggested word *important* would be in keeping with the meaning of the paragraph and should be substituted for *lowest*. Therefore, the CORRECT answer is choice C.

15. If really good practice in the elimination of preventable injuries is to be achieved and held in any establishment, top management must refuse full and definite responsibility and must apply a good share of its attention to the task.  15.____
    A. accept  B. avoidable  C. duties  D. problem

16. Recording the human face for identification is by no means the only service performed by the camera in the field of investigation. When the trial of any issue takes place, a word picture is sought to be distorted to the court of incidents, occurrences, or events which are in dispute.  16.____
    A. appeals  B. description  C. portrayed  D. deranged

17. In the collection of physical evidence, it cannot be emphasized too strongly that a haphazard systematic search at the scene of the crime is vital. Nothing must be overlooked. Often the only leads in a case will come from the results of this search.
    A. important
    B. investigation
    C. proof
    D. thorough

17.____

18. If an investigator has reason to suspect that the witness is mentally stable, or a habitual drunkard, he should leave no stone unturned in his investigation to determine if the witness was under the influence of liquor or drugs, or was mentally unbalanced either at the time of the occurrence to which he testified or at the time of the trial.
    A. accused    B. clue    C. deranged    D. question

18.____

19. The use of records is a valuable step in crime investigation and is the main reason every department should maintain accurate reports. Crimes are not committed through the use of departmental records alone but from the use of all records, of almost every type, wherever they may be found and whenever they give any incidental information regarding the criminal.
    A. accidental    B. necessary    C. reported    D. solved

19.____

20. In the years since passage of the Harrison Narcotic Act of 1914, making the possession of opium amphetamines illegal in most circumstances, drug use has become a subject of considerable scientific interest and investigation. There is at present a voluminous literature on drug use of various kinds.
    A. ingestion    B. derivatives    C. addiction    D. opiates

20.____

21. Of course, the fact that criminal laws are extremely patterned in definition does not mean that the majority of persons who violate them are dealt with as criminals. Quite the contrary, for a great many forbidden acts are voluntarily engaged in within situations of privacy and go unobserved and unreported.
    A. symbolic    B. casual    C. scientific    D. broad-gauged

21.____

22. The most punitive way to study punishment is to focus attention on the pattern of punitive action: to study how a penalty is applied, too study what is done to or taken from an offender.
    A. characteristic    B. degrading    C. objective    D. distinguished

22.____

23. The most common forms of punishment in times past have been death, physical torture, mutilation, branding, public humiliation, fines, forfeits of property, banishment, transportation, and imprisonment. Although this list is by no means differentiated, practically every form of punishment has had several variations and applications.
    A. specific    B. simple    C. exhaustive    D. characteristic

23.____

24. There is another important line of inference between ordinary and professional criminals, and that is the source from which they are recruited. The professional criminal seems to be drawn from legitimate employment and, in many instances, from parallel vocations or pursuits.
    A. demarcation   B. justification   C. superiority   D. reference

    24._____

25. He took the position that the success of the program was insidious on getting additional revenue.
    A. reputed   B. contingent   C. failure   D. indeterminate

    25._____

## KEY (CORRECT ANSWERS)

1. A
2. B
3. B
4. C
5. D

11. D
12. D
13. A
14. C
15. A

6. C
7. D
8. D
9. A
10. C

16. C
17. D
18. C
19. D
20. B

21. D
22. C
23. C
24. A
25. B

# TEST 3

DIRECTIONS: Each question or incomplete statement is followed by several suggested answers or completions. Select the one that BEST answers the question or completes the statement. *PRINT THE LETTER OF THE CORRECT ANSWER IN THE SPACE AT THE RIGHT.*

Questions 1-5.

DIRECTIONS: Questions 1 through 5 are to be answered on the basis of the following.

You are a supervising officer in an investigative unit. Earlier in the day, you directed Detectives Tom Dixon and Sal Mayo to investigate a reported assault and robbery in a liquor store within your area of jurisdiction.

Detective Dixon has submitted to you a preliminary investigative report containing the following information:

- At 1630 hours on 2/20, arrived at Joe's Liquor Store at 350 SW Avenue with Detective Mayo to investigate A & R.
- At store interviewed Rob Ladd, store manager, who stated that he and Joe Brown (store owner) had been stuck up about ten minutes prior to our arrival.
- Ladd described the robbers as male whites in their late teens or early twenties. Further stated that one of the robbers displayed what appeared to be an automatic pistol as he entered the store, and said, *Give us the money or we'll kill you.* Ladd stated that Brown then reached under the counter where he kept a loaded .38 caliber pistol. Several shots followed, and Ladd threw himself to the floor.
- The robbers fled, and Ladd didn't know if any money had been taken.
- At this point, Ladd realized that Brown was unconscious on the floor and bleeding from a head wound.
- Ambulance called by Ladd, and Brown was removed by same to General Hospital.
- Personally interviewed John White, 382 Dartmouth Place, who stated he was inside store at the time of occurrence. White states that he hid behind a wine display upon hearing someone say, *Give us the money.* He then heard shots and saw two young men run from the store to a yellow car parked at the curb. White was unable to further describe auto. States the taller of the two men drove the car away while the other sat on passenger side in front.
- Recovered three spent .38 caliber bullets from premises and delivered them to Crime Lab.
- To General Hospital at 1800 hours but unable to interview Brown, who was under sedation and suffering from shock and a laceration of the head.
- Alarm #12487 transmitted for car and occupants.
- Case Active.

Based solely on the contents of the preliminary investigation submitted by Detective Dixon, select one sentence from the following groups of sentences which is MOST accurate and is grammatically correct.

1.  A. Both robbers were armed.
    B. Each of the robbers were described as a male white.
    C. Neither robber was armed.
    D. Mr. Ladd stated that one of the robbers was armed.

    1.____

2.  A. Mr. Brown fired three shots from his revolver.
    B. Mr. Brown was shot in the head by one of the robbers.
    C. Mr. Brown suffered a gunshot wound of the head during the course of the robbery.
    D. Mr. Brown was taken to General Hospital by ambulance.

    2.____

3.  A. Shots were fired after one of the robbers said, *Give us the money or we'll kill you.*
    B. After one of the robbers demanded the money from Mr. Brown, he fired a shot.
    C. The preliminary investigation indicated that although Mr. Brown did not have a license for the gun, he was justified in using deadly physical force.
    D. Mr. Brown was interviewed at General Hospital.

    3.____

4.  A. Each of the witnesses were customers in the store at the time of occurrence.
    B. Neither of the witnesses interviewed was the owner of the liquor store.
    C. Neither of the witnesses interviewed were the owner of the store.
    D. Neither of the witnesses was employed by Mr. Brown.

    4.____

5.  A. Mr. Brown arrived at General Hospital at about 5:00 P.M.
    B. Neither of the robbers was injured during the robbery.
    C. The robbery occurred at 3:30 P.M. on February 10.
    D. One of the witnesses called the ambulance.

    5.____

Questions 6-10.

DIRECTIONS: Each of Questions 6 through 10 consists of information given in outline form and four sentences labeled A, B, C, and D. For each question, choose the one sentence which CORRECTLY expresses the information given in outline form and which also displays PROPER English usage.

6.  Client's Name: Joanna Jones
    Number of Children: 3
    Client's Income: None
    Client's Marital Status: Single

    6.____

    A. Joanna Jones is an unmarried client with three children who have no income.
    B. Joanna Jones, who is single and has no income, a client she has three children.
    C. Joanna Jones, whose three children are clients, is single and has no income.
    D. Joanna Jones, who has three children, is an unmarried client with no income.

7. Client's Name: Bertha Smith                                           7.____
   Number of Children: 2
   Client's Rent: $1050 per month
   Number of Rooms: 4

   A. Bertha Smith, a client, pays $1050 per month for her four rooms with two children.
   B. Client Bertha Smith has two children and pays $1050 per month for four rooms.
   C. Client Bertha Smith is paying $1050 per month for two children with four rooms.
   D. For four rooms and two children client Bertha Smith pays $1050 per month.

8. Name of Employee: Cynthia Dawes                                       8.____
   Number of Cases Assigned: 9
   Date Cases were Assigned: 12/16
   Number of Assigned Cases Completed: 8

   A. On December 16, employee Cynthia Dawes was assigned nine cases; she has completed eight of these cases.
   B. Cynthia Dawes, employee on December 16, assigned nine cases, completed eight.
   C. Being employed on December 16, Cynthia Dawes completed eight of nine assigned cases.
   D. Employee Cynthia Dawes, she was assigned nine cases and completed eight, on December 16.

9. Place of Audit: Broadway Center                                       9.____
   Names of Auditors: Paul Cahn, Raymond Perez
   Date of Audit: 11/20
   Number of Cases Audited: 41

   A. On November 20, at the Broadway Center 41 cases was audited by auditors Paul Cahn and Raymond Perez.
   B. Auditors Raymond Perez and Paul Cahn has audited 41 cases at the Broadway Center on November 20.
   C. At the Broadway Center, on November 20, auditors Paul Cahn and Raymond Perez audited 41 cases.
   D. Auditors Paul Cahn and Raymond Perez at the Broadway Center, on November 20, is auditing 41 cases.

10. Name of Client: Barbra Levine                                        10.____
    Client's Monthly Income: $2100
    Client's Monthly Expenses: $4520

    A. Barbra Levine is a client, her monthly income is $2100 and her monthly expenses is $4520.
    B. Barbra Levine's monthly income is $2100 and she is a client, with whose monthly expenses are $4520.

C. Barbra Levine is a client whose monthly income is $2100 and whose monthly expenses are $4520.
D. Barbra Levine, a client, is with a monthly income which is $2100 and monthly expenses which are $4520.

Questions 11-13.

DIRECTIONS: Questions 11 through 13 involve several statements of fact presented in a very simple way. These statements of fact are followed by 4 choices which attempt to incorporate all of the facts into one logical statement which is properly constructed and grammatically correct.

11. I. Mr. Brown was sweeping the sidewalk in front of his house.
    II. He was sweeping it because it was dirty.
    III. He swept the refuse into the street.
    IV. Police Officer gave him a ticket.

    Which one of the following BEST presents the information given above?
    A. Because his sidewalk was dirty, Mr. Brown received a ticket from Officer Green when he swept the refuse into the street.
    B. Police Officer Green gave Mr. Brown a ticket because his sidewalk was dirty and he swept the refuse into the street.
    C. Police Officer Green gave Mr. Brown a ticket for sweeping refuse into the street because his sidewalk was dirty.
    D. Mr. Brown, who was sweeping refuse from his dirty sidewalk into the street, was given a ticket by Police Officer Green.

12. I. Sergeant Smith radioed for help.
    II. The sergeant did so because the crowd was getting larger.
    III. It was 10:00 A.M. when he made his call.
    IV. Sergeant Smith was not in uniform at the time of occurrence.

    Which one of the following BEST presents the information given above?
    A. Sergeant Smith, although not on duty at the time, radioed for help at 10 o'clock because the crowd was getting uglier.
    B. Although not in uniform, Sergeant Smith called for help at 10:00 A.M. because the crowd was getting uglier.
    C. Sergeant Smith radioed for help at 10:00 A.M. because the crowd was getting larger.
    D. Although he was not in uniform, Sergeant Smith radioed for help at 10:00 A.M. because the crowd was getting larger.

13. I. The payroll office is open on Fridays.
    II. Paychecks are distributed from 9:00 A.M. to 12 Noon.
    III. The office is open on Fridays because that's the only day the payroll staff is available.
    IV. It is open for the specified hours in order to permit employees to cash checks at the bank during lunch hour.

The choice below which MOST clearly and accurately presents the above idea is:
- A. Because the payroll office is open on Fridays from 9:00 A.M. to 12 Noon, employees can cash their checks when the payroll staff is available.
- B. Because the payroll staff is only available on Fridays until noon, employees can cash their checks during their lunch hour.
- C. Because the payroll staff is available only on Fridays, the office is open from 9:00 A.M. to 12 Noon to allow employees to cash their checks.
- D. Because of payroll staff availability, the payroll office is open on Fridays. It is open from 9:00 A.M. to 12 Noon so that distributed paychecks can be cashed at the bank while employees are on their lunch hour.

Questions 14-16.

DIRECTIONS: In each of Questions 14 through 6, the four sentences are from a paragraph in a report. They are not in the right order. Which of the following arrangements is the BEST one?

14. I. An executive may answer a letter by writing his reply on the face of the letter itself instead of having a return letter typed.
    II. This procedure is efficient because it saves the executive's time, the typist's time, and saves office file space.
    III. Copying machines are used in small offices as well as large offices to save time and money in making brief replies to business letters.
    IV. A copy is made on a copy machine to go into the company files, while the original is mailed back to the sender.

    The CORRECT answer is:
    A. I, II, IV, III   B. I, IV, II, III   C. III, I, IV, II   D. III, IV, II, I

15. I. Most organizations favor one of the types but always include the others to a lesser degree.
    II. However, we can detect a definite trend toward greater use of symbolic control.
    III. We suggest that our local police agencies are today primarily utilizing material control.
    IV. Control can be classified into three types: physical, material, and symbolic.

    The CORRECT answer is:
    A. IV, II, III, I   B. II, I, IV, III   C. III, IV, II, I   D. IV, I, III, II

16. I. They can and do take advantage of ancient political and geographical boundaries, which often give them sanctuary from effective policy activity.
    II. This country is essentially a country of small police forces, each operating independently within the limits of its jurisdiction.
    III. The boundaries that define and limit police operations do not hinder the movement of criminals, of course.
    IV. The machinery of law enforcement in America is fragmented, complicated, and frequently overlapping.

The CORRECT answer is:
A. III, I, IV   B. II, IV, I, III   C. IV, II, III, I   D. IV, III, II, I

17. Examine the following sentence, and then choose from below the words which should be inserted in the blank spaces to produce the best sentence.
The unit has exceeded _____ goals and the employees are satisfied with _____ accomplishments.
A. their, it's   B. it's; it's   C. its, there   D. its, their

18. Examine the following sentence, and then choose from below the words which should be inserted in the blank spaces to produce the best sentence.
Research indicates that employees who _____ no opportunity for close social relationships often find their work unsatisfying, and this _____ of satisfaction often reflects itself in low production.
A. have; lack   B. have; excess   C. has; lack   D. has; excess

19. Words in a sentence must be arranged properly to make sure that the intended meaning of the sentence is clear.
The sentence below that does NOT make sense because a clause has been separated from the word on which its meaning depends is:
A. To be a good writer, clarity is necessary.
B. To be a good writer, you must write clearly.
C. You must write clearly to be a good writer.
D. Clarity is necessary to good writing.

Questions 20-21.

DIRECTIONS: Each of Questions 20 and 21 consists of a statement which contains a word (one of those underlined) that is either incorrectly used because it is not in keeping with the meaning the quotation is evidently intended to convey, or is misspelled. There is only one INCORRECT word in each quotation. Of the four underlined words, determine if the first one should be replaced by the word lettered A, the second one replaced by the word lettered B, the third one replaced by the word lettered C, or the fourth one replaced by the word lettered D.

20. The alleged killer was occasionally permitted to excercise in the corridor.
A. alledged   B. ocasionally   C. permited   D. exercise

21. Defense counsel stated, in affect, that their conduct was permissible under the First Amendment.
A. council   B. effect   C. there   D. permissable

Question 22.

DIRECTIONS: Question 22 consists of one sentence. This sentence contains an incorrectly used word. First, decide which is the incorrectly used word. Then, from among the options given, decide which word, when substituted for the incorrectly used word, makes the meaning of the sentence clear.

22. As today's violence has no single cause, so its causes have no single scheme. 22.____
    A. deference    B. cure    C. flaw    D. relevance

23. In the sentence, *A man in a light-grey suit waited thirty-five minutes in the ante-room for the all-important document*, the word IMPROPERLY hyphenated is    23.____
    A. light-grey           B. thirty-five
    C. ante-room           D. all-important

24. In the sentence, *The candidate wants to file his application for preference before it is too late*, the word *before* is used as a(n)    24.____
    A. preposition         B. subordinating conjunction
    C. pronoun             D. adverb

25. In the sentence, *The perpetrators ran from the scene*, the word *from* is a    25.____
    A. preposition    B. pronoun    C. verb    D. conjunction

## KEY (CORRECT ANSWERS)

| | | | |
|---|---|---|---|
| 1. | D | 11. | D |
| 2. | D | 12. | D |
| 3. | A | 13. | D |
| 4. | B | 14. | C |
| 5. | D | 15. | D |
| 6. | D | 16. | C |
| 7. | B | 17. | D |
| 8. | A | 18. | A |
| 9. | C | 19. | A |
| 10. | C | 20. | D |

| | |
|---|---|
| 21. | B |
| 22. | B |
| 23. | C |
| 24. | B |
| 25. | A |

# PREPARING WRITTEN MATERIAL

# PARAGRAPH REARRANGEMENT
# COMMENTARY

The sentences that follow are in scrambled order. You are to rearrange them in proper order and indicate the letter choice containing the correct answer at the space at the right.

Each group of sentences in this section is actually a paragraph presented in scrambled order. Each sentence in the group has a place in that paragraph; no sentence is to be left out. You are to read each group of sentences and decide upon the best order in which to put the sentences so as to form a well-organized paragraph.

The questions in this section measure the ability to solve a problem when all the facts relevant to its solution are not given.

More specifically, certain positions of responsibility and authority require the employee to discover connection between events sometimes, apparently, unrelated. In order to do this, the employee will find it necessary to correctly infer that unspecified events have probably occurred or are likely to occur. This ability becomes especially important when action must be taken on incomplete information.

Accordingly, these questions require competitors to choose among several suggested alternatives, each of which presents a different sequential arrangement of the events. Competitors must choose the MOST logical of the suggested sequences.

In order to do so, they may be required to draw on general knowledge to infer missing concepts or events that are essential to sequencing the given events. Competitors should be careful to infer only what is essential to the sequence. The plausibility of the wrong alternatives will always require the inclusion of unlikely events or of additional chains of events which are NOT essential to sequencing the given events.

It's very important to remember that you are looking for the best of the four possible choices, and that the best choice of all may not even be one of the answers you're given to choose from.

There is no one right way to solve these problems. Many people have found it helpful to first write out the order of the sentences, as they would have arranged them, on their scrap paper before looking at the possible answers. If their optimum answer is there, this can save them some time. If it isn't, this method can still give insight into solving the problem. Others find it most helpful to just go through each of the possible choices, contrasting each as they go along. You should use whatever method feels comfortable and works for you.

While most of these types of questions are not that difficult, we've added a higher percentage of the difficult type, just to give you more practice. Usually there are only one or two questions on this section that contain such subtle distinctions that you're unable to answer confidently. And you then may find yourself stuck deciding between two possible choices, neither of which you're sure about.

# EXAMINATION SECTION
# TEST 1

DIRECTIONS: The sentences that follow are in scrambled order. You are to rearrange them in proper order and indicate the letter choice containing the CORRECT answer. *PRINT THE LETTER OF THE CORRECT ANSWER IN THE SPACE AT THE RIGHT.*

1. Fire Marshal Adams has arrested a man for pulling a false alarm. He has recorded the following items of information about the incident in his notebook for use in his subsequent report:
    I. I was on surveillance at a frequently pulled false alarm box located at Edison Street and Harvard Road.
    II. At 1605 hours, I observed the white male, with long brown hair and a mustache, wearing black pants and a red shirt, pull the fire alarm box.
    III. I interviewed the officer of the first due ladder company, Lt. Morgan - L-37, who informed me that a search of the area disclosed no cause for an alarm to be transmitted.
    IV. A man wearing a red shirt, black pants, with long brown hair and a mustache came out of Ryan's Pub, located at Edison Street and Harvard Road, and walked directly to the alarm box.
    V. I stopped the man about five blocks away at 33rd Street and Harvard Road and asked him why he pulled the fire alarm box, and he replied, *Because I felt like it.*

    The MOST logical order for the above sentences to appear in the report is

    A. I, IV, II, III, V  
    B. I, II, III, IV, V  
    C. I, IV, III, II, V  
    D. I, IV, V, II, III

1.____

2. A fire marshal is preparing a report regarding Tom Jones, who was a witness to an arson fire at his apartment building. Following are five sentences which will be included in the report:
    I. On July 16, I responded to the fire building, address 2020 Elm Street, to interview Tom Jones.
    II. Tom Jones described the *super* (name unknown) as a middle-aged male with beard, six feet tall, wearing a blue jumpsuit.
    III. Tom Jones stated that he saw the *super* of the building next door set the fire.
    IV. After being advised of his constitutional rights at the 44th Precinct detective's squad room, the *super* confessed.
    V. I interviewed the *super* and took him to the precinct for further investigation.

    The MOST logical order for the above sentences to appear in the report is

    A. I, II, III, V, IV  
    B. I, II, III, IV, V  
    C. I, III, II, IV, V  
    D. I, III, II, V, IV

2.____

151

3. A fire marshal is preparing a report on a shooting incident which will include the following five sentences:
    I. I ran around the corner and observed a man pointing a gun at another man.
    II. I informed the man I was a police officer and that he should drop his gun.
    III. I was on the corner of 4th Avenue and 43rd Street when I heard a gunshot coming from around the corner.
    IV. The man turned around and pointed his gun at me.
    V. I fired once, shooting him in the chest and causing him to fall to the ground.
   The MOST logical order for the above sentences to appear in the report is

    A. I, III, IV, II, V       B. IV, V, II, I, III
    C. III, I, II, IV, V       D. III, I, V, II, IV

4. Fire Marshal Smith is writing a report. The report will include the following five sentences:
    I. I asked the woman for a description of the man and his location in the building.
    II. When I said, *Don't move, Five Marshal,* the man dropped the can containing a flammable liquid.
    III. I transmitted on my handie-talkie for fire companies to respond.
    IV. A woman approached our car and said there was a man pouring a liquid, which she thought to be gasoline, on a staircase at 123 East Street.
    V. Upon entering that location, I observed a man spilling a liquid on the floor.
   The MOST logical order for the above sentences to appear on the interview sheet is

    A. IV, I, V, II, III       B. I, IV, III, V, II
    C. V, II, IV, I, III       D. IV, III, I, V, II

5. Fire Marshal Fox is completing an interview report for a fire in the kitchen of an apartment at 1700 Clayton Road. The following five sentences will be included in the interview report:
    I. This is the first fire in which Mrs. Brown has ever been involved.
    II. A neighbor smelled the food burning and called the Fire Department.
    III. Mrs. Brown has been a tenant in Apt. 4C for 7 years.
    IV. Mrs. Brown was very tired and laid down to rest and fell asleep.
    V. Mrs. Brown was cooking beef stew in the kitchen after coming home from work.
   The MOST logical order for the above sentences to appear in the report is

    A. II, III, I, IV, V       B. III, V, IV, II, I
    C. I, III, II, V, IV       D. III, V, I, IV, II

6. A fire marshal is completing a report of an arson fire. The report will contain the following five statements made by a witness:
    I. I heard the sound of breaking glass; and when I looked out my window, I saw orange flames coming from the building across the street.
    II. I saw two young men on bicycles rapidly riding away, one with long blond hair, the other had long brown hair.
    III. He made a threat to get even when he was being evicted.
    IV. The young man with long blond hair was evicted from the fire building last week.
    V. The two young men rode in the direction of Flowers Avenue.
   The MOST logical order for the above statements to appear in the report is

A. I, II, V, IV, III                B. I, II, IV, V, III
C. III, I, V, II, IV                D. III, I, II, IV, V

7. A fire marshal is preparing a report regarding an eleven-year-old who was burned in a fire at the Midtown School for Boys. The report will include the following five sentences:
    I. The child described the fire-setter as a male with glasses, five feet tall, wearing a blue uniform.
    II. On December 12, I responded to Hill Top Hospital to interview a child who was burned in a fire at the Midtown School for Boys.
    III. The male perpetrator made a full confession in front of the Assistant District Attorney at the precinct.
    IV. I responded to the school, after interviewing the boy, and found a security guard who fit the description.
    V. I interviewed the security guard and took him to the precinct for further questioning.

    The MOST logical order for the above sentences to appear in the fire report is

    A. I, IV, V, II, III            B. IV, III, II, I, V
    C. II, I, IV, V, III            D. II, IV, I, V, III

8. A fire marshal is preparing a report concerning a fire in an auto body shop. The report will contain the following five sentences:
    I. The shop owner stated that he argued with a customer about the cost of a repair job.
    II. The shop owner will be the complainant in the arson case.
    III. While on surveillance, my partner and I saw the fire and called it in over the Department radio.
    IV. The customer paid the bill and left saying, *I'll fix you for charging so much.*
    V. According to witnesses, the customer returned to the shop and threw a Molotov cocktail on the floor.

    The MOST logical order for the above sentences to appear in the report is

    A. I, IV, V, II, III            B. III, I, IV, V, II
    C. V, I, IV, III, II            D. III, V, I, IV, II

9. Security Officer Mace is completing an entry in her memo-book. The entry has the following five sentences:
    I. I observed the defendant removing a radio from a facility vehicle.
    II. I placed the defendant under arrest and escorted him to the patrolroom.
    III. I was patrolling the facility parking lot.
    IV. I asked the defendant to show identification.
    V. I determined that the defendant was not authorized to remove the radio.

    The MOST logical order for these sentences to be entered in Officer Mace's memo-book is

    A. I, III, II, IV, V            B. II, V, IV, I, III
    C. III, I, IV, V, II            D. IV, V, II, I, III

10. Security Officer Riley is completing an entry in his memo-book. The entry has the following five sentences:
    I. Anna Jones admitted that she stole Mary Green's wallet.
    II. I approached the women and asked them who they were and why they were arguing.
    III. I arrested Anna Jones for stealing Mary Green's wallet.
    IV. They identified themselves and Mary Green accused Anna Jones of stealing her wallet.
    V. I was in the lobby area when I observed two women arguing about a wallet.
    The MOST logical order for these sentences to be entered in Officer Riley's memo-book is

    A. II, IV, I, III, V
    B. III, I, IV, V, II
    C. IV, I, V, II, III
    D. V, II, IV, I, III

11. Assume that Security Officer John Ryan is completing an entry in his memobook. The entry has the following five sentences:
    I. I then cleared the immediate area of visitors and staff.
    II. I noticed smoke coming from a broom closet outside Room A71.
    III. Sergeant Mueller arrived with other officers to assist in clearing the area.
    IV. Upon investigation, I determined the smoke was due to burning material in the broom closet.
    V. I pulled the corridor fire alarm and notified Sergeant Mueller of the fire.
    The MOST logical order for these sentences to be entered in Officer Ryan's memo-book is

    A. II, III, IV, V, I
    B. II, IV, V, I, III
    C. IV, I, II, III, V
    D. V, III, II, I, IV

12. Security Officer Hernandez is completing an entry in his memobook. The entry has the following five sentences:
    I. I asked him to leave the premises immediately.
    II. A visitor complained that there was a strange man loitering in Clinic B hallway.
    III. I went to investigate and saw a man dressed in rags sitting on the floor of the hallway.
    IV. As he walked out, he started yelling that he had no place to go.
    V. I asked to see identification, but he said that he did not have any.
    The MOST logical order for these sentences to be entered in Officer Hernandez's memobook is

    A. II, III, V, I, IV
    B. III, I, II, IV, V
    C. IV, I, V, II, III
    D. III, I, V, II, IV

13. Officer Hogan is completing an entry in his memobook. The entry has the following five sentences:
    I. When the fighting had stopped, I transmitted a message requesting medical assistance for Mr. Perkins.
    II. Special Officer Manning assisted me in stopping the fight,
    III. When I arrived at the scene, I saw a client, Adam Finley, strike a facility employee, Peter Perkins.
    IV. As I attempted to break up the fight, Special Officer Manning came on the scene.
    V. I received a radio message from Sergeant Valez to investigate a possible fight in progress in the waiting room.

    The MOST logical order for these sentences to be entered in Officer Hogan's memobook is

    A. II, I, IV, V, III
    B. III, V, II, IV, I
    C. IV, V, III, I, II
    D. V, III, IV, II, I

14. Police Officer White is preparing a crime report concerning the burglary of Mr. Smith's home. The report will contain the following five sentences:
    I. Upon entering the house, Mr. Smith noticed that the mortgage money, which had been left on the kitchen table, had been taken.
    II. An investigation by the reporting Officer determined that the burglar had left the house through the first floor rear door.
    III. Further investigation revealed that there were no witnesses to the burglary.
    IV. In addition, several pieces of jewelry were missing from a first floor bedroom.
    V. After arriving at home, Mr. Smith discovered that someone had broken into the house by jimmying the front door.

    The MOST logical order for the above sentences to appear in the report is

    A. V, IV, II, III, I
    B. V, I, III, IV, II
    C. V, I, IV, II, III
    D. V, IV, II, I, III

15. Police Officer Jenner responds to the scene of a burglary at 2106 La Vista Boulevard. He is approached by an elderly man named Richard Jenkins, whose account of the incident includes the following five sentences:
    I. I saw that the lock on my apartment door had been smashed and the door was open.
    II. My apartment was a shambles; my belongings were everywhere and my television set was missing.
    III. As I walked down the hallway toward the bedroom, I heard someone opening a window.
    IV. I left work at 5:30 P.M. and took the bus home.
    V. At that time, I called the police.

    The MOST logical order for the above sentences to appear in the report is

    A. I, V, IV, II, III
    B. IV, I, II, III, V
    C. I, V, II, III, IV
    D. IV, III, II, V, I

16. Police Officer LaJolla is writing an Incident Report in which back-up assistance was required. The report will contain the following five sentences:
    I. The radio dispatcher asked what my location was and he then dispatched patrol cars for back-up assistance.
    II. At approximately 9:30 P.M., while I was walking my assigned footpost, a gunman fired three shots at me.
    III. I quickly turned around and saw a White male, approximately 5'10", with black hair, wearing blue jeans, a yellow T-shirt, and white sneakers, running across the avenue carrying a handgun.
    IV. When the back-up officers arrived, we searched the area but could not find the suspect.
    V. I advised the radio dispatcher that a gunman had just fired a gun at me, and then I gave the dispatcher a description of the man.
    The MOST logical order for the above sentences to appear in the report is
    A. III, V, II, IV, I
    B. II, III, V, I, IV
    C. III, II, IV, I, V
    D. II, V, I, III, IV

17. Police Officer Engle is completing a Complaint Report of a burglary which occurred at Monty's Bar. The following five sentences will be included in the Complaint Report:
    I. The owner said that approximately $600 was taken, along with eight bottles of expensive brandy.
    II. The burglar apparently gained entry to the bar through the window and exited through the front door.
    III. When Mr. Barrett returned to reopen the bar at 1:00 P.M., he found the front door open and items thrown all over the bar.
    IV. Mr. Barrett, the owner of Monty's Bar, said he closed the bar at 4:00 M. and locked all the doors.
    V. After interviewing the owner, I conducted a search of the bar and found that a window in the back of the bar was broken.
    The MOST logical order for the above sentences to appear in the report is
    A. II, IV, III, V, I
    B. IV, III, I, V, II
    C. IV, II, III, I, V
    D. II, V, IV, III, I

18. Police Officer Revson is writing a report concerning a vehicle pursuit. His report will include the following five sentences:
    I. I followed the vehicle for several blocks and then motioned to the driver to pull the car over to the curb and stop.
    II. I informed the radio dispatcher that I was in a high-speed pursuit.
    III. When the driver ignored me, I turned on my siren and the driver increased his speed.
    IV. The vehicle hit a tree, and I was able to arrest the driver.
    V. While on patrol in Car #4135, I observed a motorist driving suspiciously.
    The MOST logical order for the above sentences to appear in the report is
    A. V, I, III, II, IV
    B. II, V, III, I, IV
    C. V, I, II, IV, III
    D. II, I, V, IV, III

19. Crime Reports are completed by Police Officers. One section of a report contains the following five sentences:
    I. The man, seeing that the woman had the watch, pushed Mr. Lugano to the ground.
    II. Frank Lugano was walking into the Flame Diner on Queens Boulevard when he was jostled by a man in front of him.
    III. A few minutes later, Mr. Lugano told a police officer on foot patrol about a man and a woman taking his watch.
    IV. As soon as he was jostled, a woman reached toward Mr. Lugano's wrist and removed his expensive watch.
    V. The man and woman, after taking Mr. Lugano's watch, ran around the corner.

    The MOST logical order for the above sentences to appear in the report is

    A. II, IV, I, III, V  
    B. II, IV, I, V, III  
    C. IV, I, III, II, V  
    D. IV, II, I, V, III

20. Detective Adams completed a Crime Report which includes the following five sentences:
    I. I arrived at the scene of the crime at 10:20 A.M. and began to question Mr. Sands about the security devices he had installed.
    II. Several clearly identifiable fingerprints were found.
    III. A Fingerprint Unit specialist arrived at the scene and immediately began to dust for fingerprints.
    IV. After questioning Mr. Sands, I called the Fingerprint Unit.
    V. On Friday morning at 10 A.M., Mr. Sands, the owner of the High Fashion Fur Store on Fifth Avenue, called the precinct to report that his safe had been broken into.

    The MOST logical order for the above sentences to appear in the Crime Report is

    A. I, V, IV, III, II  
    B. I, V, III, IV, II  
    C. V, I, IV, II, III  
    D. V, I, IV, III, II

---

# KEY (CORRECT ANSWERS)

1. A
2. D
3. C
4. A
5. B

6. A
7. C
8. B
9. C
10. D

11. B
12. A
13. D
14. C
15. B

16. B
17. B
18. A
19. B
20. D

# TEST 2

DIRECTIONS: The sentences that follow are in scrambled order. You are to rearrange them in proper order and indicate the letter choice containing the CORRECT answer. *PRINT THE LETTER OF THE CORRECT ANSWER IN THE SPACE AT THE RIGHT.*

1. Police Officer Ling is preparing a Complaint Report of a missing person. His report will contain the following five sentences:

    I. I was greeted by Mrs. Miah Ali, who stated her daughter Lisa, age 17, did not return from school.
    II. I questioned Mrs. Ali as to what time her daughter left for school and what type of clothing she was wearing.
    III. I notified the Patrol Sergeant, searched the building and area, and prepared a Missing Person Complaint Report.
    IV. I received a call from the radio dispatcher to respond to 9 Maple Street, Apartment 1H, on a missing person complaint.
    V. Mrs. Ali informed me that Lisa was wearing a grey suit and black shoes, and departed for school at 7:30 A.M.

    The MOST logical order for the above sentences to appear in the report is

    A. IV, I, V, II, III
    B. I, IV, V, III, II
    C. IV, I, II, V, III
    D. III, I, IV, II, V

    1.\_\_\_\_

2. Police Officer Dunn is preparing a Complaint Report which will include the following five sentences:

    I. Mrs. Field screamed and fought with the man.
    II. A man wearing a blue ski mask grabbed Mrs. Field's purse.
    III. Mrs. Field was shopping on 34th Street and Broadway at 1 o'clock in the afternoon.
    IV. The man then ran around the corner.
    V. The man was white, five feet six inches tall with a medium build.

    The MOST logical order for the above sentences to appear in the report is

    A. I, V, II, IV, III
    B. III, II, I, IV, V
    C. III, IV, V, I, II
    D. V, IV, III, I, II

    2.\_\_\_\_

3. Police Officer Davis is preparing a written report concerning child abuse. The report will include the following five sentences:

    I. I responded to the scene and was met by an adult and a child who was approximately four years old.
    II. I was notified by an unidentified pedestrian of a possible case of child abuse at 325 Belair Terrace.
    III. The adult told me that the child fell and that the police were not needed.
    IV. I felt that this might be a case of child abuse, and I requested that a Sergeant respond to the scene.
    V. The child was bleeding from the head and had several bruises on the face.

    The MOST logical order for the above sentences to appear in the report is

    A. II, I, V, III, IV
    B. I, II, IV, III, V
    C. I, III, IV, II, V
    D. II, IV, I, V, III

    3.\_\_\_\_

4. The following five sentences will be part of a memobook entry concerning found property:
    I. Mr. Gustav said that while cleaning the lobby he found six credit cards and a passport.
    II. The credit cards and passport were issued to Manuel Gomez.
    III. I went to the precinct to give the property to the Desk Officer.
    IV. I prepared a receipt listing the property, gave the receipt to Mr. Gustav, and had him sign my memobook.
    V. While on foot patrol, I was approached by Mr. Gustav, the superintendent of 50-12 Maiden Parkway.

    The MOST logical order for the above sentences to appear in the memobook is

    A. V, I, II, IV, III
    B. I, II, IV, III, V
    C. V, I, III, IV, II
    D. I, IV, III, II, V

5. Police Officer Thomas is making a memobook entry that will include the following five sentences:
    I. My partner obtained a brief description of the suspects and the direction they were heading when they left the store.
    II. Edward Lemkin was asked to come with us to search the immediate area.
    III. I transmitted this information over the radio.
    IV. At the corner of 72nd Street and Broadway, our patrol car was stopped by Edward Lemkin, the owner of PJ Records.
    V. He told us that a group of teenagers stole some merchandise from his record store.

    The MOST logical order for the above sentences to appear in the report is

    A. V, IV, I, III, II
    B. IV, V, I, III, II
    C. V, I, III, II, IV
    D. IV, I, III, II, V

6. Police Officer Caldwell is completing a Complaint Report. The report will include the following five sentences:
    I. When I yelled, *Don't move, Police,* the taller man dropped the bat and ran.
    II. I asked the girl for a description of the two men.
    III. I called for an ambulance.
    IV. A young girl approached me and stated that a man with a baseball bat was beating another man in front of 1700 Grande Street.
    V. Upon approaching the location, I observed the taller man hitting the other man with the bat.

    The MOST logical order for the above sentences to appear in the report is

    A. IV, V, I, II, III
    B. V, IV, II, III, I
    C. V, I, III, IV, II
    D. IV, II, V, I, III

7. Police Officer Moore is writing a memobook entry concerning a summons he issued. The entry will contain the following five sentences:
   I. As I was walking down the platform, I heard music coming from a radio that a man was holding on his shoulder.
   II. I asked the man for some identification.
   III. I was walking in the subway when a passenger complained about a man playing a radio loudly at the opposite end of the station.
   IV. I then gave the man a summons for playing the radio. V. As soon as the man saw me approaching, he turned the radio off.

   The MOST logical order for the above sentences to appear in the memobook entry is

   A. III, V, II, I, IV
   B. I, II, V, IV, III
   C. III, I, V, II, IV
   D. I, V, II, IV, III

8. Police Officer Kashawahara is completing an Incident Report regarding fleeing suspects he had pursued earlier. The report will include the following five sentences:
   I. I saw two males attempting to break into a store through the front window.
   II. On Myrtle Avenue, they ran into an alley between two abandoned buildings.
   III. I yelled to them, *Hey, what are you guys doing by that window?*
   IV. At that time, I lost sight of the suspects and I returned to the station house.
   V. They started to run south on Wycoff Avenue heading towards Myrtle Avenue.

   The MOST logical order for the above sentences to appear in the report is

   A. I, V, II, IV, III
   B. III, V, II, IV, I
   C. I, III, V, II, IV
   D. III, I, V, II, IV

9. Police Officer Bloom is completing an entry in his memo-book regarding a confession made by a perpetrator. The entry will include the following five sentences:
   I. I went towards the dresser and took $400 in cash and a jewelry box with rings, watches, and other items in it.
   II. There in the bedroom, lying on the bed, a woman was sleeping.
   III. It was about 1:00 A.M. when I entered the apartment through an opened rear window.
   IV. I spun around, punched her in the face with my free hand, and then jumped out the window into the street.
   V. I walked back to the window carrying the money and the jewelry box and was about to go out when all of a sudden I heard the woman scream.

   The MOST logical order for the above sentences to appear in the memobook entry is

   A. I, III, II, V, IV
   B. I, V, IV, III, II
   C. III, II, I, V, IV
   D. III, V, IV, I, II

10. Police Officer Webster is preparing an Arrest Report which will include the following five sentences:
    I. I noticed that the robber had a knife placed at the victim's neck.
    II. I told the robber to drop the knife.
    III. While on patrol, I observed a robbery which was in progress.
    IV. I grabbed the robber, placed him in handcuffs, and took him to the precinct.
    V. The robber dropped the knife and tried to flee.

    The MOST logical order for the above sentences to appear in the report is

    A. I, II, V, IV, III
    B. III, I, II, V, IV
    C. III, II, IV, I, V
    D. I, III, IV, V, II

11. Police Officer Lee is preparing a report regarding someone who apparently attempted to commit suicide with a gun. The report will include the following five sentences:
    I. At the location, the woman pointed to the open door of Apartment 7L.
    II. I called for an ambulance to respond.
    III. The male had a gun in his hand and a large head wound.
    IV. A call was received from the radio dispatcher regarding a woman who heard a gunshot at 936 45th Avenue.
    V. Upon entering Apartment 7L, I saw the body of a male on the kitchen floor.

    The MOST logical order for the above sentences to appear in the report is

    A. IV, I, V, III, II
    B. I, III, V, IV, II
    C. I, V, III, II, IV
    D. IV, V, III, II, I

12. Police Officer Modrak is completing a memobook entry which will include the following five sentences:
    I. The victim, a male in his thirties, told me that the robbery occurred a few minutes ago.
    II. My partner and I jumped out of the patrol car and arrested the suspect.
    III. We responded to an armed robbery in progress at Billings Avenue and 59th Street.
    IV. On Chester Avenue and 68th Street, the victim spotted and identified the suspect.
    V. I told the victim to get into the patrol car and that we would drive him around the area.

    The MOST logical order for the above sentences to appear in the memobook is

    A. III, I, V, IV, II
    B. I, III, V, II, IV
    C. I, IV, III, V, II
    D. III, V, I, II, IV

13. Police Officer Rodriguez is preparing a report concerning an incident in which she used her revolver. Her report will include the following five sentences:
    I. Upon seeing my revolver, the robber dropped his gun to the ground.
    II. At about 10:55 P.M., I was informed by a passerby that several people were being robbed at gunpoint on 174th Street and Walton Avenue.
    III. I was assigned to patrol on 174th Street and Ghent Avenue during the evening shift.
    IV. I saw a man holding a gun on three people, took out my revolver, and shouted, *Police, don't move!*
    V. After calling for assistance, I went to 174th Street and Walton Avenue and took cover behind a car.

    The MOST logical order for the above sentences to appear in the report is

    A. II, III, IV, V, I
    B. IV, V, I, III, II
    C. III, II, V, IV, I
    D. II, IV, I, V, III

14. Police Officer Davis is completing an Activity Log entry which will include the following five sentences:
    I. A radio car was dispatched and the male was taken to Greenville Hospital.
    II. Several people saw him and called the police.
    III. A naked man was running down the street waving his arms above his head and screaming, *Insects are all over me!*
    IV. I arrived on the scene and requested an ambulance.
    V. The dispatcher informed me that no ambulances were available.
    The MOST logical order for the above sentences to appear in the Activity Log is

    A. III, IV, V, I, II
    B. II, III, V, I, IV
    C. III, II, IV, V, I
    D. II, IV, III, V, I

15. Police Officer Peake is completing an entry in his Activity Log. The entry contains the following five sentences:
    I. He went to his parked car only to find he was blocked in.
    II. The owner of the vehicle refused to move the van until he had finished his lunch.
    III. Approximately 30 minutes later, I arrived on the scene and ordered the owner of the van to remove the vehicle.
    IV. Mr. O'Neil had an appointment and was in a hurry to keep it.
    V. Mr. O'Neil entered a nearby delicatessen and asked if anyone in there drove a dark blue van, license plate number BUS 265.
    The MOST logical order for the above sentences to appear in the Activity Log is

    A. II, III, I, IV, V
    B. IV, I, V, II, III
    C. V, IV, I, III, II
    D. II, I, III, IV, V

16. Police Officer Harrison is preparing a report regarding a 10-year-old who was sexually abused at school. The report will include the following five sentences:
    I. The child described the perpetrator as a white male with a mustache, six feet tall, wearing a green uniform.
    II. On September 10, I responded to General Hospital to interview a child who was sexually abused.
    III. He later confessed at the station house.
    IV. After I interviewed the child, I responded to the school and found a janitor who fit the description.
    V. I interviewed the janitor and took him to the station house for further investigation.
    The MOST logical order for the above sentences to appear in the report is

    A. II, IV, I, V, III
    B. I, IV, V, II, III
    C. II, I, IV, V, III
    D. V, III, II, I, IV

17. Police Officer Madden is completing a report of a theft. The report will include the following five sentences:
    I. I followed behind the suspect for two blocks.
    II. I saw a man pass by the radio car carrying a shopping bag.
    III. I looked back in the direction he had just come from and noticed that the top of a parking meter was missing.
    IV. As he saw me, he started to walk faster, and I noticed a red piece of metal with the word *violation* drop out of the shopping bag.
    V. When I saw a parking meter in the shopping bag, I apprehended the suspect and placed him under arrest.

    The MOST logical order for the above sentences to appear in the report is

    A. I, IV, II, III, V
    B. II, I, IV, V, III
    C. II, IV, III, I, V
    D. III, II, IV, I, V

17.____

18. Police Officer McCaslin is preparing a report of disorderly conduct which will include the following five sentences:
    I. Police Officer Kenny and I were on patrol in a radio car when we received a dispatch to go to the Hard Rock Disco on Third Avenue.
    II. We arrived at the scene and found three men arguing loudly and obviously intoxicated.
    III. The dispatcher had received a call from a bartender regarding a dispute.
    IV. Two of the men left the disco shortly before we did.
    V. We calmed the men down after managing to separate them.

    The MOST logical order for the above sentences to appear in the report is

    A. I, II, V, III, IV
    B. III, I, IV, II, V
    C. II, I, III, IV, V
    D. I, III, II, V, IV

18.____

19. Police Officer Langhorne is completing a report of a murder. The report will contain the following five statements made by a witness:
    I. The noise created by the roar of a motorcycle caused me to look out of my window.
    II. I ran out of the house and realized the man was dead, which is when I called the police.
    III. I saw a man driving at high speed down the dead-end street on a motorcycle, closely followed by a green BMW.
    IV. The motorcyclist then parked the bike and approached the car, which was occupied by two males.
    V. Two shots were fired and the cyclist fell to the ground; then the car made a u-turn and sped down the street.

    The MOST logical order for the above sentences to appear in the report is

    A. I, II, IV, III, V
    B. V, II, I, IV, III
    C. I, III, IV, V, II
    D. III, IV, I, II, V

19.____

20. Police Officer Murphy is preparing a report of a person who was assaulted. The report will include the following five sentences:
    I. I responded to the scene, but Mr. Jones had already fled.
    II. She was bleeding profusely from a cut above her right eye.
    III. Mr. and Mrs. Jones apparently were fighting in the street when Mr. Jones punched his wife in the face.
    IV. I then applied pressure to the cut to control the bleeding.
    V. I called the dispatcher on the radio to send an ambulance to respond to the scene.

The MOST logical order for the above sentences to appear in the report is

A. III, II, IV, I, V
B. III, I, II, IV, V
C. I, V, II, III, IV
D. II, V, IV, III, I

20.____

## KEY (CORRECT ANSWERS)

| | | | |
|---|---|---|---|
| 1. | C | 11. | A |
| 2. | B | 12. | A |
| 3. | A | 13. | C |
| 4. | A | 14. | C |
| 5. | B | 15. | B |
| 6. | D | 16. | C |
| 7. | C | 17. | C |
| 8. | C | 18. | D |
| 9. | C | 19. | C |
| 10. | B | 20. | B |

# THE BUILDING AND ITS MAKEUP

## TABLE OF CONTENTS

| | Page |
|---|---|
| **BUILDING CONSTRUCTION** | 1 |
| Introduction | 1 |
| General Construction Principles | 1 |
| Types of Building Construction | 2 |
| Building Materials and Contents | 3 |
| Building Code Requirements | 7 |
| Involvement of Ceilings | 8 |
| Building Elements | 8 |
| Interior Finish | 9 |
| **MATERIALS** | 11 |
| Introduction | 11 |
| Properties of Materials | 11 |
| Classes of Materials | 12 |
| **UTILITY SYSTEMS** | 17 |
| Introduction | 17 |
| Heating, Ventilation and Air Conditioning | 18 |
| Electrical | 21 |

# THE BUILDING AND ITS MAKEUP

**BUILDING CONSTRUCTION**

**Introduction**

In many cases the design, construction, and use of the building contributes to the initiation and severity of serious building fires. For these reasons, a knowledge of buildings, how they are constructed, and with what kinds of materials, is important to the fire investigator.

A knowledge and use of the correct terminology of building construction also is important in the writing of accurate reports, as well as in courtroom appearances. As an example, the investigator should know and be able to describe the similarities and the differences between spandrels, beams, and girders.

Sometimes in getting at the fire cause, it is necessary to "reconstruct" the arrangement and condition of the room or area of fire involvement to understand the development and spread of the fire. To do this "reconstruct", it is necessary to know what kinds of building materials and construction were likely to have been present prior to the fire damage. (Where there are similar rooms or areas available in the same or similar buildings, such as in hotels or garden apartments, a method to "reconstruct" is to examine undamaged units.)

**General Construction Principles**

The fire investigator should be familiar with the basic principles of building construction.

The initial concern of fire resistance provisions in building codes is that the building should not collapse as a result of a fire. Secondarily, the structure should limit the fire to an area of acceptable size.

Some elements of the system are more vulnerable to fire than others. When a fire occurs, the building is only as stable as the weakest (to fire) element.

All loads must be transmitted continuously to ground. This is accomplished by a multitude of structural components and connections in the structure. The importance of the connections varies. In some cases, the failure of a connection may have only a local effect. In other cases, the failure may be catastrophic in that a building collapse may occur.

Principal structural materials are wood, masonry (stone, brick, and concrete block), steel and reinforced concrete.

The principal elements of structures are walls, columns, and beams. Walls and columns carry the loads of the building down to the earth. Beams carry the loads generated on each floor of the building to the columns or walls.

Walls may be load-bearing, that is, carrying a load other than themselves, or be nonload-bearing, typically partitions and exterior veneer walls.

Columns carry vertical loads to the ground or foundation. Because columns take up space, suspension rods or cables in tension are sometimes used to "hang" certain loads in a building.

The system must, however, provide for the tensile load to be carried over into a column or wall and delivered to the earth in compression.

Floors and roofs are supported on beams and girders as well as on walls. A girder is a beam which supports other beams. Since beams must resist both tension (usually in the bottom of the beam) and compression forces (usually in the top), solid beams contain excess material. In many cases, the load can be carried on a lighter unit called a truss, which eliminates excess material. A trussconsists of a series of specially connected and designed load-carrying elements and open spaces, which makes it more vulnerable to fire and thus more likely to collapse than an equivalent solid beam.

**Types of Building Construction**

There are five basic construction types. Various building codes subdivide these types further (see table 1) The five types are:

**Table 1 Types of Construction According to Model codes***

| Construction Type | Basic Building Code, by Type (BOCA) | Standard Building Code, by Type (SBC) | Uniform Building Code, by type (UBC) | National Building Code, by Type (NBC) |
|---|---|---|---|---|
| Fire Resistive | 1A | I | I | A |
|  | 1B | II | I | B |
| Noncombustiable Protected | 2A |  | II (4 hr) |  |
|  | 2B | IV (1 hr) | II (1 hr) | Protected Noncombustiable |
| None combustible Unprotected | 2C | IV | II (N) | Unprotected Noncombustiable |
| Heavy Timber | 3A | III | IV (HT) | Heavy Timber |
| Ordinary Protected | 3B | V (1 hr) | III (1hr) |  |
| Ordinary Unprotected | 3C | V | III (N) | Ordinary |
| Wood Frame Protected | 4A | VI (1hr) | V (1hr) |  |
| Wood Frame Unprotected | 4B | VI | V (N) | Wood Frame |

* This Table indicates the type assigned by the respective codes to various construction types. It is not intended to indicate that different codes necessarily have identical requirements for any specific type.

*Fire Resistive*
*Noncombustible*
*Heavy Timber*
*Ordinary Wood Frame*
*Wood Frame*

The investigator's report should use the terminology of the appropriate local code.

Note that the commonly used word "fireproof" does not appear in the list of types, though it may appear in some codes. When designers first considered fire as a problem they believed that all fire problems would be eliminated by constructing the building of noncombustible material. Such buildings were called "fireproof" and the misnomer has persisted. Early "fireproof" buildings were found deficient when put to the test of actual fires since all noncombustible materials will lose strength at sufficiently high temperatures. As technology improved, the term "fire resistive" emerged.

*Fire Resistive* buildings are ones in which specimens of the major structural components have been rated by standard fire endurance tests during which collapse and passage of fire, where appropriate, were resisted for prescribed periods of time. No direct relationship should be assumed between the "time" of the controlled test and an uncontrolled hostile fire. Whereas each of the elements of the building may meet fire resistance criteria, it is most unlikely that the building as a whole was ever analyzed for the total impact of a potential fire, and "the whole may be less than the sum of the parts". Fire resistance does not guarantee life safety. Fire resistance is not necessarily related to fire loss; in fact, while achieving its designed fire resistance, the structure may be damaged severely. Fire resistive assemblies are not necessarily noncombustible. Floors and walls of wood and gypsum board are assigned fire resistance ratings by UL (Underwriters Laboratories Inc.), even though the assemblies are combustible.

Depending upon how the fire resistance is achieved, different buildings of the same fire resistance rating may exhibit different characteristics in similar fires. For instance, a fire resistive floor of reinforced concrete absorbs considerable heat. A steel joist floor and ceiling assembly, of equal fire resistance, will not absorb as much heat. This can affect the propagation of a fire, as every Btu absorbed by the structure is one less available to keep the fire growing. As a second example, a rated reinforced concrete floor may act as a very effective smoke barrier. An equally rated floor and ceiling assembly with an integral air handling system could provide a path for travel of smoke and gases. This property is not considered in the test rating.

*Noncombustible* buildings are ones in which the walls, partitions and structural members are of noncombustible construction not qualifying as fire resistive construction.

*Heavy Timber* construction buildings have masonry exterior walls and heavy timber interiors. The concept is that the heavy timber is slow to ignite and burns at a slow enough rate that collapse may be delayed. The concept fails once the fire involves the building and the fire suppression forces cannot sustain an interior attack. The massive amount of timber then simply becomes a tremendous fire load.

*Ordinary Construction* buildings have masonry exterior walls and lightly constructed combustible interiors. The principal benefit of the masonry walls is to reduce the conflagration potential. The interior is expected to collapse in a fire and may be required by code to be so designed, the so-called fire cuts on wood joists are an example.

*Wood Frame* buildings are basically of wood construction. A noncombustible veneer, such as brick, does not change the nature or classification of the building.

### Building Materials and Contents

Code regulations which limit the type and size of construction are predicated on the type of building, the type of occupancy anticipated, and the anticipated level of potential fire risk.

Estimates of the potential fire risk are based to a large extent on the fire load (or fuel load). For buildings of combustible construction the basic fire load is the building itself, thus such buildings are usually limited by code in area and height. In addition, for all buildings the weight of combustible contents per unit of floor area must be considered. Fire loads are usually expressed in the term pounds (of ordinary combustibles) per square foot. All weights are commonly converted to the equivalent of ordinary combustibles such as wood which has a heat value of about 8,000 Btu/lb. For instance, plastics which have a heat value of about 16,000 Btu/lb are converted at the rate of 1 lb of plastic to 2 lb ordinary combustibles.

Typical ranges of fire loads for the more common occupancy classes are shown in table 2. However, fire loads can vary considerably according to the occupancy the specific location in the building, and, other factors.

**Table 2 Typical Fire Loads**

| Occupancy Classification | Typical Range of Fire Loads lb/sq ft |
|---|---|
| Residential | 5 to 10 |
| Educational | 5 to 10 |
| (Library) | (10 to 40) |
| Institutional | 3 to 10 |
| Assembly | 5 to 10 |
| Business (office) | 5 to 10 |
| (File, Storage) | (10 to 40) |
| Mercantile | 10 to 20 |
| Industrial | 10 to 35 |
| Storage | 10 to 100 |
| Hazardous | * |

* No typical values available. Risk based on factors other than fire load

Structural fire protection requirements in building codes are based on fire resistance or fire endurance ratings expressed in hours. The ratings are basedon fire tests performed on the structural or compartmenting (separating) building components according to the NFPA 251 (ASTM E 119) standardized test procedure, The exposure is such that a temperature of 1000°F (538°C) is reached in 5 min, 1700°F (927°C) in 1 hr, 1850°F (1010°C) in 2 hrs, 2000°F (1093°C) in 4 hrs and 2300°F (1260°C) in 8 hrs. These temperatures-vs.-time points produce a curve which is referred to as the fire endurance standard time-temperature curve. The test is conducted in a special test furnace and continued until one of several criteria of failure, as appropriate, is reached: (a) structural failure (inability to sustain the applied load), (b) integrity failure (development of a crack or opening through which flames or hot gases may pass during the fire test, or a hose stream test) or, (c) insulation failure (heat transmission sufficient to raise the temperature on the unexposed surface by 250°F (139°C) average).

Although the standard fire test curve represents only one type of fire exposure, it serves as a useful means for the comparative rating of individual columns, beams, walls, partitions, and floor and ceiling assemblies. Again, it should be stressed that although the ratings are expressed in hours, the relationship between the rating hours and hours of an actual fire assault on a building may differ.

A relationship between fire load and equivalent fire endurance period was developed many years ago based on experimental burnouts of combustibles in special masonry test buildings and is shown in table 3. Table.3 indicates that the burning of a fire load of 10 lbs of ordinary combustibles per square foot (or 80,000 Btu/sq ft) is the approximate equivalent of 1 hour of the standard fire test ASTM E 119.

If these figures are used cautiously and broadly, rather than precisely, it is possible to estimate whether, in a given fire, the fire load was grossly excessive for the fire resistance of the building. Consider a building with floors rated two-hour fire-resistive. Such a building might reasonably be expected to successfully resist a fire involving a design fire load of 160,000 Btu/sq ft average. On the other hand, an investigator may estimate that in the affected area of an actual fire, the fire load was 300,000 Btu/sq ft average. It can be reasonably concluded that the fire area was overloaded from the fire endurance point of view, even though the total structural loading may have been within permissible limits.

Table 3. Fire Load versus Equivalent Fire Endurance Period in Standard Fire Test

| Fire Load 1b sq ft | Equivalent Fire Endurance Period hr |
|---|---|
| 5 | ½ |
| 7 ½ | ¾ |
| 10 | 1 |
| 15 | 1 ½ |
| 20 | 2 |
| 30 | 3 |
| 40 | 4 ½ |
| 50 | 6 |
| 60 | 7 ½ |

Structural members and floors are made fire resistive in a variety of ways.

Reinforced concrete has inherent fire resistance. This inherent fire resistance can be increased to the desired level by increasing the concrete cover over the "reinforcing" steel. If the depth of the concrete cover is not as specified, early failure may result.

Steel must be protected from the harmful effects of elevated temperatures (loss of strength, elongation and heat transmission). Protection can be accomplished in several ways, including encasement, sprayed fireproofing, membrane protection or by using water- filled columns. In a particular building more than one way may be used.

*Encasement.* Each structural steel member is encased in an insulating cover; hollow tile, poured concrete, concrete block, wire lath and plaster or gypsum board are typically used.

*Sprayed "Fireproofing".* In this case structural steel members are spraye or trowele with plaster containing inorganic fibers or cement. One common material formerly used, asbestos, is held responsible for health hazards due to inhalation in many buildings. In some cases this has caused its removal, sometimes without any provision for replacing the necessary fire resistance. Sprayed "fireproofing" may be poorly done and in many cases is found to have fallen off or been removed by other building trades

***Membrane Protection.*** Large areas, such as entire floors, are protected by a membrane,"consisting typically of a wire lath and plaster ceiling or a suspended ceiling of individual panels. The problem is that, like all membranes, a single penetration may reduce the effectiveness of the entire membrane. Wire lath and plaster membranes are designed to be permanent and generally left in place but individual acoustical tile (panel) ceilings are readily removable.

The entire floor and ceiling assembly is fire rated as a unit. The presumption is that the unit is installed the same way as the unit tested. Even if this is accomplished, the ceiling tiles may be removed for many reasons. The fact that the ceiling tiles are part of the fire resistance of the building is unknown to many building owners and operators and fire inspectors. Untested penetrations as for sound system speakers are another weakness. Any tampering with the ceiling opens the entire floor area up to attack by fire. The void space between the ceiling and the floor above represents a potential for lateral fire spread between every floor of the building. There can be a substantial fire load in the void due to plastic insulation and piping, and lightweight merchandise is sometimes found stored in the void.

In one case, fire in one occupancy entered the void and extended downward to combustible shelves and contents in the next occupancy, This was detected early enough to clearly show what had happened. Had the extension not been detected, all appearances would have been of two separate fires. In fact, the fire was incendiary and successfully prosecuted. Failure to describe the development of the fire accurately might have led to a loss of the case.

Current lists of fire rated constructions and assemblies are maintained by Underwriters Laboratories -- the American Insurance Association -- and the Factory Mutual System.

Almost any structure has some degree of fire resistance, even though it is itself combustible. Table 4 is provided to enable the investigator to develop estimated fire resistance values for some common wall and floor assemblies. It consists of two parts. In the first part values are given for some common materials used as membranes (the surface finish). The second part gives values for framing members

For example, using table 4, unprotected open web steel joists are assigned a value of 7 minutes. With 1/2" gypsum wallboard properly attached and sealed, the combination could be assigned a time of 22 minutes (7 minutes for the steel joists, 15 minutes for the gypsum wallboard).

A wood stud wall with 1/2" gypsum board on both sides could be assigned a value of 50 minutes (20 minutes for the studs plus 15 minutes for each layer of the wallboard). It should be stated here again that the times referred to are estimates of how long the structure in question would continue to meet the standards of ASTM E 119 (NFPA 251) when tested in accordance with that standard. There is no necessary relationship to elapsed time in a hostile fire.

**Table 4   Time Assigned to wallboard membranes**

| | Description of Finish | Time Assigned to Membrane in Minutes |
|---|---|---|
| (i) | ½ in Fiberboard | 5 |
| (ii) | $3/8$ in Douglas Fir Plywood Phenolic bonded | 5 |
| (iii) | ½ in Douglas Fir Plywood Phenolic bonded | 10 |
| (iv) | $5/8$ in Douglas Fir Plywood Phenolic bonded | 15 |
| (v) | $3/8$ in Gypsum Wallboard | 10 |
| (vi) | ½ in Gypsum Wallboard | 15 |
| (vii) | $5/8$ in Gypsum Wallboard | 30 |
| (viii) | Double $3/8$ in gypsum Wallboard | 25 |
| (ix) | ½ + $3/8$ in Gypsum Wallboard | 35 |
| (x) | Double ½ in Gypsum Wallboard | 50(1) |
| (xi) | $3/16$ in Asb. Cem. + in Gypsum Wallboard | 40(2) |
| (xii) | $3/16$ in asb. Cem. + $1/2$ in Gypsum Wallboard | 50(2) |
| (xiii) | Composit 1/8 in Asb. Cem. $7/16$ in Fibreboard | 20 |

1) No. 16 s.w.g. 1 in sq wire mesh must be fastened between the two sheets of wallboard.
2) Values shown apply to walls only.

**Time Assigned for Contribution of Wood or Light Steel Frame**

| Description of Frame | Time Assigned to from in Minutes |
|---|---|
| i. Wood Stud walls | 20 |
| ii. Steel Stud Wall | 10 |
| iii. Wood Joist Floors and Roofs | 10 |
| iv. Open Web Steel Joist Floors and roofs | 10(07) |

**Building Code Requirements**

In many cases a building is not required by code to be fire resistive but the designer chooses to use components which resemble rated fire resistive units (or which may in fact be rated). For instance, structures recently observed in the Washington, DC area are rated as Type 3C (unprotected ordinary) under the BOCA (Building Officials and Code Administrator's International, Inc.) Basic Building Code. The floors are of bar joist construction with concrete topping on corrugated metal. The suspended ceilings need only meet Fire Hazard (flame spread) requirements. When the job is finished its appearance will be similar to a rated floor and ceiling assembly and protected with the same surface finish. Wood joists would have been acceptable under the code and the floor as installed may not be as resistive to collapse as a wood joisted floor.

In a fire investigation it may be necessary to determine whether or not a fire-resistive structure or structural element reacted to the fire in a manner consistent with its rating. This can be extraordinarily difficult. Assuming that the building was required to meet fire resistance standards, there can be several reasons for determination of the reason for failure to perform adequately. Information developed may be of use in prosecution, civil actions, code changes or fire suppression planning.

Did the building meet code requirements? This requires a thorough knowledge of code requirements at the time the building was built and access to original drawings, change orders and officially authorized variances.

Possibly, in fact, the building met modern code requirements but when given the ultimate test, the fire, the code requirements were proven inadequate. Such information, properly developed and carefully documented, is vital to translating costly experience into recommended code revisions.

Valuable information also can be developed to aid fire suppression forces in preplanning and combating future fires in the same or similar buildings. For example, the investigation may develop information that the sealant of the floor slab to the panel exterior walls was made of foamed plastic which lacks "dimensional stability" (that is, it melts). If this was permitted in one building, it may exist in other buildings built about the same time.

### Involvement of Ceilings

Fires generally burn upward. Thus, the ceilings and upper parts of walls are generally exposed to higher temperatures than the lower parts of walls and floors. Fire exposed ceilings can fail early in fires, sometimes considerably earlier than a fire test rating would indicate. The fact that a particular ceiling fell may be an important element in an investigation. It cannot be assumed that the ceiling stayed in place for as long as one might conclude from its quoted fire rating.

Recently there have been a number of cases of fires burning downward (10). Many plastics when ignited form a pool of fire on the floor. The plastic may be from building contents or it may have been installed as part of the wall or ceiling.

Material falling from the ceiling may extend the fire beyond the area of origin. Consider a noncombustible building with steel bar joists with combustible tile ceiling mounted on the bottom side of the joists. There is a gap atop the masonry partition wall equal to the height of the top chord of the joist. Heated gases passing through this gap into the adjacent space may ignite the combustible tiles on their upper side. They may fall, extending the fire beyond the masonry wall.

### Building Elements

Historically the chief consideration in building fire problems has been given to the Structural Elements of the building, but in building fires three elements can be identified:

- Structural Elements
- Nonstructural Elements
- Contents

The structural elements are those which are necessary to the stability of the building. The nonstructural elements may be more important in the development and extension of a fire than the structural elements. Nonstructural elements which contribute to the fire are independent of the type of construction and may be found in any of the five structural types discussed. For instance, a high flame spread interior finish of plywood and fiber tile may be found in any type building. The life hazard due to rapid flame spread over the surface will be the same. In the case of a combustible building the interior finish may be the kindling which ignites the structure. In the case of a noncombustible or fire-resistive structure, the structure will not be ignited, but substantial damage may be done to structural elements.

Nonstructural elements can include the electrical system, interior finish on ceilings, walls, and floors, air handling systems, openings from floor to floor such as shafts, stairways, interior courts, and combustible exterior surfaces and insulation.

In the majority of fires the initial fuel is the contents. Only rarely is the building directly ignited.

**Interior Finish**
Up to World War II there was only one significant interior finish, plaster installed over either wood lath or metal lath. It is noncombustible and, when properly installed, provides a degree of fire resistance for combustible structural elements. If the plaster is penetrated and if wood lath is present, the wood lath may provide substantial fuel.

The interior finish of the building may be the most important single element in the development and spread of a fire. In a number of cases interior finish has been a major factor in the rapid spread of fire and resultant loss of life.

Interior finish may be applied to the ceiling, walls or floors. Building codes have applied specific limitations on the flame spread classification of wall and ceiling materials. Floor coverings are less likely to be regulated but flame spread over carpeting, for example, has been an important factor in a number of serious fires. Standards and techniques for measuring carpeting flame spread have been developed recently and these regulations have begun to appear in the codes.
There are a number of ways in which the restriction of high flame spread interior finishes can be circumvented which do not appear in the code regulations. Materials which would not be permitted by the code if attached to the building may appear in significant amounts as furniture, in exhibits, as free standing office dividers, and in merchandise displays.

Alterations are sometimes accomplished without a building permit and buildings properly built have been altered with the use of high flame spread ceiling or wall materials.

Even the building permit does not guarantee safety. Consider a building with a combustible acoustical tile ceiling. It is planned to "modernize" the room by installing a ceiling grid with tiles and light fixtures mounted below the existing ceiling. A local code may require the new tiles to meet flame spread requirements but there is no requirement to remove the old combustible ceiling hidden in the void. Such a hidden ceiling can generate heat and gases which can move upward through available openings.

The investigator must try to get an accurate description of the wall and ceiling surfaces before the fire. Often only very slight clues are available, for example, nails holding scraps of furring strip to joists may indicate that there was a combustible acoustical ceiling. Adhesive beading on a wall may indicate where paneling had been secured with adhesive. Small pieces may be found behind unburned baseboard.

Table 5 contains a listing of selected materials commonly used for interior finish in buildings and a rough classification according to flame spread rating by ASTM E 84. This tabulation is intended only as a general guide and the reader should not assume that all material of the same

**Table 5 Approximate Spread Raing (E-84 Tunnel Test)**

Ceilings

| | |
|---|---|
| Gypsum Plaster | 0 |
| Sprayed Mineral-base plaster | 0-20 |
| Enameled metal | 0-20 |
| Mineral fiber tile | 10-25 |
| Glass or mineral fiber bord or title, coated | 10-40 |
| Wood-base acousical tile (flame proofed) | 20-75 |
| Wood-base acoustical tile (untreated) | 75-300 |

Walls

| | |
|---|---|
| Brick, concrete, asbestos-cement board, ceremic tile, gypsum plaster | 0 |
| Enameled st eel, aluminum | 0-20 |
| Gypsum board, various facings | 10-50 |
| Wood, fiberboard (flame-retardant treated) | 20-75 |
| Plastic Paneling (flame-retardant-treated) | 20-75 |
| Wood, at least 0.5 in thick, various species | 70-200 |
| Plywood paneling | 70-300 |
| Hardoard | 100-250 |
| Cork | 100-250 |
| Cloth, paper, wood veneer, fiberboard (untreated) | 200-500 |
| Shellac finish on wood | 500+ |

Floors*

| | |
|---|---|
| Concrete, terrazzo | 0 |
| Vinyl Asbestos Tile | 10-50 |
| Red oak | 100 |
| Linoleum | 100-300 |
| Carpeting** | 50-600 |

---

\* Use of E 84 Tunnel Test on Floor Covering Materials is no longer recommended. See other Methods, for example, NFPA 253 and ASTM E648

\*\* Depends on type of face fiber, uunderlayment, method of attachment if glued down, loose, etc.

---

all materials of the same generic type will perform in a similar manner. Furthermore, although a flame spread classification rating or label denotes that a test has been performed on a sample of the material, there is no assurance that the material will not contribute in a major way to the spread of a fire in an actual building situation. A fire investigator should not hesitate to request that tests be performed on samples of unburned material removed from the building where the finish material appears to have contributed significantly to the fire.

In removing materials for testing the investigator should understand how the test is done so that proper samples will be obtained. If it is possible that criminal proceedings will develop, the samples must be treated as any other criminal evidence.

ASTM E 84, the Steiner Tunnel Test, is the usual basis for legal regulation of flame spread. The sample required is about 22 in width and 24 ft (565 mm x 7.32 m) in length. It may not be easy to get a sample of this size, but it may be necessary.

The fact that the method of attachment is important to the actual flame spread of combustible tiles was discovered when a full size sample of tiles glued to gypsum board showed a much greater flame spread than the same tiles, removed from the board for shipment

ASTM E 162 requires a sample only 6 x 18 in (15 x 46 cm). Samples this size is easier to get. For some materials, results from this test can be correlated in a general way with ASTM E 84 but no direct relationship should be assumed. The information developed can be useful in developing better code requirements. If the question of discrepancy in the installed material is going to be criminally significant, the prosecutor should be made aware of the difference in these tests because it might be critical to the case that the test be performed under the same conditions as the code requires, which would almost invariably be ASTME 84.

Carpeting should first be tested to the requirements of FF 1-70 (11), al so known as the "pill test". The "pill test" only measures the ignitability of the carpet from small flame sources, such as a dropped, burning match. If the carpet passed the "pill test", and it was thought to have contributed significantly to the fire, it may be useful to test the flame spread properties of the carpet, properties which are not involved in the "pill test". One flame spread test procedure is that given in NFPA 253, Standard Method of Test for Critical Radiant Flux of Floor Covering Systems Using a Radiant Heat Energy Source. For this test, samples 10 x 42 in (25 x 107 cm) are required. If a pad was used with the carpet, this pad should be included with the carpet in the test.

Nearly all carpets will spread fire if the exposure is sufficiently intense. However, some carpets spread fire under less heat exposure than others. If a pad is used under a carpet, the pad generally will cause an increase in the carpet's flame spread characteristics. The purpose of conducting the NFPA 253 test is to determine whether the carpet spreads fire easily or is more resistant to this spread than other carpets. The results of NFPA 253 will be a number called the critical radiant flux (CRF). To compare this number against other carpets, one should then refer to reference which lists the CRF's for many different types of carpets, with and without padding.

## MATERIALS

### Introduction

Knowledge of the effect of fire and high temperature on all types of materials -- construction, interior finish, furnishings and contents is essential to the job of the fire investigator. In searching through a burned building, the investigator should make note of the materials which were relatively unaffected as well as those which burned, charred and melted. The historical patterns of fires in buildings should be recognized and comparative differences or similarities noted.

### Properties of Materials

There are many properties of materials which determine their response to fire and high temperature, as well as the contribution they may make to the growth of a fire. The principal fire properties of organic materials are heat of combustion and ignition temperature. Other thermal and mechanical properties include heat conductivity: ·specific heat (heat absorption capacity), melting and softening points, coefficient of expansion (elongation due to heating), shrinkage, cracking, etc. Some typical thermal properties are listed in table 6.

The high thermal conductivity of metals can be a means of spreading fire, for example, through sheets, ducts, joints, connectors and fasteners. Specific heat (or more accurately volumetric heat capacity) is a measure of the capacity to absorb and store heat. A material with a high heat capacity will heat up slower and may keep the maximum air temperatures lower but it will also retain the heat longer. Where high temperatures exists, thermal radiation is important and shiny surfaces (aluminum, steel, mirrors) may reflect the heat to other surfaces. While reflective surfaces would be expected to remain cooler, in most cases smoke deposition, oxidation and other changes often occur on shiny surfaces so that they eventually absorb as well as most other materials. Melting and softening points are obvious indicators of fire scene temperatures, provided allowance is made for fallen ceilings (which may protect materials at floor level), heat sinks (metals, for example, or water) and exposure to heat prior to the fire.

### Classes of Materials

*Masonry.* In common usage, this term includes precast or cast-in-place concrete, concrete and cinder block, brick, stone, cement and clay tiles (terra cotta). Under fire exposure, many masonry walls will remain intact. However, due to thermal expansion caused by severe heating of the exposed surface (usually the interior surface), ordinary brick, block and stone walls may sometimes lean out at the top and collapse. The integrity of masonry walls depends to a large extent on the quality of the mortar bond at the joints. Collapse also may occur for other reasons, including failure of a non-masonry supporting element, thermal expansion of floors, beams or trusses, or impact loading due to collapse of a floor, a roof, another building, or an explosion. A brick veneer wall depends for its integrity on the wooden structural wall to which it is fastened. If the wooden wall is damaged, the brick wall may collapse.

## Table 6 Typical Thermal Properties of Selected Materials

| Materials | Density Lbs/Cu Ft | Thermal [1] Conductivity Btu-in Hr ft2 °F | Spefic [2] Heat Btu/lb °F | Percent Increase in Length for each 100° Temp Rise | Melting Point °F |
|---|---|---|---|---|---|
| Air | 0.06 | 0.2 | 0.24 | | |
| Water | 62 | 5 | 1.0 | 0.01 | 32 |
| Aluminum | 165 | 1400 | 0.22 | 0.14 | 1220 |
| Brass | 530 | 720 | 0.09 | 0.11 | 1650 |
| Copper | 560 | 2600 | 0.09 | 0.09 | 1980 |
| Cast iron | 440 | 320 | 0.13 | 0.06 | 2466-2550 |
| Steel | 490 | 310 | 0.12 | 0.06-0.15[3] | 2370-2550 |
| Glass | 160 | 6 | 0.20 | 0.04-0.06 | 2600 |
| Brick | 120 | 5 | 0.22 | 0.05 | -- |
| Concrete, normal | 140 | 9-12 | 0.16-0.25 | 0.06-0.08 | -- |
| Weight | 120 | 4 | 0.2 | | |
| Asbestos-cement | 45 | 1.1 | 0.30-0.55 | 0.03-0.05 | -- |
| board | 32 | 0.8 | 0.33-0.45 | 0.02-0.03 | -- |
| Wood (oak, maple) | 65 | 1.0 | 0.33 | -- | -- |
| Wood (fir, pine) | 35 | 0.8 | 0.29 | -- | -- |
| Hardboard | 15 | 0.35 | 0.30 | -- | -- |
| Plywood | 70 | 3-6 | 0.23 | -- | -- |
| Fiberboard (wood | 50-60 | 1.5 | 0.26 | -- | -- |
| or cane) | 0.6 | 0.5 | 0.2 | -- | -- |
| Plaster | 3 | 0.3 | 0.2 | -- | -- |
| Gypsum Board | 3 | 0.3 | 0.25 | -- | -- |
| Glass fiber batt | | | | | |
| | - | 1-2 | 0.2-0.3 | 0.3-1.0 | -- |
| Mineral wool | - | 0.7-1.0 | 0.32-0.35 | 0.3-0.4 | -- |
| Plastics, rigid | 2 | 0.26 | 0.32 | 0.3-04 | -- |
| Vinyls | 2 | 0.18 | 0.38 | 0.4 | -- |
| Styrene | | | | | |
| Polystyrene foam | | | | | |
| Polyurethand foam | | | | | |

Note: Values listed are estimated values at ordinary temperatures, or over typical temperature ranges in fires, if available.

    Actual values vary considerably with temperature, particularly where moisture is involved.

[1] The number of Btu transmitted in one hour, through one square foot, one inch thick, for each degree of temperature difference.

[2] Specific Heat is the number of Btu required to increase the temperature of one pound of the material one degree F.

[3] Steel elongation increases at higher temperatures.

*Concrete.* Concrete is typically composed of portland cement, sand and coarse aggregate, for example, gravel, stone, cinders, slag, shale, vermiculite. The proportions may vary, for example, from 1:1:3 for columns to 1:3:6 for foundations. Concrete has high compressive strength but low tensile or shear strength. When exposed to elevated temperature under load, the compressive strength decreases and is one-half of its normal value at a temperature of about 1100°F (593°C). When exposed to rapidly rising temperatures, concrete is susceptible to spalling which is the (sometimes violent) loss of surface material. Spalling is attributed to the rapid generation of steam and depends upon moisture content (generally above 5%) in the concrete, type of aggregate and compressive load. Spalling is more likely in concrete which has not had sufficient time to lose its initial water of hydration, a process which continues for years in heavy concrete sections.

Ordinary concrete contains no steel reinforcement (or only light reinforcement). Concrete blocks may be made from cement sand and gravel, or from cement and sand alone, or from cement, sand and cinders.

Reinforced concrete is a composite mixture in which steel rods or bars are used to provide tensile and flexural strength. Fire may cause the concrete to spall away from the reinforcing steel. The strength of the concrete structural element depends upon the close bond between the steel and the concrete. Damaged concrete may be structurally unsafe. The tendons used in prestressed concrete totally lose their prestress at 800°F (427°C).

*Steel.* Steel has high tensile and compressive strength and is used in buildings in many sizes, shapes and products. Steel loses strength at elevated temperatures. When used as a structural member its yield, tensile and compressive strengths decrease to one-half of its normal value at a temperature of about 1000 to 1100°F (538° to 593°C). The color of heated iron and steel is sometimes used as a measure of temperature (see table 7). Steel is used in rolled or built-up members, in bar and thin sheet "C" joists, as channels, tees and angles, and as a variety of connectors such as nails, screws, bolts, hangars, and gusset plates. The fire characteristics of the steel, including high heat conductivity, substantial thermal expansion and decrease in yield strength at high temperatures, may be critical factors in a fire. For instance, a 20 ft steel member will elongate almost 2 in when heated to 1000°F (538°C). If restrained, it will buckle to accommodate the expansion. The buckling may cause structural collapse and may be well removed from the point of origin of the fire.

*Gypsum.* Gypsum is used both for plaster and for manufactured wall boards. Gypsum is one of the few materials which absorb heat from a fire, rather than contributing to the fire. It performs well in fires. It is widely used in fire-resistive assemblies. If the question of fire resistance is an issue, careful examination of the rear of several full sections should be made to determine if the board has a label or marking indicating it was listed by UL (Underwriters Laboratories Inc.) or FM (Factory Mutual Research Corp.). If the board is listed, then the installation should be compared with the code requirements, particularly in type and spacing of nails, cement cover over the nails, taping of all joints and firestopping of the structure.

*Wood.* Lumber is sawn wood used for construction purposes, although the word timber is often applied to large cross sectional pieces of lumber. Under fire exposure, wood undergoes dehydration, followed normally by a burning and/or charring process. Charred wood has readily defined layers or zones. The charring rate is roughly 0.025 or 1/40 in/min, but varies significantly with species, density and moisture content. The relatively thin wood members of frame construction may lose structural strength rapidly on fire exposure. Thick structural members may retain their strength for long periods but the structure itself may fail because of failure of the connections.

**Table 7 Approximate color of Glowing Hot, Solid Objects**

| Appearance | Temperature | |
|---|---|---|
| | °F | °C |
| No emission detectable | Less than 885 | Less than 475 |
| Dark red | 885-1200 | 475-650 |
| Dark red to cherry red | 1200-1380 | 650-750 |
| Cherry red to bright cherry red | 1380-1500 | 750-815 |
| Bright cherry red to orange | 1500-1650 | 815-900 |
| Orange to yellow | 1650-200 | 900-1090 |
| Yellow to light yellow | 2000-2400 | 1090-1315 |
| Light yellow to white | 2400-2800 | 1315-1540 |
| Brighter white | higher than 2800 | Higher than 1540 |

Wood cannot be "fire proofed" or made "noncombustible". However, it can be treated to reduce its rate of burning by a variety of surface treatments and impregnations with mineral salts. Pressure impregnation is one of the most effective methods of reducing surface flame spread, rate of heat release and smoke generation. If there is an apparent poor performance of impregnated or surface-treated wood, samples should be removed and tested for adequacy of the treatment.

*Plastics*. This term refers to a group of organic substances (resins) of high molecular weight which can be shaped or molded into finished solid products. Cellulosic plastics, which include cellulose acetate, ethyl cellulose, methyl cellulose and cellulose nitrate, are produced by chemical modification of cellulose. Some plastic products are blends, combinations or composites with unique properties; some can be compounded to be thermoplastic or thermosetting.Thermosetting plastics are those which undergo chemical reaction and cure during molding and do not melt. Some thermoplastics melt at temperatures only slightly above 212°F (100°C) and may form liquid pools and burn intensely in a manner similar to flammable liquids. Examples of the two types of plastics and quoted values of service temperatures and ignition temperatures are given in table 8. These temperatures may not relate directly to actual performance of products in fires, since the test methods do not take into account specimen size, heat transfer properties, aging, etc.

The fire performance of plastics depends upon type, use and leve) of exposure. Some plastics form a char structure which may inhibit further burning, but most plastics will burn rapidly and generate heat, smoke and potentially toxic gases at fire temperatures. The plastics may be almost completely consumed, and the investigator should investigate for the presence of plastics in fires which reached high intensity early.

**Table 8 Pastics**

| | Typical Uses | Continuous Service Temp [1] °F | Ignition Temp [2] Flash °F | Ignition Temp [2] Self °F | Decomposition Temp Range °F |
|---|---|---|---|---|---|
| **Thermoplastics** | | | | | |
| ABS | Piping, refrigerators, telephones | 175-212 | -- | -- | -- |
| Acrylic/Methyl Methacrylate | Glazing, light diffusers, furnishing | 170-23 | 540-570 | 830-860 | 340-570 |
| Cellulose Nitrate | Throwaway test tubes | 120-160 | 285 | 285 | -- |
| Polyamide (Nylon) | Carpeting, clothing, appliances | 180-250 | 790 | 795 | 590-715 |
| Polycarbonate | Glazing, appliances, light diffusers | 250 | -- | 930 | -- |
| Polyethylene | Containers, vapor barriers | 160-230 | 645 | 660 | 635-840 |
| Polypropylene | Wire insulation, appliances, piping | 190-280 | 650 | 730 | 625-770 |
| Polystyrene | Appliances, furnishings, thermal insulation (foam) | 140-175 | 650-680 | 910-925 | 570-750 |
| Polytetrafluorethylene (Teflon) | Cooking utensils, wire insulation | 500 | -- | 985 | 950-1000 |
| Polyurethane | Furniture cushioning, coating, thermal Insulation (foam) | 250-300 | 590 | 780 | -- |
| Polyvinyl chloride | Floor and wall covering, wire insulation, piping, Upholstery, clothing, coating | 150-175 | 735 | 850 | 390-570 |
| **Thermosetting** | | | | | |
| Alkyd | Paints, lacquers | 350 | | | |
| Epoxy | Protective coating, reinforced plastics | 210 | -- | -- | |
| Melamine | Tableware, laminates | 280 | 885-930 | 1150-1190 | |
| Phenolic | Laminates, appliances | 250-350 | | 900 | |
| Polyester | Partitions (Glass-reinforced), boats | 350-525 | 635-750 | 810-910 | |
| Silicone | Electrical Insulation, coatings, grease | 120 | -- | -- | |
| Urea Formaldehyde | Thermal insulation | | | | |

Flame retardants added in manufacture may be used to reduce the ease of ignition and flammability of some plastics.

*Insulation.* The principal types of thermal insulation used in buildings are (1) mineral wool batts, blankets and fibrous loose fill, (2) foamed plastics, (3) inorganic (vermiculite, perlite) loose fill, (4) organic (wood or cane fiber) boards and (e) organic (macerated paper) loose fill.

Batts and blankets may be supplied with an integral vapor barrier (asphalt-treated or aluminum-foil-faced Kraft paper) which is intended for application to the warm-in-winter surface of the wall or ceiling interior finish board. The paper facing"is flammable and should never be left exposed. The batts are held together with a combustible binder. Plastic foam, which is combustible, should never be left exposed and most building codes require that a layer of 1/2 in (1.3 cm) gypsum board or equivalent barrier protection be provided.

Loose fill cellulosic insulation is commonly made of ground-up paper with chemicals added to reduce flammability. The more common chemicals used are boric acid, borax, and various sulfates and phosphates and these are added in amounts ranging generally from 15 to 30% by weight. If the chemicals are not added properly, they may segregate and leave portions of untreated paper. Loose fill insulation may be poured or blown into attics or blown into walls. Unless care is taken to maintain clearances around light and heat fixtures, and around flues and other heated surfaces and heat-producing appliances, smoldering of the cellulosic insulation may occur.

## UTILITY SYSTEMS

### Introduction

Brief descriptions of the types of utility systems found in buildings are provided. Those features and materials of the various systems which have resulted in fires and fire spread are discussed. The principal utility systems are:

1. Plumbing systems;
2. heating, ventilation, and air conditioning systems;
3. electrical systems.

### Plumbing Systems

Plumbing systems include water supply and waste removal (sewage). Water supply systems, as the wording indicates, supply water to the building's fixtures and equipment. Sewage systems remove the waste products, usually accompanied by water for ease in movement, from the building.

Piping for both water supply and waste removal systems may be either metallic (copper, steel, or cast iron) or nonmetallic (plastics such as chlorinated polyvinyl chloride, polyvinyl chloride and acrylonitrile-butadiene-styrene, or CPVC, PVC, and ABS, respectively).

In some code jurisdictions, gas piping is included under the local plumbing code provisions and, as such, is a plumbing system. Piping for gas supply systems includes wrought iron (black pipe) and zinc-coated pipe (galvanized).

The major concerns with plumbing systems from a fire standpoint are with:

1. Piping, if metallic, providing an accidental ground for stray electrical currents;
2. piping, if nonmetallic, providing a fuel for nearby fires with the resultant spread of the fire;
3. penetration of fire-resistive walls and floors without proper protection (firestopping) leading to the spread of the fire;
4. leaks or ruptures in fuel gas piping and the possibility of ignition of the leaking gas.

Gas leaks have contributed too many accidental fires. The leak does not have to be within the building to pose a fire problem. Gas from leaks in the underground piping outside of a building has been known to follow the piping through the wall of the building and contact an ignition source within the structure. Also, gas leaking outside of the building has been known to have entered the sewage system and flowed back into the building through untrapped floor drains, reach an ignition source within the building and explode. Natural gas and liquefied petroleum gas have no natural odor. They are odorized artificially. The odorant may be removed as gas leaks through the earth or it may be absorbed in the scale in the inside of the pipeline. As a consequence, the absence of any reported gas odor does not necessarily mean that gas was not present. Gas leaks in the underground gas utility systems which result in accidents should be reported to the National Transportation Safety Board. While the Board must investigate any accident in which a fatality occurs, the Board also will assist in the investigation of any serious gas utility accident.

The major concerns from fire in plumbing systems are with:
(1) leakage from joints, especially in gas piping or sewer systems,where sewer wastes may produce methane; and (2) improperly constructed penetrations of fire-rated assemblies by the piping or appurtenances. Under fire exposure certain installations of plastic piping, either water or waste, may contribute to spread of fire or emit toxic gases.

### Heating, Ventilation and Air Conditioning

*Heating.* The basic types of heating systems are hot water, steam, hot air and electricity. Hot water and steam systems utilize water usually heated by coal, gas, or oil-fired boilers. The hot water or steam is conveyed to radiators and/or convectors by piping. In hot-air systems, the air is heated by coal, oil, or gas-fired burners, or electric-resistance heaters, and conveyed throughout the building through ducts. Electrical heating systems generally utilize either radiant panels (resistance heating cables) built into the floor or ceiling or baseboard heating coils (convective panels) with electrical service supplied directly to the heating units.

*Ventilation.* Mechanical ventilation is provided either in conjunction with the air conditioning systems, or is in the form of ventilating fans installed in exterior walls or roofs and exhausting directly to the outdoors or into exhaust shafts which lead to the outdoors. Supply or makeup air is usually obtained through grills in doors or exterior walls, or by air leakage through openings.

*Air Conditioning.* There are two primary types of air conditioning: (1) central systems with distribution ducts or piping, utilizing compression or absorption-type refrigeration equipment or (2) packaged room or zonal air conditioners with free air discharge.

Central air conditioning systems utilize electricity, natural gas, or fuel oil to operate the compressors and a refrigerant as coolant in the coils and condensers. Either cooled air is circulated through ducts or chilled water is circulated through piping to individual room or zone convectors.

Individual packaged room or zonal units are generally electrically operated with closed refrigerant circuits self-contained within the units and may, depending on the conditions of usage, take fresh air from the outside or recirculate the inside air.

Heating, ventilation and air conditioning systems may be the cause of the original fire or the systems may contribute to the growth and spread of the fire. Fire initiation may include:

1. Explosive ignition due to the accumulation of gas or oil vapors within the equipment from failure of equipment controls;
2. ignition of fuel gases or oils from leaks in the piping or in the equipment;
3. ignition of combustibles near flue pipes, combustion chambers, and radiant heating units.

In air duct systems, most codes require fire dampers at points where ducts pierce fire-resistive walls and floors (where not in a shaft). In fire investigations, it is sometimes important to determine whether these dampers operated properly. As noted below, air conditioning and ventilation systems are sometimes designed to perform specific functions, such as smoke removal from the area of the fire. It is sometimes necessary for the fire investigator to determine whether such a system was installed and whether the system operated as intended.

*Smoke Movement*

The explanation of heated smoke and gases rising and mushrooming under the roof, if not vented, is adequate for simple structures. In tall buildings a number of factors may cause the movement of smoke to locations far beyond the area of origin, without necessarily affecting the areas in between.

Smoke movement may be caused by:
1. Thermal energy of the fire;
2. wind;
3. stack effect;
4. air handling system;
5. special built in smoke removal equipment;
6. openings in the building;
7. atmospheric conditions.

**Wind.** The wind exerts a pressure on one side and suction on the opposite side of the building. It may be powerful enough to overcome any of the other forces discussed here. It may change direction a number of times during the fire. It may blow in different directions at different levels of a high-rise building, particularly in congested areas where "canyon effects" may occur. The effect of the wind is increased when openings occur in the building. It is important to note that the wind at the fire may not have conformed to the information recorded at the nearest official weather station.

**Stack Effect.** This is due to differences between the inside and outside temperatures. The greater the difference, the greater the stack effect. Under cold weather conditions, normal air flow in the lower part of the building is from floors into shafts. The flow will decrease on successively higher floors until there is a "neutral zone", one or more floors where the flow is minimal. In the absence of wind, this generally will be from 1/3 to 1/2 the height of the building. Above the neutral zone the flow reverses, from the shafts onto the floors, with the pressure (and thus the flow) increasing with height. The greatest flow therefore is from the lowest floors into the shafts and out from the shafts onto the highest floors. Thus top floor occupants sometimes may be the first to report a lower floor fire. In air conditioned buildings on a hot summer day, the flow may be reversed, that is downward. It should be kept in mind that the stack effect exists due to temperature difference and height. The fire does not cause it, the fire gases simply are transported by it. As an example of stack effect on fire gases, a rubbish fire on the ninth floor of a high-rise building under construction ignited PVC (polyvinyl chloride) air conditioning connectors. The fumes greatly distressed workmen on the 35th floor. They started to walk down the stairs but the stairwell was so full of noxious fumes that they got out at the 25th floor. They smashed the glass windows to get relief. This movement of gases from a lower to an upper floor was due to stack effect.

*Air Conditioning.* The investigator should determine the effect of the system on the fire. If the system was supposed to react to the fire in some way, the suggestions in the next paragraph are pertinent.

*Special Smoke Removal Equipment* In some buildings special equipment is provied to vent the fire area. It may be triggered automatically or manually. In other buildings the air conditioning system may have been designed to assist in controlling the spread of smoke.

There are two questions the investigator can ask:

"Did the special smoke removal equipment operate as designed? If it did operate as designed, were the results adequate?"

*Openings in the building.* Openings in the building, particularly large ones, can disrupt stack effect, multiply the wind effect, and disrupt the operation of mechanical equipment. When and why openings occurred might be important information as the fire investigation develops.

*Atmospheric Conditions.* When the temperature of the atmosphere is constantly decreasing as height increases, the condition is called "lapse". Under "lapse" conditions smoke will move up and away from the fire. If there is a layer of air warmer than the air below, this layer is called the "inversion layer". It acts as a roof to rising smoke. A high rise building may penetrate an inversion layer. This causes substantial differences in the smoke situation above and below the layer.

*Wood-Burning Stoves and Furnaces*

In recent years, there has been a growth in the use of wood-burning stoves and furnaces to provide either primary or supplemental heating. Such equipment, if not installed with adequate clearances to nearby combustible materials is potential sources of accidental fires. The burning of wood leads to the production of creosote which tends to deposit in the flue pipes and chimneys. This is particularly true of the newer so-called air-tight stoves. Operation of these stoves at low-firing rates enhances the production of creosote. The buildup of creosote in the flue pipes and chimneys can lead to a severe fire in the flue and chimney as the creosote is combustible. Flues and chimneys, be they masonry or the newer all-fuel triple-wall metal variety, should be able to withstand a total burnout. However, they may not due to deficiencies which may have been built in or have occurred with the passage of time.

# ELECTRICAL

### Electrical service consists of the following:

1. Service drop wires, either overhead or underground (from the public utilities' lines to the building);

2. service-entrance wires (from outside of building to equipment on the inside);

3. meter;

4. service entrance switch (to disconnect entire installation from public utilities' lines);

5. panel boards providing fuse or circuit breaker protection as well as disconnect means for each of the individual branch circuits;

6. grounding system;

7. distribution system - individual circuits, for lighting, appliance, and equipment operation.

There are six different types of wiring systems in common use. They are: (1) rigid conduit; (2) thin wall conduit; (3) flexible conduit; (4) nonmetallic-sheathed cable; (5) armored cable; and (6) knob-and-tube (which is seldom used today). Electrical codes are very specific with regard to where each of these systems may be used.

Junction boxes and outlet boxes are required at every location where wiring is spliced or insulation is removed, and at fixture locations.

In older buildings, electrical installations may have been made without outlet boxes at all splices and where insulation had been removed. In these locations, and where the wiring has been run in joist or stud spaces, dust, cobwebs and other easily ignitable materials may be present. If the splices and joints have not been properly made, there is a possibility of either short circuits or overheating of wire junctions thus leading to fire.

Another common cause of electrical fires, particularly in single-family dwellings, is the replacement of fuses of one rating with those of higher rating, that is, replacement of 15 ampere fuses with 20 or 30 ampere fuses. This practice may result in the overloading of the electrical wiring causing overheating and breakdown of insulation, and, if in close proximity to combustibles, eventually to smoldering and possible flaming ignition.

# THE SCIENCE OF FIRE

## Chemistry and Physics of Fire

## CONTENTS

| | Page |
|---|---|
| FRIENDLY AND UNFRIENDLY FIRES | 1 |
| FUEL, OXYGEN, IGNITION SOURCE | 1 |
| CHEMISTRY OF FIRE | 1 |
|     Introduction | 1 |
|     Gaseous Fuels | 2 |
|     Liquid Fuels | 2 |
|     Solid Fuels | 4 |
|     Oxygen Requirements for Combustion | 5 |
|     Heats of Combustion and Maximum Flame Temperatures | 6 |
|     Products of Combustion | 7 |
|     Reference | 8 |
| HEAT TRANSFER IN FIRES | 8 |
|     Introduction | 8 |
|     Convective Heat Transfer | 8 |
|     Conductive Heat Transfer | 8 |
|     Radiant Heat Transfer | 9 |
|     Other Methods of Fire Extension | 10 |
| FIRE DEVELOPMENT | 10 |
|     Introduction | 10 |
|     Ignition | 10 |
|     Flame Sptread | 12 |
|     Effect of Enclosure | 13 |
|     Flashover | 14 |

# THE SCIENCE OF FIRE
## Chemistry and Physics of Fire

### FRIENDLY AND UNFRIENDLY FIRES

Combustion may be defined as a chemical and physical reaction between a fuel and oxygen from the air which generates heat. Combustion usually produces light, smoke, and combustion gases as well. Controlled combustion, or friendly fires, has been of enormous benefit to mankind but when uncontrolled can be a terribly destructive force. Many destructive, or unfriendly fires, grow out of controlled, useful combustion.

### FUEL, OXYGEN, IGNITION SOURCE

Three conditions are necessary to have a fire: a fuel must be present; it must be in contact with oxygen (usually from the air), and there must be a source of energy to raise the temperature of the fuel and oxygen to a point where they react rapidly (ignite). Fuels and oxygen coexist safely everywhere in nature. As an example, gasoline, which forms a highly flammable mixture in air, is handled safely in enormous quantities every day in the United States. Only when an ignition source, such as a spark, heat or flame, is present can a fire result.

### CHEMISTRY OF FIRE

#### Introduction

Fuels may be classified as gases, liquids, or solids. Each behaves differently in fires. Most fuels are organic in nature; that is, they are made up of carbon and hydrogen. They may be natural products such as coal, oil, or plant materials. Or, they may be products derived from these sources, such as coke, gasoline, lumber, paper, or the wide range of chemicals and plastics produced by industry.

When organic fuels burn with an abundant supply of air the principal products are carbon dioxide and water vapor.

Nitrogen-containing plastics, such as nylon, produce nitrogen gas among the products of combustion in addition to carbon dioxide and water vapor. Similarly, plastics containing chlorine, such as polyvinyl chloride, produce hydrogen chloride, an acid gas, when they burn along with the carbon dioxide and water.

When combustion takes place in a limited air supply, as is the case . in building fires, combustion will be incomplete. Incomplete combustion produces toxic gases such as carbon monoxide and hydrogen cyanide (from nitrogen-containing materials), along with other irritating and toxic gases and smoke particles.

In burning buildings incomplete combustion is the rule, with a large variety and quantity of toxic, flammable, even explosive, gases being generated. Overall, then, there is no "perfect combustion" in a building fire.

### Gaseous Fuels

Fuel gases, such as natural gas, since they mix readily with air, present a very serious fire hazard. They are readily ignited by a very small ignition source, such as a spark. As they flow freely, they can reach remote ignition sources. Once ignited, the flame spreads rapidly through the fuel/air mixture, generating high temperatures, igniting other combustibles, and creating a destructive pressure wave (explosion).

Fuel gas/air mixtures will burn only if their composition lies within certain limits. If the fuel concentration is too low (below the lower or lean limit, and often called the lower explosive limit, L.E.L.) insufficient fuel is present to sustain the flame. If the fuel concentration is too great (the upper or rich limit and often called the upper explosive limit, U.E.L.) not enough oxygen is present in the mixture for combustion. The region between the upper and lower limits is called the flammable range. From a fire safety standpoint, generally it is only the lower limit that is of practical interest since a mixture above the upper limit will always have to pass through the flammable range to bring the mixture to within safe limits.

### Liquid Fuels

When the surface of a combustible or flammable liquid is exposed to the air, some of it converts to a vapor and mixes with the air. In a closed container the concentration of vapor in the air reaches an equilibrium value (the saturated vapor pressure), which depends on the composition of the liquid and the temperature. The vapor pressure of a liquid increases with increases in temperature until, at the boiling point of the liquid, the vapor pressure is just equal to-atmospheric pressure and rapid vaporization (boiling) occurs.

The combustion of a liquid actually takes place in this fuel/air mixture above the liquid surface rather than at the surface of the liquid. In this respect, it resembles the combustion of a gaseous fuel. For ignition to take place, the concentration of fuel vapor in air must exceed the lower flammability limit; that is, the temperature of the liquid must be high enough for the equilibrium vapor concentration to be within the flammable range.

The minimum temperature at which vaporization is sufficient to produce a flammable liquid fuel/air mixture is called the flash point of the liquid. It is measured by gradually heating a sample of the liquid in contact with the air and periodically bringing a small ignition flame near the surface . The minimum temperature at which a flash of flame spreads over the surface is recorded as the flash point. It is one of the most important properties in determining the fire hazard of a liquid.

The initial flash seen when the ignition source is brought near to the liquid surface may consume the fuel in the fuel/air mixture and the flash will die out. At a slightly higher temperature, vaporization of the liquid is sufficient to sustain the flame. This temperature at which the sustained flame is observed is called the fire point. The flash point is more widely used than the fire point to characterize the flammability properties of a liquid.

A liquid fuel is not readily ignited by a small ignition source if the liquid's temperatures is below its flash point, but it can be ignited by a larger ignition source which is capable of heating the surface of the liquid to the flash point. Once ignited, radiation from the fire will increase the temperature of the liquid, increasing the rate of vaporization and the intensity of the fire.

Liquid sprays and mists (for example, from a leak under pressure) are more easily ignited and burn more vigorously than the bulk liquid because of the larger surface area per unit volume in contact with air. An example of this is the pressurized oil burner of an oil-fired heating plant.

Another measured property of liquid fuels is ignition temperature, also referred to as autoignition temperature. The ignition temperature of a liquid fuel is that temperature to which the fuel, in air, must be heated to ignite spontaneously. The ignition temperature of a specific substance can vary widely depending upon many conditions. The following information is quoted from reference (2):

> "Ignition temperatures observed under one set of conditions may be changed substantially by a change of conditions. For this reason, ignition temperatures should be looked upon only as approximations. Some of the variables known to affect ignition temperatures of flammable liquids and gases are percentage composition of the vapor or gas-air mixture, shape and size of the space where the ignition occurs, rate and duration of heating, kind and temperature of the ignition source, catalytic or other effect of materials that may be present, and oxygen concentration. As there are many differences in ignition temperature test methods, such as in size and shape of containers, method of heating and ignition source, it is not surprising that different ignition temperatures are reported for the same substance by different laboratories.
>
> As illustration of the effects of test methods, the ignition temperatures of hexane determined by three different methods were 437° F, 637° F, and 950° F, respectively. The effect of percentage composition is shown by the following ignition temperatures for pentane: 1,018.4° F for 1.5 per cent pentane in air, 935.6° F for 3.75 per cent pentane, and 888.8F for 7.65 per cent pentane. The following ignition temperatures for carbon disulfide demonstrate the effect of size of space containing the ignitible mixture: in a 200 ml (milliliter) flask the ignition temperature was 248° F; in a 1,000 ml flask 230° F; and in a 10,000 ml flask 205° F. That materials of the container walls in which the flammable mixture is in contact may affect the ignition temperature is illustrated by ignition temperature determinations for benzene conducted in various containers: 1,060° F in a quartz container, 1,252° F in iron, and 1,330° F in zinc."

These variations in ignition temperatures for a given liquid fuel should be kept in mind by the investigator should he encounter a fire where ignition of a liquid fuel by an external heat source is thought to be involved.

Flash points are used to provide for legal regulation of liquid fuels. Liquids with flash points below 100F (38° C) are classified as "flammable" under most codes, while those with flash points above 100°F (38° C) are classified as "combustible". Regulations for the handling and storage of "combustible" liquids, for instance, are more lenient than for "flammable" liquids. There is much misunderstanding of these terms. People accustomed to obtaining information from handbooks and tables, often take the published figures as physical constants, which they are not. They are merely observed phenomena and are truly valid only for the sample tested in the apparatus in which tested.

Floor wax, nominally "combustible", ignited from the spark of a floor resulting in a large fire. Tests of a similar material gave an actual flash point of 74° F (23° C). A flammable liquid mixture, such as alcohol and water, may or may not ignite under ordinary temperatures depending upon the percentage (or proof) of alcohol. Whiskey will ignite; wine will not. However, if the wine is heated, it will ignite. The relationship between the fire point and proof of various alcoholic beverages is shown in table 1.

Table 1 Fire Points for Various Alcoholic Beverages

| Beverage | Fire Point °F | °C |
|---|---|---|
| Whiskey | | |
| 80 proof[2] | 100 | 38 |
| 100 proof | 95 | 35 |
| Gins | | |
| 80 proof | 100 | 38 |
| 95 proof | 98 | 37 |
| Rums | | |
| 80 proof | 100 | 38 |
| 140 proof | 80 | 27 |
| Brandies | | |
| 80 proof | 100 | 38 |
| 140 proof | 80 | 27 |
| Wines | | |
| 20 proof (10%) | above 180 | 83 |
| 40 proof (20%) | 135 | 57 |

[1]Fire points typically are only a few degrees higher than flashpoint.
[2]For alcohol percentage, divide proof by two.

Published characteristics of flammable liquids must be used with caution in attempting to determine what part a particular flammable liquid played in the development of a fire.

Solid Fuels

The combustion of solid fuels is more complex than the combustion of a liquid or gas. For example, as wood is heated certain gases are given off. The wood is decomposing even though flaming has not yet developed. The reaction moves from the surface into the wood. Gas continues to evolve. The wood is still absorbing heat (endothermic reaction). When enough gas is emitted (temperatures of about 600° to 900° F or 316° to 482° C are required), the gas ignites. The wood is now burning and contributing heat to the fire (exothermic reaction).

Surface area is important in the burning of solids. Materials with large surface-to-volume ratios, such as paper or wood shavings, are readily ignited by a match while a solid block of wood may be difficult to ignite. As plywood and plywood paneling burn, the plywood layers separate increasing the surface area. The total amount of fuel is not increased, but increasing the surface area increases the rate of burning.

For a long time it was thought that the damage to structural elements would be equal in fires where the total amount of heat generated was equal. More recent work indicates that short, hot fires may be more destructive to some materials than long, cooler fires, even though the total amount of heat given off is the same.

Many solid fuels, particularly plastics, will volatilize and burn almost completely when subjected to high temperatures. Other materials, particularly those made from wood, may be only partially volatilized and leave behind a carbon-rich char. The carbon is non-volatile but it will react with oxygen which diffuses to the solid surface, giving off a large amount of heat and causing the solid surface to glow brightly (glowing combustion). The glowing combustion of charcoal is an example. This is a relatively slow process and may continue for a long time after the more volatile flame-producing gases are used up.

Because of the low volatility of most solid fuels, flame spread over surfaces in the downward direction is relatively slow. Flame spread in the upward direction, where the fuel is heated by the rising flaming gases, is much more rapid. Flame spread in the horizontal direction falls between these two extremes. The flame spread, however, may be influenced by a variety of other factors, for example, reradiation from nearby surfaces or air flows.

### Oxygen Requirements for Combustion

Since oxygen combines with fuel in the combustion process, the size of a fire may be limited by either the amount of fuel available or by the amount of oxygen which can reach the fire.

Oxygen will usually be supplied to the fire from the surrounding air. Air normally contains 20.9 percent of oxygen by volume or 23.2 percent by weight. The remainder (79.1%) consists of nitrogen and traces of other gases. Nitrogen is not consumed in the combustion process. One cubic foot of air contains 0.0175 lbs of oxygen (0.28 kg/m$^3$). The amount of oxygen required to burn a fuel will depend on the nature of the fuel. Hydrocarbons, such as gasoline, have the highest oxygen requirement, needing approximately 3.5 lbs of oxygen per pound of fuel or 200 cubic feet of air per pound of fuel. Paper has a much lower oxygen requirement, needing approximately 1.2 lbs of oxygen per pound of fuel or 69 cubic feet of air per pound of fuel. Most other common fuels will have oxygen requirements between these limits.

As an example of what this means, consider a fire started in a pile of paper in a closed room 10 by 10 by 8 ft (3.2 x 3.2 x 2.5 m). The 800 cubic-foot-room will initially contain about 14 lb (30.8 kg) of oxygen, sufficient to burn less than 12 lb (26.4 kg) of paper. The actual amount of fuel consumed, however, would be less since the fire will go out when the oxygen concentration drops to around 8 or 10 percent. The rest of the oxygen would remain unconsumed.

Thus, a fire in a tightly-closed compartment will go out due to lack of sufficient oxygen and will not grow to a dangerous size. Most fires, however, will have access to an unlimited air supply through open doors, windows and other openings. In such circumstances the fire will continue to burn until all of the fuel is consumed, unless the fire is extinguished.

### Heats of Combustion and Maximum Flame Temperatures

The complete combustion of a pound (or gram) of a specific fuel yields a fixed quantity of heat. This quantity is known as the heat of combustion and will differ for different fuels. Among the common fuels, hydrocarbons (such as gasoline) have the higher heats of combustion while oxygen-containing fuels such as paper (cellulose) have lower values. Heats of combustion for typical fuels are listed in table 2.

The heat given off in a fire goes first to heat the gases coming off and then the nitrogen and any excess oxygen in the air. When the supply of oxygen is exactly sufficient to consume the fuel present, the flame temperature will be at a maximum. Maximum flame temperatures for typical fuels are listed in table 3. If the air supply is insufficient to burn the fuel completely, not all of the heat available will be released and the flame temperature will be reduced. If an excess of air is present, part of the heat will go to heat this excess air and again the flame temperature will be reduced.

The maximum flame temperature is probably never reached in a fire. Usually, the temperature will be much less due to mixing of the cooler surrounding air with the flame gases, incomplete combustion, and the loss of heat through windows and doors as well as to walls, ceilings, floors and room contents.

Table 2   Approximate heats of combustion of typical fuels

| Fuel. | Heat of Combustion | |
|---|---|---|
| | kcal/g | Btu/lb |
| Methyl Alcohol | 5.3 | 9,600 |
| Ethyl Alcohol | 7.1 | 12,800 |
| Isopropyl Alcohol | 7.9 | 14,200 |
| Ethylene Glycol | 4.5 | 8,100 |
| Octane | 11.4 | 20,500 |
| Benzene | 10.0 | 18,000 |
| Gasoline | 11.5 | 20,700 |
| Kerosine | 11.0 | 19,800 |
| Fuel Oil | 10.5 | 18,900 |
| Crude Oil | 10.8 | 19,500 |
| Rubber | 10.8 | 19,500 |
| Wood | 4.2 - 5.0 | 7,600 - 9,000 |
| Paper | 4.5 | 8,100 |
| Polyethylene | 11.1 | 20,000 |
| Polystyrene | 9.9 | 17,800 |
| Polyurethane | 6.2 | 11,200 |
| Polyvinyl Chloride | 4.0 | 7,200 |

Table 3   Maximum flame temperatures of typical gaseous fuels in air

| Fuel | Flame Temperature | |
|---|---|---|
| | °F | °C |
| Methane (natural gas) | 3400 | 1871 |
| Propane (LPG) | 3500 | 1927 |
| Octane (gasoline) | 4050 | 2232 |
| Acetylene | 4350 | 2399 |
| Hydrogen | 3700 | 2038 |
| Benzene | 4150 | 2288 |

Products of Combustion.

The products of combustion from a hostile fire are as great a threat to humans as is direct exposure to the fire. The combustion products from all fires are toxic; the level of toxicity will depend on the concentration, the type of fuel, and the specific conditions of the fire. In a hot fire with a good air supply, the principal products will be carbon dioxide and water vapor. Carbon dioxide is mildly toxic while water vapor is not. The low oxygen content of the fire gases, due to the consumption of the oxygen in the fire, may make them dangerous, even in the absence of significant quantities of toxic gases. Around a free-burning fire, however, material being heated is generating quantities of toxic and combustible gases. Carbon dioxide in fires is always accompanied by some carbon monoxide. The ratio of carbon monoxide to carbon dioxide increases as the oxygen supply is decreased. Carbon monoxide is highly toxic and is the direct cause of a majority of fire deaths. A concentration of 3,000 ppm (parts per million) can cause death in half an hour while higher concentrations will cause correspondingly more rapid death.

When the supply of air to a fire is limited, combustion will be incomplete and, in addition to carbon monoxide, large quantities of other combustion products, including hydrocarbons and soot particles, will be produced. This mixture of products will contain insufficient oxygen for further combustion but can accumulate in a building. When additional oxygen (air) is introduced (if the window breaks or the door opens), rapid combustion can occur. A sudden and dangerous pressure rise, called the back-draft, is created. The back-draft resulting from the rapid combustion may be reported as an explosion by witnesses to the fire. (However, the investigator should be aware that there are other sources of explosions in fires, such,,as aerosol cans, which may mislead witnesses.)

Incomplete combustion also produces a variety of toxic and irritating gases, in addition to carbon monoxide. Nitrogen-containing materials such as wool, nylon and polyurethane, can produce highly toxic hydrogen cyanide and nitrogen oxides. Sulfur-containing materials, such as wool and rubber, produce sulfur dioxide. Chlorine-containing materials, such as polyvinyl chloride, produce hydrogen chloride, a choking, irritating gas. When dissolved in water, hydrogen chloride forms hydrochloric acid, a corrosive liquid which attacks metal surfaces. All fuels can produce aldehydes such as formaldehyde and acrolein. These are strong irritants which attack the lungs and may produce delayed respiratory complications. Toxic gases may remain at the scene of a fire after the fire has been extinguished. For this reason, breathing apparatus should be used in examining the site until it has been thoroughly ventilated. Ventilation may not, however, thoroughly clear cellars, basements and other low points. (The investigator should keep this in mind.) Fire gases may cause incapacitation of the victim before death occurs. In such cases escape is prevented and death may follow due to continued toxic gas exposure or burns from contact with the fire.

Smoke is the visible product of a fire. It consists of soot particles, partially burned fuel fragments and liquid droplets. The visible smoke serves as a warning of the presence of toxic gases, and the smoke particles themselves may contain toxic and irritating substances.

Reference

Methods for measuring the flash points of various liquids can be found in the most recent edition of the following ASTM standards:

| | |
|---|---|
| D 56 | Flash Point by TAG Closed Tester |
| D 92 | Flash and Fire Points by Cleveland Open Cup |
| D 93 | Flash Point by Pensky-Martens Closed Tester |
| D 1310 | Flash Point by TAG Open-Cup Apparatus |

## HEAT TRANSFER IN FIRES

### Introduction

Heat energy generated by a fire first heats the fire gases (flames) to a high temperature. It must then be transferred to other materials to spread the fire. This energy transfer can take place through convection, conduction and radiation, either singly or in combination.

### Convective Heat Transfer

Convective heat transfer is the movement of the hot fire gases upwards and away from the fire source. Heat flows from regions of high temperature to regions of lower temperature. The rate of flow is proportional to the temperature difference between the two regions. As these gases come in contact with solid surfaces, such as walls, ceilings and building contents, heat energy is transferred to these surfaces and the gases are cooled in turn. Since the hot gases tend to rise, the ceiling and upper walls of a room will be heated first and most strongly. The flow of convective energy will follow the flow of fire gases, the temperature decreasing with distance from the fire source.

### Conductive Heat Transfer

When a solid surface is heated by contact with hot gases, heat is carried from the surface into the interior of the solid by conduction. The conductivities of materials vary widely. Metals have high thermal conductivities (conduct heat readily), followed by other dense materials such as masonry. Porous and lightweight materials, such as wood and particle board, have still lower thermal conductivities while insulating materials, such as mineral wool or foam plastic, have very low thermal conductivities. The amount of heat absorbed by a wall, and thus the amount of cooling of the fire gases, will be greater for materials with high thermal conductivity. On the other hand, the surface temperatures of materials with low thermal conductivity or materials backed by insulation, such as a carpet with a pad, will rise more rapidly since the heat cannot be conducted rapidly from the surface to the interior. This may result in more rapid fire spread over the surface of these materials, providing they are combustible.

The rate of heat transfer to an object immersed in a flame will decrease as the temperature of the object increases until, as its temperature approaches that of the flame, the rate decreases to zero. Thus the temperature of any object in the fire can never exceed that of the flame heat source.

### Radiant Heat Transfer.

Radiant heat transfer takes place without direct contact between the heat source and the receiving surface. The transfer takes place by electromagnetic radiation or waves. Radiant heat transfer follows line-of-sight and does not turn corners. The warming of the earth's surface by the rays of the sun is one example of radiant heat transfer.

The quantity of heat transferred per unit of time by convection and conduction is approximately proportional to the difference in temperature between the heat source and the receiving surface. As a consequence, small changes in the temperature differential produce small changes in the rate of heat transferred. However, in radiant heat transfer, small changes in the temperature differential between the heat source and the receiving surface can produce large effects due to the nature of the laws of electromagnetic radiation which govern radiant heat transfer. This explains the danger from overheated stoves and heaters, particularly the black-colored, radiant-style, wood stoves currently in vogue. Clearances from combustibles that were more than adequate when fuel is burned at a low rate, rapidly become inadequate when fuel is burned at a high rate.

As in convective and conductive heat transfer, objects cannot be heated in a fire by radiation to a temperature higher than that of the flame source.

The amount of heat radiated also is a function of the area of the radiating surface. A small fire will have a relatively small radiant output. But as the fire grows, the radiation will increase. In addition, the upper part of the room will fill with a layer of hot, radiating smoke and gas, and the walls and ceiling surfaces will become heated and contribute further to the radiant energy falling on the floor and other objects in the room. Temperatures of easily-ignited materials (such as paper or fabrics) may reach the point where they burst into flame without direct contact with the fire due to this radiant heat transfer. Thus, radiation can play a very important role in the spread of a fire. Figure 5.4.4-1 depicts the effect of radiation from the hot gas layer at the ceiling on the floor and other objects in the room.

Radiation also heats the burning fuel surface, increasing the rate of burning and the intensity of the fire. Radiation from the ceiling, ahead of the fire, is important in the spread of fire along carpeting in corridors. Differences in ceiling height, however, may cause significant differences in the flame spread on identical carpets, with the radiation from lower ceilings being more pronounced than that from higher ceilings. Similarly, it is thought that one of the causes for rapid flame spread in mobile homes is the relatively short distances between vertical surfaces, which promotes high levels of radiation and reradiation.

### Other Methods of Fire Extension

Radiation, conduction, and convection are the classic methods of heat transfer and have long been cited as the methods of fire extension. This overlooks another important method of fire extension "Moving Flaming or Heated Material".

Burning shingles, when carried by the up-draft of the fire, have long been recognized as a potential method of fire extension What is not often recognized is that the same phenomenon can occur inside of a building. Take, as an example, an office where papers are scattered around on the tops of desks, file cabinets and tables. In the event of a fire in this room, burning papers are likely to be lifted by the hot plume of the fire and deposited in different locations around the room. If the fire department arrives at this point, they may conclude that there were several different fires instead of just one and suspect that the fires were incendiary. It is appropriate, therefore, for the investigator to consider what types of materials were involved in the fire and their likely behavior under fire conditions in the process of determining the fire cause and origin.

Heat transfer also can result in secondary fires, fires away from the original point of origin. This can mislead if the investigator is not aware of this phenomenon. For example, consider a chair burning in a living room. As the chair burns, the room begins to fill with hot gases from the ceiling down. There are cloth draperies on windows and these draperies extend up close to the ceiling, into the hot gas layer. Before the room flashes over, the top of the draperies ignite, burn free of the drapery rods, and fall in a burning pile onto a sofa. Assume a few minutes later, the fire department arrives and extinguishes the fire. In a casual examination of the room, the investigator might conclude that there were two fires, independent of each other, and suspect a malicious intent when such was not the case.

Figure 4

While fire usually moves upward, fire can fall down through hollow walls and cause confusion as to the point of origin. Many fires have been started by heated metal falling from cutting torches, falling, in some cases, several stories.

## FIRE DEVELOPMENT

### Introduction

The severity and duration of a fire, as well as the hazard involved and the extent of damage, will depend on many elements. The nature of the ignition source, the proximity, type, and amount of fuel present (whether there is sufficient air available to sustain the burning), are just a few of the elements determining the behavior of the fire. In spite of the seemingly endless number of variations of elements which will affect the outcome of the fire, there exist several general characteristics common to most fires, a knowledge of which will aid the fire investigator in understanding fire development.

### Ignition

The nature of the ignition source, combined with the first fuel item involved, will determine the initial fire development. For example, one extreme might be an explosion and the resulting fire from operating an electrical switch in a room filled with a natural gas/air mixture caused by a leaking gas main. At the other extreme might be a piece of combustible material located close to a furnace or stove flue. Upon being heated over weeks, months or years, the material could begin to smolder and finally burst into flame.* The ignition source for most fires would generally fall between these extremes. A cigarette dropped into the folds of an upholstered chair or bedding could cause the chair or bedding to smolder for several hours before one might observe a flame. A pan of cooking oil being heated and left unattended on a kitchen stove could ignite in a matter of minutes.

The intensity or strength of the ignition source in reference to fuel is important. A light switch is generally not thought of as an ignition source nor would a cigarette placed on a plank of ordinary lumber be considered dangerous. Yet by switching to a gas, liquid, dust or easily ignitable plastic, ignition can and does take place from quite weak ignition sources. For example, flaming ignition (the direct contact of a flame with the material or fuel), is potentially dangerous for any fuel. The temperature of an open flame, be it a match, candle, torch, fireplace, furnace, or kitchen stove, is generally higher than other sources. Obviously the larger the flame the more the heat transfer and the greater the risk of ignition.

Simple theories of ignition require only that the material reach a certain critical temperature for ignition to take place. The item can be heated indirectly (for example, with a heater) until it reaches a high enough temperature and bursts into flame (autoignition). Or, the item can be heated directly with an open flame (piloted ignition). The material is raised to the required temperature and ignited by the flame. (Autoignition generally requires higher temperatures than piloted ignition.) The two processes, indirect or direct heating, are identical. The presence of the flame simply is faster in initiating the chemical chain reactions in the combustible gases (flaming) given off by the material at these high temperatures.

In reality, ignition is a more complex process than that described above. However, the concept of raising the temperature to high enough values is an easy one to understand and provides a simple means of ranking ignition sources as to their strength. An electric spark will produce extremely high temperatures but generally only for a very short time and only in a small volume. If there is a flammable mixture surrounding the spark, then there will be an explosion. At the other extreme is heating due to spontaneous ignition, mild frictional heating, and other lower temperature heat sources.

### Flame Spread

Whatever was ignited, the next phase of the fire involves flame spread. The growth of the fire will involve both flame spread along the ignited or initial item, as well as from one item to the next. In the beginning stages of flame spread, the fire usually will be small and growing. The important elements again will be the material properties as well as the item's location. Generally, sufficient air is available in the initial stages of flame spread.

Heat transfer from the flame will raise the temperature of the unburned fuel adjacent to it causing the area of involvement to increase. As the area increases, the flames will become larger, resulting in larger heat transfer rates and larger areas of involvement. If conditions are favorable, a self-sustaining chain reaction occurs. How rapidly this takes place will change from material to material. A flame will spread across the surface of gasoline in seconds. On the other hand, a flame will not spread across an oak floor and the chain reaction will stop, unless heat is supplied from some other nearby fuel. Carpeting may react like the oak floor, like gasoline, or somewhere in between, depending on the carpet material, the presence of padding, if any, the radiation from the ceiling, and the energy of the ignition source.

Heat loss from the material is also important in flame spread. If underlayment (pad) is placed under the carpet, increasing the thermal insulation between the carpet and the floor, the flame spread rate will increase since less energy would be lost from the burning area. This is the reason it is much easier to keep two or more logs alight in a fireplace since the radiant energy given off by the logs will be "captured" by the others and not lost to the surroundings as in the case of a single log.

Location is extremely important. The results of a small waste basket fire, located at the base of a combustible wall or at the edge of a bed or sofa, will be vastly different than the same waste basket fire placed in the center of the room. In general, upward flame spread rates will be significantly higher than horizontal or downward flame spread rates due to the heating by the hot combustion products flowing upward over the unburned fuel. The more closely spaced the items or fuel elements are in a given region, the higher the potential for fire spread from one item to the next. The further a nonburning item is from a burning one, the larger the flame must be before the nonburning item will ignite.

Flame spread tests are available to rank materials as to their potential hazard, that is, how easily flame will propagate along a given sample of the item when one end is lighted. They are described in reference

### Effect of Enclosure

After the fire is started, the fire development will be determined by the room or building or, simply, the enclosure. Up until this point nothing has been said about where the fire is taking place, only that there was sufficient air available. From this point onward, fire development will be dominated by the effects of the room, building, or the enclosure.

Consider a lighted candle safely placed on a table in a room. The candle will burn continuously until it runs out of wax. It will not change conditions in the room and it will not be changed by the room. The amount of oxygen used up in the room will be made up by normal air infiltration and similarly, the combustion products will leave the room through leaks. Any heating effects in nearby items will be small.

For a larger fire, however, the effect of the enclosure will begin to be felt. There are two primary effects that will now determine the course of the fire; one is ventilation, the other is called reradiation. The fire, beyond the size of a candle, will be consuming oxygen at a much greater rate, such that normal leaks will not be sufficient. For a completely sealed room the fire will go out due to a lack of oxygen.

Doors are not always closed or even present in open-plan homes or offices. Hence, a ready supply of air is generally available to a fire and the fire will grow. Fresh air will be drawn in through the lower part of the door opening at the same time hot gases from the fire will be collecting at the ceiling, filling the upper portion of the room and spilling out under the top of the door frame. (In older buildings, transoms were often installed over doorways for ventilation and light. This permitted the room fire to spread quickly to the corridor. After several hotel fires in which transoms were a factor in fire spread many codes were changed to require the permanent closure of the transoms, and they are not installed in modern buildings.)

The second effect of the enclosure will begin to be realized. The trapped hot gases in the upper portion of the room will heat the ceiling and walls. These surfaces, together with the gases themselves, will radiate down onto the unburned fuel in the room raising the fuel to the required temperature necessary for burning. An additional acceleration process (reradiation) now will be operating making the fire spread and grow further (see figure 4).

The larger fire will draw more and more air through the doorway. If the opening is large enough relative to the potential fuel supply, the controlling mechanism for further development is the amount of fuel present, the so-called fuel-controlled or fuel-limited fire. The fire will continue to grow until all of the fuel elements are burning inside the enclosure as long as there is more than an adequate supply of air coming through the door. This fire will continue in a more or less steady manner until the fuel is consumed.

Flashover

Consider the same sized opening, with considerably more fuel than in the previous case. The fire would continue to get larger, drawing more and more air, burning more and more vigorously. Temperatures and corresponding radiation feedback would rise until rather dramatically a phenomenon known as "flashover" occurs. Items in the room not in direct contact with the original flames suddenly burst into flame due to the high radiation levels. The rate of burning for all items in the room becomes so high that the amount of air coming through the door is inadequate. Flame lengths become longer and reach out through the door in search of more air to burn the additional combustibles and the "inferno" inside becomes controlled by the amount of air entering. This is called a ventilation-controlled fire. The fire cannot get any larger in the room because all the air entering is being utilized. The fire will continue in this fashion until all the fuel is burned up.

Flashover can be abrupt, unpredictable and highly dangerous. Firefighters are warned about entering rooms or buildings not knowing the state of things. For a growing or fuel-controlled fire one might be able to crawl into the room for rescue purposes. If the room has "flashed over," the flames coming out the door will prevent entry. It is likely that the fire will extend to the corridor and adjacent parts of the building are now in grave danger. Inspection of the enclosure after a fire often will reveal the telltale signs of flashover—every combustible in the room will exhibit some degree of fire damage, if not totally destroyed, even to charring of the paint and paper on gypsum walls.

www.ingramcontent.com/pod-product-compliance
Lightning Source LLC
Chambersburg PA
CBHW081809300426
44116CB00014B/2298